Thomas Firminger Dyer

Church-lore Gleanings

Thomas Firminger Dyer

Church-lore Gleanings

ISBN/EAN: 9783337004408

Printed in Europe, USA, Canada, Australia, Japan

Cover: Foto ©Lupo / pixelio.de

More available books at **www.hansebooks.com**

CHURCH-LORE GLEANINGS.

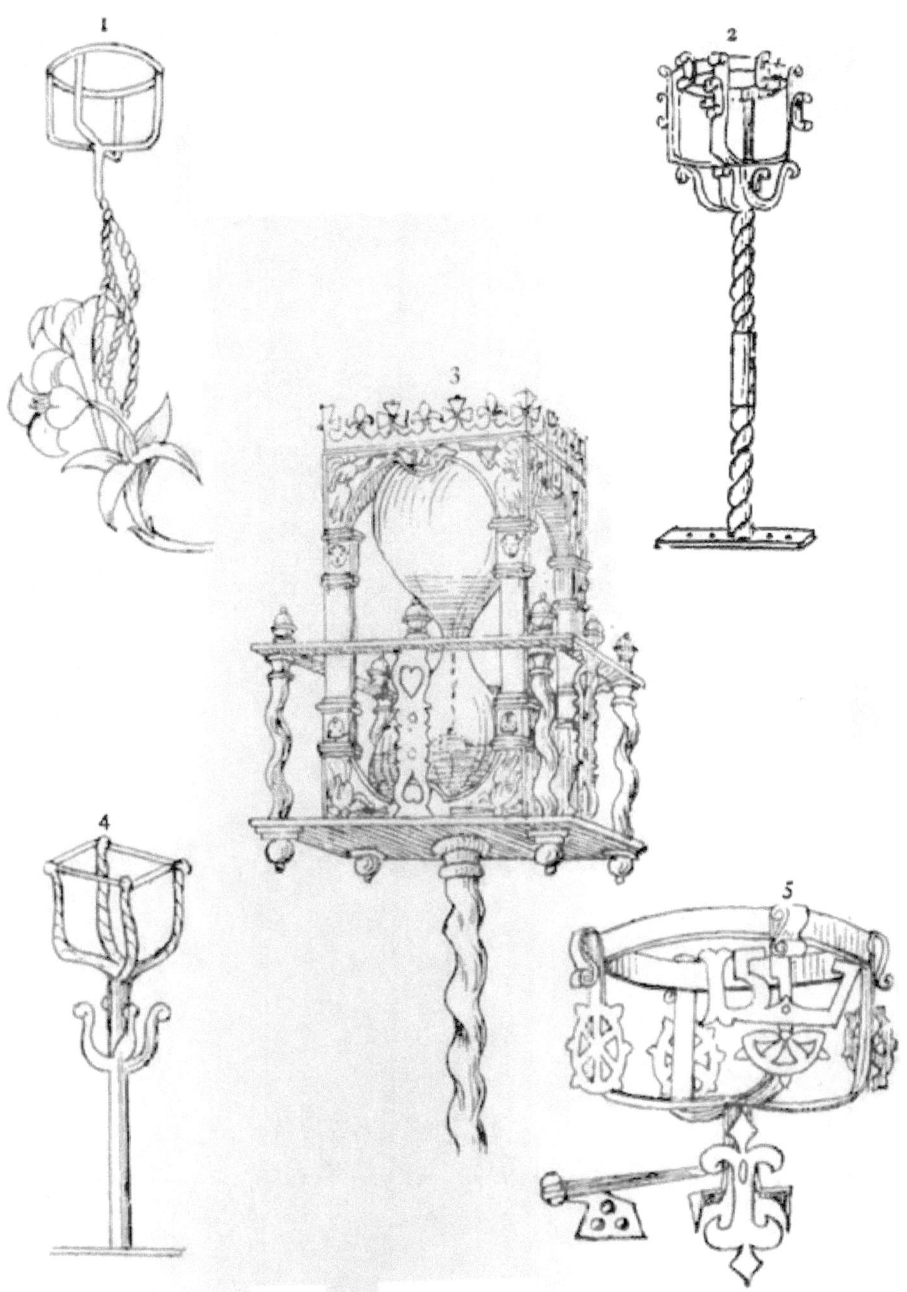

HOUR-GLASS STANDS.

1. Salhouse, Norfolk. 2. St. Michael's, St. Albans. 3. St. Alban's, Wood Street.

4. Flixton, Suffolk. 5. Leigh, Kent.

(Page 205.)

Frontispiece.

CHURCH-LORE GLEANINGS

BY

T. F. THISELTON DYER.

LONDON:

A. D. INNES AND CO.,

31 & 32, BEDFORD STREET, STRAND, W.C.

1892.

LONDON:
PRINTED BY WILLIAM CLOWES AND SONS, LIMITED,
STAMFORD STREET AND CHARING CROSS.

CONTENTS.

CHAPTER		PAGE
I.	CHURCH-BUILDING LEGENDS	1
II.	SOME CURIOUS CHURCH TRADITIONS ...	16
III.	STRANGE STORIES AND TALES OF WONDER ...	26
IV.	THE CHURCH PORCH	39
V.	CHURCH DISCIPLINE	53
VI.	CHURCH PIGEON-HOUSES	67
VII.	ACOUSTIC JARS AND HORSES' SKULLS	70
VIII.	BELLS AND BELFRIES	75
IX.	CONSECRATION CROSSES	108
X.	BAPTISMAL CUSTOMS	111
XI.	THE MARRIAGE CEREMONY	118
XII.	BURIAL CUSTOMS	128
XIII.	THE CHURCHYARD	153
XIV.	MEMORIALS OF THE DEAD—GARLANDS, FUNERAL ARMOUR, FLAGS AND BANNERS	161
XV.	THE RIGHT OF SANCTUARY	173
XVI.	PEWS AND THEIR LORE	184
XVII.	JACK OF THE CLOCK, ETC.	197
XVIII.	LYCHNOSCOPES, OR LOW SIDE WINDOWS ...	209

CONTENTS.

CHAPTER		PAGE
XIX.	THE EASTER SEPULCHRE	219
XX.	CURIOUS CHURCH PECULIARITIES	231
XXI.	CHURCHWARDENS	242
XXII.	PARISH CLERKS	251
XXIII.	PARISH BULLS AND COWS	264
XXIV.	WELLS AND WELL-CHAPELS	273
XXV.	CHURCH LIBRARIES	284
XXVI.	BOOKS IN CHAINS	296
XXVII.	SOME CHURCH SUPERSTITIONS	306
XXVIII.	HATS WORN IN CHURCH, ETC.	314
XXIX.	CHURCH-ALES AND RUSH-BEARINGS	322
XXX.	SOME CURIOUS RELICS	333
	INDEX	339

LIST OF ILLUSTRATIONS.

		TO FACE PAGE
HOUR-GLASS STANDS	... ...	*Frontispiece*
THE PEDLAR AND HIS DOG, LAMBETH CHURCH	...	18
PIGEON-HOUSES IN CHURCHES: BIRLINGHAM, NEAR PERSHORE	... ...	68
CONSECRATION CROSSES	... ...	109
LICH-GATES	... ...	155
FUNERAL WREATH, AND MAIDEN'S FUNERAL	...	162
JACK O' THE CLOCK, SOUTHWOLD	... ...	200
THE WILLINGALES, ESSEX	... ...	232
WITCH'S CALDRON, FRENSHAM CHURCH	... ...	308
ST. WILFRID'S NEEDLE, RIPON CATHEDRAL	... ...	312
FINGER-STOCKS, OR PILLORIES	... ...	335

CHURCH-LORE GLEANINGS.

CHAPTER I.

CHURCH-BUILDING LEGENDS.

MYSTERIOUS invisible agency, interfering with the work of building, has formed the subject of many curious church legends. According to the general conception, underlying most of these traditions, a supernatural obstacle—to counteract which human power was helpless—frustrated the erection of certain churches on the sites originally selected. Hence, what was built during the day was persistently removed at night-time by unseen hands; this process having been repeated until the founders of such sacred structures submitted to the will of the higher powers by adopting the spots which they evidently considered more suitable.

Many conjectures have been suggested to explain the antecedent history of this extensive group of legendary tales; but they may probably be traced back to a primitive period of ignorance and superstition, when a deep-rooted belief in all kinds of supernatural agencies originated most of those stories of wonder which survive in our midst to-day. What more natural than to invest with a halo of supernatural romance many of those churches which are situated in somewhat wild and inaccessible spots, and whose existence in such localities has often been a matter of comment and surprise !

Stories of supernatural interference, too, when told of any particular neighbourhood would, like other folk-lore stories, in process of time be adapted to other places as occasion demanded; although it has always been a difficult matter to decide when and how this happened. But as most of our counties have always been jealous of their traditions and legendary lore, it is easy to conceive how, in the old days prior to steam, when fairies, witches, and other unearthly beings were commonly supposed to have a voice in so important an event as the building of a church, similar weird and strange stories would be recorded of different localities—most of which have been preserved by the local antiquarian with more or less pride.

Curious tales, too, are told in Cornwall of the selection of sites for churches, and of their erection. It is said, for instance, when a church was finished, its patron saint stood on the tower, and taking the builder's hammer, swung it round his head, and let it take what direction it might. Wherever it fell, there was the next church to be erected. The hammer thrown for St. Madron alighted on a pleasant place. The church stands on the brow of an eminence, which slopes gradually down for about two miles to the shores of Mount's Bay.*

In many of our church legends, the devil is represented as having caused the sacred edifice to be placed on a high hill instead of at its foot; his idea being, it is said, that worshippers would be less inclined to visit it. In the village of Churchdown, about four miles from Gloucester, the church dedicated to St. Bartholomew is built on the summit of Churchdown Hill,—the ascent to it being steep and tortuous. The legend runs, that "the church was

---

* *Gentleman's Magazine* (1862), pt. i. 527.

begun to be built on a more convenient and accessible spot of ground, but that the materials used in the day were constantly taken away in the night and carried to the top of the hill, which was considered a supernatural intimation that the church should be built there." *

The site of Rochdale church was removed, we are told, from the banks of the Roach up to its elevated position. Roby, in his "Traditions of Lancashire," gives a tale entitled "The Goblin Builders," relating how "Gamel, the Saxon thane, lord of Recedham or Rached—the present Rochdale—intended to build a chapel unto St. Chadde, nigh to the banks of the Rache or Roach." But his intentions were frustrated; for three times were the foundations laid, and the same number of times conveyed by invisible hands to a more lofty site, where the present church was eventually built.† There is a similar legend connected with Holme Church, in the East Riding of Yorkshire, which is built on the top of a hill; but, in this case, the work of obstruction was the result of fairy agency. "Some persons," the story goes, "commenced to build the church at the bottom of the hill, and they were warned by the fairies to build it at the top; but they took no notice. When the church was nearly finished, it was found all in ruins. They recommenced to build, but the church was found in ruins again. And they started a third time, when it was again spoiled by the fairies. They then built it at the top." The fine Norman church of Godshill, in the Isle of Wight, was to have been in the valley; but the builders each morning found the previous day's work destroyed during the night, and the stones carried mysteriously to the top of the hill; and so they reared it on

* Rudder's "History of Gloucestershire" (1779), 339.

† See Harland and Wilkinson's "Legends and Traditions of Lancashire," 52.

that green knoll, where to-day it is an object of beauty for miles round.   And the parish church of St. Matthew, Walsall, Staffordshire, situated on a high hill above the town, was to have been built in a field called the "Church Acre," but since corrupted into "Chuckery."   The little church of Brent Tor, a lofty conical hill on the north-western borders of Dartmoor, has the same tradition, it having been intended to erect the sacred structure at the foot of the Tor, whereas it is now on the summit.   Another instance in the same county is the church at Buckfastleigh. The church hill is ascended by one hundred and forty steps, and it is said that "the devil obstructed the builders by removing the stones; and a large block, bearing the mark of the 'enemy's' finger and thumb, is pointed out on a farm about one mile distant."

Similarly, a curious legend is attached to Mayfield Church, Sussex, which was originally constructed of timber. St. Dunstan, it is said, observing that it did not stand east and west, applied his shoulders to the edifice and screwed it into its proper "orientation."   Whether the error had originated from the ignorance of the village wights, or from the malice of St. Dunstan's ancient enemy, the devil, is not certain.   It is supposed, however, to have been the latter, for it is added that, at a subsequent date, when the wooden church was replaced by a stone one, Satan used every night to set wrong what had been done the day before.   For ages the prints of his feet were shown in a neighbouring quarry, where he was accustomed to resist the workmen in procuring stones for the new edifice.*

But, in some cases, supernatural interference altered its tactics, as happened in the building of the church at Plympton St. Mary, in Devonshire, where the foundation stones were mysteriously removed from high ground to

* Sussex Archæological Society, xiii. 227.

the low land beneath it. At the village of Duffield, a few miles from Derby, there is the site of an ancient castle, formerly belonging to the Ferrars, Earls of Derby. The site is still known by the name of Castle Orchards, and at a very short distance from the hill, on which the castle stood, is another eminence, where some ancient cottages are standing. There is a tradition current in the neighbourhood, writes the late Mr. Llewellynn Jewitt,* "that the church was originally intended to be built upon this eminence; but that, after the work had been commenced and proceeded to some extent, the devil, for some unexplained reason, removed the whole of the work in one night to the site it now occupies, in a field by the side of the river Derwent, at quite the opposite side of the village. The workmen, surprised at finding that their work had all disappeared, after solemn prayers, again began laying the foundations; but to be carried away by the devil on the succeeding night. Day after day the same thing took place, and at last the arch-fiend so completely triumphed over the patience of the workmen, that they went down to the place where he had carried the material, and completed the church."

With this legend may be compared one told of the parish church at Kidderminster. It appears that the original design was to erect it on the brow of the rising ground, on the Bewdley side of the river Stour; but the day's work was always demolished in the night. As, therefore, it was evident that their plans were obstructed by the evil one, the builders "left him in full possession of his territory, and removed the site of their church to the rising ground on the opposite side of the Stour. There they finished their work without further interruption, and named the scene of their failure the 'Curst Field,' which has become corrupted into 'Cussfield.'"†

* *Notes and Queries*, 2nd series, iv. 357.
† Ibid., 19.

When the workmen were engaged in erecting the ancient church of Old Deer, in Aberdeenshire, upon a small hill called Bissau, their work was impeded by supernatural obstacles. At length the Spirit of the River was heard to say—

> "It is not here, it is not here,
> That ye shall build the Church of Deer ;
> But on Taptillery,
> Where many a corpse shall lie."

The site of the edifice was accordingly transferred to Taptillery, an eminence at some distance from the place where the building had been commenced.

Shropshire affords several examples of the same form of legend. When Worfield Church, near Bridgnorth, was built, the site selected was on the brow of a neighbouring hill; but the devil, it is said, fearing lest, if it were placed in such a conspicuous spot, the spire should attract too much attention, and draw too many worshippers to the church, carried the stones to the place where the church now stands. The site chosen for Baschurch Church, was on the top of Berth Hill,' but as long as the work was carried on here, "however hard the men worked during the day, 'something,' they knew not what, always pulled their work down again during the night, and threw the stones into the Berth Pool, until at last the disheartened people tried a fresh site, and then their work was allowed to remain." The same story is told of Stoke-upon-Tern old Church, north of Newport—rebuilt 1874—and of Broughton Church, the ruins of which may be seen in a low marshy hollow, near Yorton railway station, between Wem and Shrewsbury.*

St. Brelade's Church, Jersey, close to the tide-mark in the beautiful little bay, was to have been built on a spot

---

* Miss Jackson, "Shropshire Folklore," pp. 8, 9.

overlooking St. Peter's Valley from the summit ground of the island; but the materials were **in** the same mysterious **manner removed** to the spot on which the church was eventually built.

In many parishes where the church is at some distance from the village, or has been built in some awkward situation, we find the same kind of legends current to explain this curious peculiarity. But the inconvenient position of many old churches may probably be attributed to the fact that such structures were, in days of old, built by the lords of manors, or the great landed proprietors, who invariably erected them near their own houses, which usually stood in the middle **of** large parks, and consequently at some distance from **the** village. **In** the same way many old churches **owe** their position on the top of some high **eminence to the** circumstance that they were used for **pilgrimages,** and hence were made as difficult of access as possible. In the parish of Talland, in S.E. Cornwall, is a spot locally known as Pulpit, about which the following legend is told: "When it was decided to build the parish church, Pulpit was selected as its site, and the foundations were commenced. But on the following night a phantom voice was heard repeating these warning words—

> "'If you will my wish fulfil,
> Build the church on Talland Hill.'

And at daybreak it was found that all the stones had been removed to the spot selected by the spirit. Finding it useless to oppose the superior power, the builders ultimately erected the church on Talland Hill, near the sea-shore, and far from the centre of the parish."

The parish church of Wendover, which is **about** half **a mile** from the town, **was to** have been built in a field **known as the** "Witches' Meadow," **but the same difficulty was** encountered. Near Thornton-le-Moor, in the parish of North Otterington, Yorkshire, there is a slight eminence, on which, it is said,* in all probability stood at one time an ancient village, though no trace of either the village or its name now remains, except the designation of the adjoining fields as "the Tofts," and the socket of an old cross, known as "Perry Trough." At this place, tradition tells us, the church was to have been erected, but invisible opposition so persistently impeded the labours of the builders, that at last they gave up the idea, and erected the church at the place indicated at North Otterington, where for nigh a thousand years it has stood as the old parish church dedicated to St. Michael. A similar legend is found in the neighbouring parish of Leake, accounting for the present remote position of the ancient church of that parish. The intention was to have erected it on the top of Borrowby Bank, convenient to the village of Borrowby, but their plans were frustrated by the same agency.

The church of Over, in Cheshire, stands about a mile from the more populous part of the village, its present position being thus explained. Years ago the devil being alarmed at the religious zeal of the villagers in attending the services of their church, and fearful thereby of losing his influence over them, he determined to rob them of the sacred edifice by removing it bodily. But the prayers of the monks so far prevailed that he was obliged to drop his burden, when it fell where it now stands. A poetical version of this legend is given by Major Egerton Leigh in his " Ballads and Legends of Cheshire."

The Church of Ste. Marie du Castel, which is inconveniently situated, is said to occupy the site of a castle, which, long before the conquest of England by the Normans,

* Rev. T. Parkinson, "Legends and Traditions of Yorkshire" (1888), 120.

was the abode of a piratical chief traditionally known as "le grand Geffroy," or "le grand Sarrazin." A field almost in the centre of the parish, called "les Tuzets," is pointed out as the spot originally fixed on for the church, but the same mysterious removal of the building materials took place. Hence its present position. In this case fairies are accused of being the agents, though some say it was the work of angels.*

At Udimore, near Rye, the church was to have been built on the opposite side of the river Ree to that where it was eventually built. But unseen hands removed nightly what had been built during the day, while a ghostly voice, in warning and reproachful tones, was heard to cry, "O'er the mere! o'er the mere!" †

Among the numerous other instances in which the enemy of mankind displayed his active zeal in opposing church building, the story runs that, as the masons built up the towers of Towednack Church, near St. Ives, the devil knocked the stones down, hence its dwarfed dimensions. Similarly we learn from the *Oswestry Advertiser* (May 28, 1878) that, in days of old, "repeated attempts were made to build a church at Godrefarth, near Llanddewi, but the walls fell down as quickly as they were built; and it was not till the present time was fixed upon that a church could be erected. There is a saying that, in the building of the tower two men brought the stones from the Voelallt rock. One of them died, and the other, lamenting his dead companion, bowed three times, and the rock at once was shattered, and thereafter no difficulty was experienced in fetching the stones for the tower."

Sanderson, in his "Antiquities of Durham Abbey," gives a similar legend of the Galilee at Durham Cathedral, with

---

* See *Notes and Queries*, 2nd series, iv. 298.
† Sussex Archæological Collections, xiii. 227.

the exchange of St. Cuthbert for the devil. The story goes that preparations were made "to erect a New Work at the east angle of the said cathedral, for which seven pillars of marble were brought from beyond sea. The work, being advanced to a small height, began, through great clifts visible therein, to fall down, whence it mani-festly appeared unacceptable to God and holy St. Cuthbert, especially for the access women were to have so near his Feretory ; whereupon that work was left off, and a new one begun, and soon finished, at the west end of the said church, in which it was lawful for women to enter, there being before no holy place where they might have admittance for their comfort and consolation. It is called the Galiley by reason, as some think, of the translation thereof—being once began and afterwards removed." *

When the church at Inkberrow was rebuilt on a new site in olden days, it was supposed that the fairies took umbrage at the change, as they were believed to be averse to bells, and accordingly endeavoured to obstruct the building. But as they did not succeed, the following lamentation was occasionally heard by the startled peasantry—

> "Neither sleep, neither lie,
> For Inkbro's ting-tangs hang so nigh."

Occasionally, the opposition to church building has taken another form. When the founder of Winwick Church, Lancashire, had fixed on what he considered an appropriate spot, and after some progress had been made in the founda-tions, at night a pig was seen running hastily to the site of the new church, screaming aloud, " We-ee-wick, we-ee-wick, we-ee-wick." Then, taking up one of the stones in its mouth, the pig carried it to the spot sanctified by the death of St.

* Similar church legends are found on the continent. See Marryatt's "Jutland and the Danish Isles," ii. 358 ; Thorpe's "Northern Mythology."

Oswald, and in **this manner** removed all the **stones** which had **been laid by** the builders. The founder, considering himself justly reproved for not having selected that sacred spot as the site of the church, at once yielded to the **wise counsels** of the pig. Then it is said the pig not only decided **the** site **of** the church, but gave a name to the parish. In support **of** this tradition there is the figure of a pig sculptured on the tower of the church just above the western entrance, and also **the** following Latin doggrel—

> "Hic locus Oswalde, quondam placuit tibi valde,
> Northanumbrorum fueras Rex, nunc que Polorum,
> Regna tenes, prato passim marcelde vocato." *

There **is a** similar legend **of** "Burnley Cross **and the** Demon Pigs." It **appears that,** prior to the foundation **of** any church **in** Burnley, religious rites were celebrated on the spot **where** this ancient cross now exists. But upon **the** attempt **being** made to erect an oratory, the materials were nightly removed by supernatural agents in the form of pigs, to where St. Peter's Church was afterwards erected.† Another tradition relates that the church of Breedon, Leicestershire, which stands on a hill above the village, was to have been erected in a central situation. But when **the** builders began to build the fabric, their work was carried away by "doves" in **the** night-time, and built in **the same** manner on the hill where the church now stands.

At Alfriston the foundations of the church were originally laid **in a** field on the west side of the town, known as the Savyne Croft, but every night the stones were violently hurled over the houses into **a** field called "The Tye," where the church now stands. It is further added that a certain wise man observed in the field four oxen lying asleep, rump to rump, **in** the form of a cross—a strange incident,

---

* Harland **and** Wilkinson's "Lancashire Legends," 76, 77.
† Ibid., 8.

which suggested the cruciform arrangement which was ultimately carried out in the building.[*]

A correspondent, writing to the *Wrexham Advertiser* (April 16, 1881), gives a local legend connected with Wrexham Parish Church: "After Christianity was introduced to this country, it became necessary to have churches built; and when that question came before the inhabitants of this locality, according to tradition Bryn-y-ffynnon was the spot fixed upon, and the work was begun in earnest; but owing to something, believed then to be supernatural, what was built in the day was thrown down at night, and caused much alarm and fear among the inhabitants.

"At last valiant and sturdy men are found with sufficient courage to watch and see whether the walls were thrown down by an invisible being, or by a being possessing flesh and bones like themselves. While thus watching, the walls that were built the day before were thrown down, and the watchmen were unable to see anything near them; but, immediately afterwards, they fancied there was something hovering over their heads, which repeatedly cried, ' Bryn-y-grog,' with no other explanation. When they related the next morning what had taken place in the night, it was decided at once that Bryn-y-grog was the place the church was to be built upon. Bryn-y-grog was then the name of the place where the church now stands, but was in the possession of a person that was unwilling to part with the inheritance of his father; but upon hearing of the mysterious being crying in the air, indicating the place where the church was to be built, his heart was melted, and he agreed to give up possession, upon condition that another place was provided for him instead, and the present Bryn-y-grog was given him instead, and he carried the name with him there."

[*] Sussex Archæological Collections, xiii. 226.

"When St. Patrick," writes Mr. Kennedy, in his "Fireside Stories of Ireland" (p. 153), "was building the great church on the Rock of Cashel, the workmen used to be terribly annoyed, for whatever they put up by day was always found knocked down next morning. So one man watched, and another man watched, but about one o'clock in the night every watcher fell asleep." At last it was arranged that St. Patrick himself should sit up, and, just as the clock struck one, "what did he see but a terrible bull, with fire flashing from his nostrils, charging full drive up the hill, and knocking down every stone, stick, and bit of mortar that was put together the day before."

"'Oh, ho,' says the saint, ' I'll soon find one that will settle you, my brave bull !' Now who was this but Usheen (Oisin) that St. Patrick was striving to make a good Christian ? . . .

"The day after St. Patrick saw the bull, he up and told Usheen all about what was going on.

"'Put me on a rock or in a tree,' says Usheen, 'just by the way the bull ran, and we'll see what we can do.' So in the evening he was comfortably settled in the bough of a tree on the hill-side, and when the bull was firing away up the steep like a thunderbolt, and was nearly under him, he dropped down on his back, took a horn in each hand, tore him asunder, and dashed one of his sides so hard against the face of the wall that it may be seen there this day, hardened into stone. There was no further stoppage of the work, and in gratitude they cut out the effigy of Usheen riding on his pony, and it may be seen inside the old ruins this very day."

In other ways animals have been associated with church-building. Thus the Church of St. Neot, Cornwall, which is celebrated for its beautiful painted glass, has not escaped the influence of tradition. St. Noet, the reputed brother of King Alfred, lived some hundreds of years before the present church dedicated to him was erected. But folk-lore has it that it was built at night entirely by his own hands, and that he drew from a neighbouring quarry, by the help of reindeer, all the stones he used in the building. He is described as a man of short stature, and tradition adds that, after the church was finished, he found that he was not tall enough to reach the keyhole of the door, and could not, therefore, unlock it. To remedy this defect, he put a stone opposite (still pointed out) from which, when he stood on it, he could throw the key into the lock with unerring precision.

This legend reminds us of one told of St. Kieran,[*] who is said to have built the church which bears his name, and to have possessed extraordinary powers, little inferior to those of Orpheus and Amphion. But whilst their influence extended to the moving of the very stones, and arranging them into architectural order, his only went so far as to provide the means of doing so. The saint possessed but one ox, which during the day drew the materials for the building, and in the evening was slaughtered to feed the workmen. There is a well at the foot of the hill on which the building is erected, which still retains its character for miraculous powers. Into this well the bones of the ox were thrown each evening, and every following morning he appeared ready for his daily labour. One evening, however, when nothing but a small part of the eastern gable remained to be finished, one of the work-men, named McMahon, broke one of the shin-bones to get the marrow, and, though every care was taken to collect the splinters, the next morning the ox appeared with his leg broken, and totally incapable of continuing his share of the work. So melancholy a spectacle overcame the

* Mason's " Statistical Account of Ireland," iii. 161, 162.

patience of the saint, and he prayed that the gable should never fall till it crushed a McMahon. Most part of it, however, has fallen, and hitherto it would seem no McMahon has been the victim of its final ruin.

The church at Braunton, Devonshire, is reported to have been built by St. Branock, who was directed in a dream to erect it on a spot where he should first meet a sow with a litter of young ones. There is an ancient carving on the panel of a seat in the church, representing a litter of pigs. With this tradition, we may compare that told of Llangar Church, in the "Gossiping Guide to Wales." "There is a local legend that this church was to have been built where the Cynwyd crosses the Dee, but after the work done by day had been destroyed in the night, the builders were warned supernaturally that they must seek a spot where, on hunting, a 'Carw Gwyn' (white deer) should be started. They did so, and Llangar Church is the result. From this circumstance the church was called Llan-garw-gwyn, and from this name the transition to Llangar is easy." Numerous other similar legends exist throughout the country, but they are gradually becoming forgotten under the influence of the new life, which has been quickened in so many of our rural parishes by railway communication.

CHAPTER II.

SOME CURIOUS CHURCH TRADITIONS.

THE central feature of Southwark is the Church of the Priory of St. Mary Overie, now called St. Saviour's, the early history of which is all cased in the mists of ancient tradition. Whenever the churchwardens and vestry meet over their cups, the first cup, it is said, is to their church's patron saint, "Old Moll." This Old Moll was, according to Stow, Mary, the daughter of a ferryman, concerning whom he records the following story, which has been much discredited, connecting as it does the building of the original London Bridge with the Church of St. Mary Overie.

"A ferry being kept in the place where now the bridge is builded, at length the ferryman and his wife deceasing, left the same ferry to their only daughter, a maiden named Mary, who with the goods left her by her parents, as also with the profits of the said ferry, builded an House of Sisters on the place where now standeth the east part of St. Mary's Church, above the quire where she was buried, unto which house she gave the oversight and profits of the ferry. But afterwards, the said house of sisters being converted into a college of priests, the priests builded the bridge of timber, as all the other bridges of this great land were, and, from time to time, kept the same in good reparation, till at length, considering the great charges which were bestowed in the same, there was, by the aid of the citizens and others, a bridge builded with stone."

There is still existing at the Church of St. Overie, a skeleton effigy, which some affirm to be that of Audery the ferryman, father of the immortal Moll.* The story amusingly tells how the miserly old man counterfeited death in order that his household might forego a day's victuals, thinking their sorrow would make them, at least, fast so long. But no sooner had the ferryman been laid out, wrapped in a sheet, with one taper burning at his head, and another at his feet, than the half-starved servants, overjoyed at seeing their master apparently dead, danced with delight around his body, broke open the larder, and fell to feasting and merry-making. For a short time, the old ferryman restrained his feelings; but, suddenly springing from his bed, he rushed forth to chastise his servants, when one of them, thinking it was the devil himself, struck his master dead.

The corpse of the old miser was denied Christian burial —for he had been deemed by the clergy a wicked and excommunicated man ; but the friars of Bermondsey Abbey, in the absence of their father abbot, were bribed to give the body " a little earth for charity." The abbot, on his return, enraged at this act of the friars, had the corpse dug up and thrown on the back of an ass, which was then turned out of the abbey gates. The animal carried the body up Kent Street, and eventually shook it off near the small pond once called St. Thomas à Waterings, where it was roughly interred.† Mary, the fair-haired heiress of the ferryman's wealth, shrouding her beauty in a cowl, retired into a cloister for life, and devoted her money to the establish-

---

* The effigy is really supposed to be of fifteenth century.

† It has been suggested that the religious house was originally founded in honour of St. Audrey, or Etheldreda of Ely. A probable derivation of Overie is from " Over the rie," that is, " Over the water."

ment of a House of Sisters, as mentioned above. Thus runs the tale of the early history of St. Mary Overie, being one, however, upon which little or no reliance can be placed.*

The parish of Lambeth has long been proverbial for the familiar legend of the " Pedlar and his dog." The story runs that a piece of land known as "Pedlar's Acre" was bequeathed to the parish by a grateful pedlar on condition that the picture of himself and his dog should be preserved for ever in painted glass in one of the windows of the parish church. This piece of ground, consisting of one acre and seventeen poles, adjoins to the river, and is situate near to the east end of the Surrey abutment of Westminster Bridge. It first occurs as the possession of the parish in 1504, when the rents arising from it were carried to the churchwarden's accounts. It was then called the "Church Hoppys" or " Hope" (signifying an isthmus or neck of land projecting into the river, or an enclosed piece of marsh land), which name it retained in 1623, when it was denominated the Church Osiers, probably from its swampy situation. It was first called Pedlar's Acre in a lease granted by Dr. Hooper, the rector, and the churchwardens, dated August 6, 1690. It is now built over.†

At what time the memorial was put up in Lambeth Church is uncertain, but such a portrait existed in 1608, there being in the churchwardens' account for that year an entry of " two shillings paid to the glazier for the window where the picture of the pedlar stands." A "new glass pedlar" was put up in 1703 at the expense of £2, and the curious picture may still be seen in the church. Whatever truth there may be in this popular tradition, it should be added that the parish register records the fact of the land in question

---

* "Old and New London," ii. 9 ; vi. 20, 21.

† John Tanswell, "History of Lambeth" (1858), 104.

THE PEDLAR AND HIS DOG, LAMBETH CHURCH.

Page 18.

having been bequeathed by some person unknown.* On Pedlar's Acre was formerly a public-house, with the sign of a pedlar and a dog, and on a pane of glass in one of the windows in the tap-room the following lines were written with a diamond—

> " Happy the pedlar whose portrait we view,
> Since his dog was so faithful, and fortunate too ;
> He at once made him wealthy, and guarded his door,
> Secured him from robbers, relieved him when poor.
> Then drink to his memory, and wish fate may send
> Such a dog to protect you, enrich, and befriend."

An early legend connected with the Church of All Hallows Barking, relates to Edward I. That king, it is said, had a vision which commanded him to erect an image of the Virgin at All Hallows Barking, under the promise that if he did so, visited it five times every year, and kept the chapel in repair, he should be victorious over all nations, and should ascend the throne when his father died. To the truth of this vision Edward swore before the Pope, and obtained a dispensation of forty days' penance for all true penitents who should contribute towards the lights, ornaments and repairs of the chapel, and should pray for the soul of King Richard, whose heart was, it is said, buried before the high altar. The pilgrims and worshippers of Our Lady of Barking continued numerous till the Reformation abolished the practice.

The following tradition relating to the building of the Church of St. Moorin, Morwenstowe, Devon, has been preserved among some old manuscripts belonging to the Coffins of Portledge. " Moorwinstow, its name, is from St. Moorin. The tradition is, that when the parishioners were about to build their church, this saint went down under the cliff and

* There is a similar tradition of a pedlar being a benefactor to the parish of Swaffham, in Norfolk.

chose a stone for the font, which she brought up upon her head. In her way, being weary, she lay down the stone and rested herself, out of which place sprang a well, from thence called St. Moorin's Well. Then she took up the stone, and carried it to the place where now the church standeth. The parishioners had begun their church in another place, and there did convey this stone, but what was built by day was pulled down by night, and the materials carried to this place. Whereupon they forbare, and built it in the place they were directed to by an order." *

The situation of the Church of St. Antony in Kirrier, Cornwall, is very peculiar, and is accounted for by the following tradition. It is said that soon after the Conquest, as some Normans of rank were crossing from Normandy into England, a tempest drove them on the Cornish coast, where they were in momentary danger of destruction. In their distress they called on St. Antony, and vowed, if he would save them from shipwreck, they would build a church in his honour on the spot where they should first land. The ship was wafted into the Durra Creek, and there the pious Normans as soon as possible fulfilled their vow. A similar legend is told of Gunwalloe Parish Church, which tradition says was erected as a votive offering by one who here escaped from shipwreck, "Where he had miraculously escaped from the fury of the waves, he vowed that he would build a chapel in which the sounds of prayer, and praise to God, should blend with the never-ceasing voice of those waves from which he had so narrowly escaped. So near to the sea is the church, that at times it is reached by the spray. The waves have frequently broken away the walls of the churchyard." But, according to another tradition, it is said that the builders intended to erect the church nearer the centre of the parish, at Hingey, but the materials

* *The Antiquary* (1890), **144, 145.**

by some mysterious agency were removed during the night to the present site.*

Local tradition says that when the architect of Shottesbrooke Church, six miles from Maidenhead, was placing the last stone on the top of the spire, he called for wine to drink the king's health. After drinking it he immediately fell to the ground, was dashed to pieces, and buried on the spot; also that a coffin-shaped stone was placed over his remains, the interjection "O! O!" which he uttered when dying, being the only thing engraven upon it.†

A curious old story tells how the priests of St. German's persuaded Sir John de Daunay to build a church on his lands at Sheviock. He commenced the work, but, notwithstanding his great wealth, his heart failed him, and he curtailed the fair proportions on which he had at first decided. His wife, Lady Emelyn, was enraged at this; and, prompted, it is said, by the devil in visible presence, she resolved to build a barn which should exceed in beauty the house of God. The barn rose with astonishing rapidity, and the work proceeded as if the most lavish expenditure had been bestowed upon it. The church progressed but slowly, and was a very inferior structure to the barn, the devil, it is commonly supposed, having assisted Lady Daunay in her wicked work. ‡ In Gilbert's "Cornwall," this legend is thus told: "There runneth a tale among the parishioners how one of the Daunay family's ancestors undertook to build the church, and the wife the barn adjoining; and they, casting up accounts on finishing their work, the barn was found to have cost $1\frac{1}{2}d$. more than the church."

An amusing tradition belongs to the detached tower of

* *Gentleman's Magazine* (1862), ii. 25, 539.
† Murray, Berks, 40.
‡ Hunt's "Popular Romances of West of England," 442.

the church of West Walton, Norfolk, near Wisbech. During the early days of that church the fenmen were very wicked, and the evil one hired a number of people to carry the tower away. They set it well on their shoulders, but could not get it over the churchyard wall, and they ran round and round with it until they found themselves unable to get it out of consecrated ground at all, and so they left it at the gate.

The north transept of York Cathedral has long been famous for the five very lofty and narrow lancets, best known as the "Five Sisters"—a name which, it has been suggested, arose from the equal dimensions of the five windows. According to Gent's "York Cathedral" there is a tradition that five maiden sisters were at the expense of these lights—the painted glass in them, representing a kind of embroidery or needlework, might perhaps give occasion for this story. According to another story, four young orphans, wards of St. Mary's Abbey, agreed to fill the lancets with memorial glass, in patterns taken from their embroidery frames, which they had long laid aside for sorrow, in remembrance of a dead sister. Here they are reported to have knelt and prayed, until, one by one, they passed away and were laid in a common grave. This window has also been called the Jewish window, but for what reason is unknown, although it has been conjectured that the cost of the window may have been defrayed by exactions from the Jews of York.[*]

It may be noted there are numerous traditions scattered here and there over the country, recording how we are indebted to the co-operation of sisters for some of the churches which still exist.

The parish churches of Albrighton and Donington, Shrop-

---

[*] R. J. King, "Handbook to the Northern Cathedrals" (1869), pt. i. 22.

shire, stand curiously near together "on the high banks, overhanging one of the picturesque dingles containing a pretty sheet of water, which are common in that part of the country. The two churches are of different styles and dates, but legend tells that they were built by two sisters in a spirit of rivalry, and that this is the reason why Donington Church is so far from any village, and so much in one corner of the parish." *

A similar legend was formerly current of the churches of Owthorne and Withernsea, Yorkshire, known as the "Sister Churches." They were said to have been built by two sisters, who at first said that a single church would be sufficient for the adjoining manors, but they quarrelled as to the respective merits of a tower or spire, and each sister at last built her own church.

Similarly, the churches of Putney and Fulham, which stand opposite each other on the banks of the Thames, are said to have been built by the individual manual labour of two sisters. They possessed but one tool between them, so they agreed to work and to rest alternately for an hour. The plan of transferring the tool was to fling it across the river; so when the hour for work arrived to the lady of Putney, she called out lustily to her sister, " Put it high ;" while the Fulham lady's watchword was, " Heave it full home."

A strange legend is told of the building of Linton Church, which is situated on a little knoll of fine compact sand, without any admixture of stone or even pebbles, and widely different from the soil of the neighbouring heights. The sand has, however, hardened into stone, yet the particles are so coherent that the sides of newly opened graves appear smooth as a wall, and this to the depth of fifteen feet. This singular phenomenon is thus accounted for by the local tradition. "Many years ago," runs the legend, "a

* Miss Jackson's "Shropshire Folklore," 100.

young man killed a priest in this place and was condemned to suffer death for murder, and sacrilege. His doom seemed inevitable, but by the intervention of his two sisters his life was granted him on condition that they should sift as much sand as would form a mound on which to build a church. The maidens readily undertook the task, and in process of time the church was built, although, it is added, one of the sisters died immediately after her brother's liberation, either from the effects of past fatigue, or overpowering joy. *

A note in Beesley's " Banbury " records that "the three churches of Bloxham, Adderbury, and King's Sutton were built by three masons, who were brothers; that the devil served them each as a labourer; and that one day he fell down with a hod of mortar and made Crouch Hill."

A local tradition represents Ormskirk Church, Lancashire, as having been erected at the cost of two maiden ladies (? sisters) named Orm, who, being unable to decide whether it should be a tower or a spire, accommodated their differences by giving it both. But Roby discredits the story, remarking that the old ladies might each have had her way, by building a tower and surmounting it by a spire. A more probable tradition states that the spire was attached to the original edifice, and that, on the suppression of Burscough Priory, the tower was built for the reception of eight of the bells taken thence, the remainder of the priory bells being removed to Croston church.

Another Lancashire tradition states that, during the building of Ashton-under-Lyne Church, whilst the workmen were one day amusing themselves at cards, a female unexpectedly presented herself. She asked them to turn up an ace, promising, in case of compliance, that she would build several yards of the steeple, upon which they luckily turned up the ace of spades. But, says Roby in his "Tra-

* Henderson's "Folklore of Northern Counties," 298.

ditions of Lancashire," this tale may owe its origin to the following circumstance : " Upon the marriage of Sir Thomas Assheton with the daughter of Ralph Stayley, a considerable accumulation of property was the consequence. This might induce him to repair the church, and perform sundry other acts of charity, and beneficence. Whilst the work was going on, Lady Elizabeth Assheton, it is not improbable, surprised the workmen at their pastime, and might desire that her arms should be fixed in the steeple, impaled with those of her husband. The shape of an escutcheon, having a considerable resemblance to a spade ace, in all likelihood gave origin to the fable."

In the south transept of Gloucester Cathedral is the so-called " Prentice's Bracket " in form, representing a builder's square. Two figures support it, curiously placed, the lower with a bag at his waist. It is traditionally said to be a memorial of the master-builder and his son, or prentice, but was, in all probability, a bracket for light.* At Lincoln, the south window is called the Prentice Window, from a tradition which has been told in reference to the " princes pillar " of Roslyn Chapel, and the spire of Norrey, that it was erected by an apprentice in the absence of his master, who on his return, being fired with a sudden impulse of jealousy, killed the unfortunate youth with a blow of his mallet. Furthermore, " the country folk," says Fuller, " have a tradition that the master-workman built Salisbury and his man Chichester ; whilst the one served as a guide across the interminable plains, the other is the only cathedral spire visible at sea." †

* R. J. King, " Handbooks to Cathedrals of England " (1864).
† See Mackenzie Walcott's " Traditions and Customs of Cathedrals," 222, 223.

CHAPTER III.

STRANGE STORIES AND TALES OF WONDER.

LEGENDS commemorative of supernatural and ghostly deeds have clustered round many of our cathedrals and parish churches.   In connection with Durham Cathedral the story goes that years ago a phantom army suddenly appeared, and rescued a certain devout worshipper from the hands of assassins, just as he had finished his orisons for the repose of departed souls.   Unexpectedly surprised, he fled into the burial ground for refuge, when "the graves bristled with swords and spears, starting out of the earth in his defence, and the long-buried captains for whom he had prayed rose up and came together clad in armour, their weapons in their fleshless hands, but without a sound, and so the ghostly band closed round him against his terrified enemies." *   A similar story is told of St. Bristan, a bishop of Winchester, who was in the habit of singing a psalter at midnight in the churchyard for repose of departed souls.   On one occasion, at the completion of his devotions, "up from the graves came the voices of the dead, and a great army, numberless, making answer, ' Amen.' "

A strange tale is told by an old writer † of a remarkable

* Mackenzie Walcott, "Traditions and Customs of Cathedrals " (1872), 214.

† Barthol. de Cotton, 457, 458.

event which happened about the close of the thirteenth century, in **Hereford** Cathedral. To quote his words, "it was a marvel almost inconceivable," for "a demon **in the choral** act of a canon sat in a stall after matins had **been sung, and** a canon came up to him to inquire the reason of his sitting there, thinking that he was one of his brother **canons.** The demon was dumb, and said not a word. The canon **was** beyond measure terrified, thinking it was the foul **fiend** himself; but he conjured it by the holy name of St. **Thomas** of Cantilupe not to stir from that place ; **he at once brought** assistance and bound it." The late Prebendary Mackenzie Walcott, who quotes this story, says **it** was harmless compared to the wrestling match **at** night between **St.** Wolstan and the **devil, in the gown of his servant, before the** very altar of **Worcester** Cathedral, leaving the prior breathless and **exhausted after** three **bouts.** The fiend vanished, but **"the sight of** that servant's face ever after **made** his stout-hearted antagonist tremble and turn pale."

Stories of strange encounters with terrible animals are still remembered in some parishes, memorials of which, **it is** said, are occasionally preserved in effigies and monuments.

The monster-slaying hero, for instance, makes his appearance in an old legend connected with Berrington Church, near Shrewsbury. In the south aisle there is a cross-legged effigy, representing some unknown knight of the **late** fourteenth, or early fifteenth, century. The **Rev. W. A.** Leighton, visiting the church, inquired of the parish clerk if **he** had ever heard whom the figure represented. "No," **said he;** "but **the** people of the neighbourhood always called him 'Owd Scriven **o'** Brompton.' **The** story goes that once upon **a time** when Scriven was going from Brompton to visit his lady-love at Eaton Mascott—two hamlets in Berrington parish,—just **by** the stile at the bottom of **the** 'Banky Piece,' he met with **a great** lion, 'the terror of the neighbourhood.'   But Owd Scriven happened to have his sword with him, and he attacked the lion, and, after a terrible tussle, overcame the beast, and cut him in two. And," added the clerk, " you may see a lion, cut in half just the same, lying under the feet of the image, and on the man's face you may see where the lion gave Owd Scriven a terrible scratch with his forepaw, and tore away half his cheek." *

In Nunnington Church, Yorkshire, there is an ancient tomb, by traditional account said to be that of Peter Loschy, a famous warrior, whose last exploit was killing a huge serpent or dragon, which infested the country round about.†
A similar legend is current at Slingsby, in the same county, where the villagers point to the effigies of Wyvill and his dog yet remaining in their church.   The story runs, as told by Roger Dodsworth, the antiquary, that " between Malton and Slingsby there was some time a serpent that lived upon prey of passengers, and which this Wyvill and his dog did kill, when he received his death wound.   There is a great hole half a mile from the town, round within, three yards broad and more, where the serpent lay.   In which time the street was turned a mile on the south side, which does still show itself if any takes pains to survey it."

Another story of the same kind tells how at Sexhow, a small hamlet four miles from Stokesley in Cleveland, a terrible worm or dragon one day made its appearance, and had so voracious an appetite that it took the milk of nine cows daily to satisfy its cravings.   When "not sufficiently fed, the hissing noise it made alarmed all the county round about, and its breath was so strong as to be absolutely poisonous, and those who breathed it died."   But "at length the 'monster's' day of doom dawned.   A knight

* " Transactions of the Shropshire Archæological Society," iii. 149.
† See " Leisure Hour," May, 1878 ; Parkinson's " Legends and Traditions of Yorkshire," 170–173.

clad in complete armour passed that way, whose name or country no one knew, and, after a hard fight, he slew the monster, and left it dead upon the hill, and then passed on his way. The inhabitants of the hamlet of Sexhow took the skin of the monster worm and suspended it in the church, over the pew belonging to the hamlet of Sexhow, where it long remained a trophy of the knight's victory, and of their own deliverance from the terrible monster."

In commemoration of another curious dragon legend, the owner of the manor of Sockburn, held under the bishopric of Durham, was required by the terms of his feudal tenure to meet every new bishop of that See upon the centre of the bridge at Croft which spans the river Tees, that separates Yorkshire from Durham, and there present before him an ancient sword, at the same time repeating these words : " My Lord Bishop, I here present before you the falchion wherewith the champion Conyers slew the worm, dragon, or the fiery-flying serpent, which destroyed man, woman, and child, in memory of which the king then reigning gave him the manor of Sockburn to hold by this tenure, that upon the first entrance of every bishop of Durham into the county, this falchion should be presented." Upon which the bishop took the weapon into his hand, and immediately returned it, wishing the Lord of Sockburn health and long enjoyment of his manor. This service is said to date from the time of Bishop Pudsey, who purchased from Richard I., for himself and his successors, the title of Earl of Sadberge. The falchion, it may be noted, appears in painted glass in a window of Sockburn Church, and, together with the worm, is sculptured in marble on the tomb of the ancestor of the Conyers family. A fragment of verse, too, well known in the neighbourhood, tells of— *

* Mr. Henderson thinks these lines may be safely ascribed to Mr. Sartees. See " Folklore of Northern Counties " (1876), 284, 285.

> " Sockburn, where Conyers so trusty
> A huge serpent did dish up,
> That had else ate the Bishop ;
> But now his old falchion's grown rusty, grown rusty."

This legend relating to Sockburn is not unlike one told of the Pollard worm. It appears that long ago a huge worm —probably a wild boar—inhabited the woods of Bishop Auckland, all attempts to kill or drive it away being in vain. After several knights and others who went to encounter it had been slain, the king issued a proclamation that whoever brought the boar's head to Westminster should receive a reward, and the bishop promised he would give a princely guerdon to any champion who was brave enough to get rid of this monster. Accordingly, a member of the Pollard family, after ascertaining its usual track, ascended a large beech tree, and shook down a quantity of ripe beechmast, patiently awaiting the creature's approach.

As he foresaw, it was arrested by the rich repast, and having eaten voraciously for some time, it moved away drowsily. At this crisis its antagonist suddenly appeared from his hiding-place, and, after a desperate struggle, vanquished his foe, severing the boar's head from the trunk. Worn out with fatigue, the brave hero fell into a deep sleep, but on awaking found the boar's head was gone, and with it the proof of his victory. But, undaunted, he rode off to Auckland, arriving at the gate just as the bishop was sitting down to dinner. After he had made known his exploit, the good bishop, true to his promise, sent word that he might take for his guerdon as much land as he could ride round during the hour of dinner. Thereupon the Pollard turned his horse's head and rode round Auckland Castle, thus making it, and all it contained, his own. His claim was acknowledged by the bishop, who gladly redeemed castle, goods, and chattels on the best terms he could granting the champion a freehold estate, still known as the Pollard's lands, with this condition annexed: the possessor was to meet every Bishop of Durham on his first coming to Auckland Castle, and to present him with a falchion, saying, "My Lord, I, on behalf of myself, as well as several others, possessors of Pollards' lands, do humbly present your lordship with this falchion at your first coming here, wherewith, as the tradition goeth, he slew of old a mighty boar which did much harm to man and beast. And by performing this service we hold our lands." *

Then there is the story of the Linton worm, the sculptured effigy of which may still be seen, with the champion who slew it, at the south-western extremity of Linton Church.

A stone, writes Mr. Henderson,† evidently of great antiquity, is built into the wall. It is covered with sculpture in low relief, and bears figures which, though defaced by time, can yet be made out pretty clearly. A knight on horseback, clad in a tunic or hauberk, with a round helmet, urges his horse against two large animals, the foreparts of which only are visible, and plunges his lance into the throat of one. Behind him is the outline of another creature, apparently of a lamb. The heads of the monsters are strong and powerful, but more like those of quadrupeds than of serpents. Popular tradition connects this representation with the Linton worm, and avers that the inscription below it—now quite defaced—ran thus—

> "The wode laird of Larristone
> Slew the Worme of Wormestone,
> And wan a' Linton parochine."

But whether "this effigy really represents some doughty deed by which the first Somerville won the favour of William the Lion, and was presented by him with the barony of

---

* "Folklore of Northern Counties," 287.
† Ibid, 295–297.

Linton, or visibly embodies the great conflict between Paganism and Christianity, has been a matter of dispute with antiquarians."

At Mordiford Church, Herefordshire, a dragon is represented in a painting as a winged serpent, about twelve feet long, with a large head and open mouth. It is in memory, says tradition, of a famous combat in the river Lug between a dragon and a condemned malefactor, who was promised pardon on condition that he destroyed his antagonist. He did so, but fell a victim to the poison of its breath.[*]

Hyssington Church, Shropshire, is remarkable for several cracks in the walls, caused, according to a local legend, by an enormous bull, which was the terror of the surrounding county, and which grew bigger and bigger every day. At last the people got the parson of Hyssington to exorcise him; whereupon, by constant reading of texts, the beast shrank into dimensions sufficiently small to allow of his being driven into the church. But, unfortunately, before he was completely extinguished, the parson's candle burnt out, and, ere the morning came, when the reading could be resumed, the bull swelled out again until he burst the church walls.

Miss Jackson, in her "Shropshire Folklore" (1883, 108), gives the story as taken down in 1881 from an old farmer named Hayward: "There was a very bad man lived at Bagbury Farm, and when he died it was said that he had never done but two good things in his life; and the one was to give a waistcoat to a poor old man, and the other was to give a piece of bread and cheese to a poor boy; and when this man died he made a sort of confession of this. But when he was dead his ghost would not rest, and he would get into the [farm] buildings in the shape of a bull, and roar till the boards and the shutters and the tiles would

[*] See "Folklore Record." 1878.

fly off the building, and it was impossible for any one to live near him. He never came till about nine or ten at night, but he got so rude at last that he would come about seven, or eight, at night, and he was so troublesome that they sent for twelve parsons to lay him. And the parsons came, and they got him under, but they could not lay him; but they got him in the shape of a bull all the time, up in Hyssington Church. And when they got him into the church, they all had candles, and one old blind parson, who knowed him, and knowed what a rush he would make, he carried his candle in his top-boot. And he made a great rush, and all the candles went out, all but the blind parson's, and he said, 'You light your candles by mine.' And while they were in the church, before they laid him, the bull made such a burst that he cracked the wall of the church from the top to the bottom, and the crack was left as it was for years, till the church was done up; it was left on purpose for people to see. I've seen it hundreds of times.

"Well, they got the bull down at last, into a snuff-box, and he asked them to lay him under Bagbury Bridge, and that every mare that passed over should lose her foal, and every woman her child; but they would not do this, and they laid him in the Red Sea for a thousand years."

Another version of the strange story, as told by Mr. Wright in his "Collectanea Archæologia" (vol. i. pt. i.) runs thus: "There was a wicked squire who lived at Bagley (*Bagbury*), and who made his men work over hours, swore at them, and gave them nothing to drink. At last one of them wished that he might be turned into a bull, and the wish took effect. But such a monstrous and wicked bull as he, did more harm than a dozen wicked squires; and, as there were no churches or parsons in that county then, the people were entirely at his mercy. At length Hyssington Church was built, and the people resolved to try and get the parson to talk to the bull and quiet him. So they assembled all round for miles, and drew closer and closer till they got him up to the church. The parson read texts to him all the way, and he continually grew smaller and tamer. Once inside the church, the parson began to preach, and the bull was slowly but steadily decreasing, when night came on before the work was finished. Only a small bit of candle could be found, and when it was burnt out the parson could see no longer, and was obliged to stop reading. The bull was then about the size of a dog, but as soon as the parson ceased he began to grow again, till he was larger than before. The church was not big enough to hold him, and the walls cracked around him. Next day the parson came again, and this time the people brought a good store of candles, and the reading went on without interruption, till the bull was so small that they could bind him up in a boot, which one of the congregation gave up for the purpose. They then buried him deep under the door-stone, where he lies to this day. There are believers in this story who affirm that were the stone to be loosened the bull would come forth again, by many degrees worse than he was at the first, and that he could never be laid again."

A curious illusion which has, at different times, excited a good deal of interest and excitement, is the phantom nun of Holy Trinity Church, Micklegate, York ; a full description of which is given by Mr. Baring Gould in his "Yorkshire Oddities." According to a legendary explanation of this strange scene, it is said that during the suppression of religious houses before the Reformation, a party of soldiers came to sack the convent attached to this church. But having forced an entry, they were confronted by the abbess, —a lady of great courage and devotion—who declared that they should only pass in over her body, and that should they slay her, and succeed in their errand of destruction, her spirit would haunt the place, until the time came that their sacrilegious work was expiated by the rebuilding of the holy house." *

Among the many accounts published of this apparition, we quote the following from the *Ripon and Richmond Chronicle* (May 6, 1876): "In the middle of the service, my eyes, which had hardly once moved from the left or north side of the [east] window, were attracted by a bright light, formed like a female, robed and hooded, passing from north to south with a rapid gliding motion outside the church, apparently at some distance. There are four divisions in the window, all of stained-glass; but at the edge of each runs a rim of plain transparent glass, about two inches wide, and adjoining the stone-work. Through this rim especially could be seen what looked like a form transparent, but yet thick (if such a term can be used) with light. The robe was long and trailed. About half an hour later it again passed across from north to south, and having remained about ten seconds only, returned with what I believed to have been the figure of a young child, and stopped at the last pane but one, and then vanished. I did not see the woman again ; but a few seconds afterwards the woman reappeared, and completed the passage behind the last pane very rapidly."

It is said to appear very frequently on Trinity Sunday, and to bring two other figures on to the scene, another female, called the nurse, and the child. Similarly at one of the windows of the Abbey Church, Whitby, was seen on certain occasions

> " The very form of Hilda fair,
>   Hovering upon the sunny air."

---

* Rev. Thomas Parkinson, "Yorkshire Legends and Traditions" (1888), p. 144.

an effect, it is said, of light and mist which is still sometimes visible.

In connection with the building of Durham Cathedral, a curious legend is told about an effigy which lies near the north porch; and Sir William Brereton, who travelled in the county in 1685, thus writes: "In the churchyard is the tomb of him that was steward, and disbursed the money when the church was erected, of whom it is reported that his money being paid over-night, his glove was by a spirit filled and supplied, so that, though it was empty over-night, it was replenished next morning. His hand is made holding a glove stuffed with money, and by this means was that great work built." But, according to another version of this legend, the figure is said to be in memory of a certain brave and daring man, who leaped from the great tower to the ground to win a purse of gold.

Then there is the familiar story of the milkmaid and the dun cow, which are carved on the north front of the cathedral. The story, as commonly told, is that, while St. Cuthbert was still undetermined as to his final resting-place, " it was revealed to Eadmer, a virtuous man, that he should be carried to Dunholme, where he should find a place of rest. His followers were in distress, not knowing where Dunholme lay; but as they proceeded, a woman, wanting her cow, called aloud to her companion to know if she had seen her, when the other answered that she was in Dunholme. This was happy news to the distressed monks, who thereby knew that their journey's end was at hand, and the saint's body near its resting-place. As a sequel to this story, it appears that the after-riches of the See of Durham gave rise to the proverb, "The dun cow's milk makes the prebends' wives go in silk."

In the porch of St. Mary Redcliffe Church, Bristol, is, or was, preserved a whale's bone, popularly reputed to be the rib of a monster **cow, which once supplied the whole city** with milk. **There are sundry** versions of this story. **At** Grimsargh, **near** Preston, Lancashire, tradition says that in a time of drought the inhabitants were supported on the milk **of a** gigantic dun cow, until an avaricious old woman milked her into a sieve, through which the milk passed into **a** succession of vessels constantly removed. At last the **cow** died, either of exhaustion, or of distress on discovering the imposture; and she was buried in a spot known as the Cow Hill, where it is said that huge bones have been **dis-**interred. A Warwickshire legend tells of a dun cow having been driven mad by the over-milking of a witch.[*]

Many curious stories are told of the appearance **of his** Satanic majesty in the course of a thunderstorm, **the truth** of which **was fully** credited in olden **days.**

Stow records, **for instance, a** strange legend, telling us **how the devil** came **down** to the belfry of St. Michael's, Cornhill, in **a** storm **of** lightning: "Upon St. James's night, certain men in the loft nest under the bells, ringing of a peal, a tempest of lightning and thunder did arise. An ugly-shapen sight appeared to them coming in **at the** south window, and lighted on the north. For fear **whereof** they all fell down, and lay as dead for the time, letting **the** bells ring and cease of their own accord. When the ringers came to themselves, they found certain stones of **the** north window **to be** raised and scratched, as if **they** had been **so** much butter printed with a lyon's claw; **the same** stones were fastened there again, **and** so remain **till** this **day.** I have seen them oft, and have put **a** feather **or** small stick into the holes where the claws had entered three or four inches deep." **In** August, **1577, a** terrible thunderstorm occurred at Bungay whilst the people were in church; during which, according **to a** contemporary pamphlet, "a

[*] C. Hardwick, "**Traditions,** Superstitions, **and** Folklore," **112.**

black dog, or the divel in such a likeness," ran down the body of St. Mary's, "with great swiftness and incredible haste," and wrung the necks of two men.　It is also reported that the "divel" once appeared in the somewhat inappropriate form of a Minorite friar, during a thunderstorm at Danbury, in Essex, in 1402, when the nave and great part of the chancel were destroyed.　But such "straunge shapes" have, in our days, been exorcised by lightning-conductors.

In a line due north of the east end of Walsingham Church was a portal admitting to the precincts, called the "Gateway of the Knight," from a story that a knight on horseback, pursued by his enemies, was on the point of being taken at the door, far too narrow for his passage, when he called on the Virgin for protection, and suddenly found himself safe within, horse and all.　A brass figure of a mounted knight was fastened to the portal.

There is the "Speaking Stone" at St. David's Cathedral. The little River Alan is crossed by two or more bridges * within the walls of the Close.　"These bridges," writes Mr. King, "are all ancient and interesting.　The most remarkable is that near the west front of the cathedral.　This bridge, replaced a stone known as the Llechllafar, or "Speaking Stone," described by Giraldus as a slab of marble polished by the feet of wayfarers.　It was not lawful to carry a dead body into the cemetery across this stone, which, when that indignity was on one occasion offered to it, lifted its voice in remonstrance, and split with the effort. A prophecy of Merlin foretold that a king of England, on his return from the conquest of Ireland, should die on this stone, wounded by a red-haired man.　The prediction was applied to Henry II. by a woman whose petition the king had rejected.　But before setting foot on the stone, Henry addressed it solemnly, and passed over unharmed to make his offerings before the shrine of St. David.

* "Handbook to the Cathedrals of Wales" (1873), 215.

CHAPTER IV.

THE CHURCH PORCH.

IN days of old the church porch was an important place, and many things that required publicity were usually done there. Thus it was at the church porch that the sheriff performed one of the preliminary processes in outlawry, and a writ of right was proclaimed there by his bailiffs with blast of trumpet. Upon the same principle, lists of voters, allowance of poor rates, notices of assessed taxes, etc., are still affixed on the church doors, that the parishioners may have an opportunity of seeing them if they go to church.[*]

In 1395 the Lollards fixed "their heretical conclusions on the doors of St. Paul's and Westminster, with various insolent verses. Bishop Hacket, on the doors of Lichfield, wrote up a Latin verse forbidding candidates for holy orders to wear long hair."[†]

In the same way payments of legacies and annuities in the church porch were no uncommon occurrence, and an early instance of this practice tells us how one Vincent Tuke, Vicar of Sunning, Berks, in 1592, left by will sundry sums of money, among others a legacy to each of his daughters "to be paid in the church porch." At Goosnargh in Lancashire, we find an entry of the seventeenth century

---

[*] *Notes and Queries*, 3rd series, xii. 359.
[†] "Traditions and Customs of Cathedrals," 111, 112.

relative to the transfer of some land. The deed is dated 1641, and tells how Alice Sidgreaves agrees to relinquish to James Sidgreaves certain lands on condition that he pays £130 on a certain day "att or within the south porch of the p'ishe church or chappell of Goosnargh." At Preston a similar case is recorded : "Articles of agreement, dated 20th Feb. 1650. Item, the sum of £200 to be paid at or in the south porch of the parish church of Preston, between the hours of ten and two of the clock on 20th March, 1652." Mr. North, in his "Church Bells of Leicestershire," quotes an entry dated April 14, 1462, whereby John Lea of Lutterworth, in consideration of 6s. 8d. paid to him annually in the south porch of the chapel of Market Harborough, bound himself to keep the chimes there in "good, sweet, solemn, and perfect tune of musick."

In the "Sussex Archæological Collections" (ix. 36) an extract illustrative of this custom is given from the will of John Miller, proved at Lewes, May 3, 1654. The testator leaves to his son Richard Miller certain property "upon condition that my said son Richard pay to my daughter, Anne Miller, £100 on her attaining the age of twenty-one, such sum to be paid at or in the south church porch of Chittingly." In some of the earlier deeds of property in Rye, Sussex, the rent reserved was made payable in the south porch of the church of Rye. In the will of one of the rectors of Maresfield, by which he bequeaths a small sum to be applied to educational purposes in the parish, he directs the owner of the property in Ringmer, on which it is charged, to pay it on a particular day, at twelve o'clock at noon, to the trustees, in the porch of the parish church of Maresfield.* A correspondent of *The East Anglian* (new series, i. 63) whilst making researches

---

* "Sussex Archæological Collections," xxii. 132.

at the Ipswich Probate Registry, found in the will of William Falckward, of Winston, Suffolk, yeoman, the following : "I give and bequeath to my sonne, Sill Reve, with Elizabeth, his wife, one shilling, to be paid to him or his wife, at the church porch of Winston by my executrix. Proved, 18 Oct., 1684."

Occasionally the church porch was supplied with a stone ledge, or dole-table, by way of counter, such as may be still seen in the south porch of St. Peter and St. Paul, Eye, with the remains of a suitable inscription.

In the time of Henry VII. it was no unusual occurrence to make money payments in the church itself in fulfilment of contracts. In an old deed quoted in the "Sussex Archæological Collections" (xxii. 119) we read how one John Archer, of Alfryston, left certain landed property on the understanding that his "attorneys, heirs, executors, or assigns, shall at the feast of St. Michael the Archangel in the Church of Alfriston, make payment of ten pounds sterling, and at the same feast of St. Michael then next following, in the aforesaid church, nine pounds sterling." Payment of money in a church, writes a correspondent of *Notes and Queries* (5th series, xi. 432), " is the practice in the Isle of Portland. Having completed the purchase of several strips of land, I gave notice that on a certain day I would attend in the church to pay over the purchase-money, and take in exchange the deed of 'church gift,' which was duly signed in the church, *coram populo*. The act is supposed to give due notoriety, and to have a peculiarly binding effect. I found the witnesses (not attesting), some fifteen or twenty in number, expected to have their presence acknowledged by some small payment in money."

Referring to business transactions performed in the church itself, it is worthy of note that, in times past, court rolls were occasionally kept in churches. Hallam, in his

"Middle Ages" (1872, ii. 283), translates from Hickes a document of the reign of Canute, relating to a dispute about the ownership of certain lands. The case was heard in the county court at Agelnothes-stane (which Hallam says is Alyston, in Herefordshire), and Thurkil, husband of one of the parties concerned, "rode to the church of St. Ethelbert, with the leave and witness of all the people," and had the result "inserted in a book in the church."

About 1542 John Dodington writes to William Plompton thus : "The cofer wherein your said court rowles lieth is nought, and the lock thereof not worth a pene, and it standeth in the church at Sacomp [Sacomb, county Hertford], wheare every man may come at his pleasure." In 1809 the court rolls of the Manor of Howden were kept in Howden Church.[*]

In 1326 the tithe corn of Fenham, Fenwick, and Bede was collected in the chapel of Fenham, and a manor-court, called Temple Court, was held in the Church of St. John Baptist, Dunwich, annually on the feast of All Souls. Wool was stored in one of the churches of Southampton, and a law-suit settled in St. Peter's Church, Bristol. Mr. Sparvel Bayly, in his "New Studies in Old Subjects," relates a case in Essex, where the non-resident incumbent came into the neighbourhood, and expressed a wish to perform service in his parish church. The principal farmer —the churchwarden—was consulted, but a difficulty presented itself. It was harvest-time, the weather had been showery and uncertain, and the churchwarden was obliged to reply that there had been deficiency in barn accommodation, and the church was full of wheat.

The Rev. D. R. Thomas, in his "History of the Diocese of St. Asaph" (297), writing of the town of Newmarket, in Flintshire, says, "The registers, which date from 1698,

* *Notes and Queries*, 7th series, viii. 305.

mention, under 1712, the interest of £5 given by Mr. Wynne, of Coppa'sheim, for the purchase of flannel for four old men and women, who were 'to draw lots' or 'throw dice' for it in the church porch."

A mode of punishment for robbing the churches in former days consisted in flaying the offender, and in affixing his skin to the church door. This penalty for sacrilege appears to have had the sanction of the law in the Anglo-Saxon period, when money was often paid by the offender to save his skin, called "hide gold," a ransom for one's skin.

There is an old tradition that the skin of a sacrilegious Dane was often nailed upon a church door. According to a story current in Worcester, the skin of a Dane, who stole the Sanctus bell, and was flayed in consequence, was placed on the doors of the north porch of Worcester, a portion of which remains in the crypt. Mr. Albert Wray, in the "Archæological Journal" (v. 185), thus writes on the subject: "Having heard that one of the doors of Worcester Cathedral had skin upon it, I wrote to Mr. Jabez Allies, of that city, and received a portion, and a drawing of the doors which had been removed into the crypt." And he adds that the skin on examination proved to have been taken from the body of a light-haired person. So at Westminster, the doorway leading into the revestry was lined with the tanned skin, as a memorial, it is said, of the deliverance of England from their rule ; but, in all probability, this leather, it has been suggested,* was made, as in the preceding case, from the skins of persons executed for sacrilege, and set up as a terror to less hardened thieves. Pepys in his Diary, under April 10, 1661, has this entry: "To Rochester, and there saw the cathedral . . . observing the great door of the church, as they say, covered with the skins of the Danes." Morant mentions a similar tradition re-

* "Traditions and Customs of Cathedrals," 114.

specting the Church of Copford, Essex, to the effect that the building "was robbed by the Danes, and their skins nailed to the doors."

In 1789, Sir Harry Englefield exhibited before the Society of Antiquaries, a plate of iron from the door of Hadstock Church, Essex, with a portion of human skin upon it. In 1846, the north door of Hadstock being much damaged, was removed; but part of the original woodwork, with the massive nails used to attach the skin, is preserved at Audley End.

Frequent notices of the right of refuge in the church porch occurs in old documents; a curious entry appearing in a corporation book of Norfolk, under 1662 : " Thomas Corbald, who hath a loathsome disease, have with his wife and two children layne in the Porch of St. Peter's per Mountegate above one year ; it is now ordered by the Court that he be put into some place in the Pest-houses during the pleasure of the Court, until the Lazar-houses be repaired." In an old church book in the parish of Diss, Norfolk, among the disbursements of Samuel Foulger, one of the churchwardens in 1687, is the following : " To the Wench Ellener, that laye in the Church Porch, at several times, £00 7s. 0d."

Chambered porches are found in many English churches, chiefly during the Early English and Decorative periods. It has often been asked, What was the use of these chambers? A query to which many answers have been given. Sometimes they have been designated "priests' chambers ; " and other names for them are muniment rooms, vestries, and libraries, from the local uses for which they have been employed. But the chambered porch was probably intended for the sacrist and guardian of the church—a necessary official where there were very valuable relics, and other things, to be protected. Pugin, in his

" Present State of Ecclesiastical Architecture " (1843, 20), describes the chambered porch as " usually occupied by the sacristan, and sometimes provided with tracery apertures through which the church could be watched at night." This is confirmed by the records at Southwell, which require the sacrist " to be within the church," and to be " ready to ring the bells," etc. At Lincoln, Canterbury, and Rochester, " the watcher's door and chamber are still remembered by name, which were used by men who patrolled the church at night, to see that all was safe from robbers and fire. At Worcester, Oxford, and Lichfield the galleries used for this purpose still remain." *

The chambered porch has also been called the " leper's gallery," where persons suffering from loathsome diseases could join in the divine offices without offending the congregation.   But this seems an improbable explanation ; for, as it has been pointed out, " the approach to them is generally by a stair communicating with the interior of the church, so that a leper, or other sufferer, would first have to enter the sacred building."

Occasionally the chambered porch is described as a " schoolroom," and numerous instances occur of its having been used for this purpose. The old charity school of Cheltenham was formerly carried on over the north porch of the parish church,† and the following entry occurs in the minute book of the chamber of Feoffees of Colyton, A.D. 1660 : " Ordered alsoe that Edward Clarke have notice that hee shall departe from keepinge of schole from the chamber over the church porch." ‡   A clause in the will of John Gines, citizen of London, haberdasher and schoolmaster within St. Sepulchre's Church, 1592, directs that his

---

* " Traditions and Customs of Cathedrals," 114.
† See " History of Cheltenham " (1863), pp. 156, 424.
‡ See *Notes and Queries*, 5th series, passim.

body be buried in the "lower end of the church, at the stayre foote that goeth up to my school." In St. Michael's loft in the [Priory Church, Christchurch, Hants, a school was formerly held; and a correspondent of *Notes and Queries* (5th series, xii. 37), writes : " I was at Malmesbury on Tuesday, May 27, 1879, and on ascending the stairs to the chamber above the grand Norman porch of the Abbey Church, I discovered a school of about thirty children being conducted there. It is called the Abbey School." Another correspondent, 1879 (5th series, xii. 197), says, " being at Selby Abbey Church two or three weeks ago with a friend, we scented out the bluecoat school of the place, which is carried on in a chamber over the chapel, or, as some think, chapter house, now used as a vestry. A newel staircase connects the school-room with the outer air, so the boys have no right of way through the church as they go to and from their daily tasks."

A paragraph in the manuscripts of Lord Coleraine in 1697, speaking of the church porch at Tottenham, Middlesex, says, " It has a good square room with a chimney, leaded on the top, with brick battlement for the teacher." This room has in recent years been used for the Sunday school ; as also the chambered porch at Colby Church, Norfolk ; and some years ago the one at Berkeley Church, Gloucestershire, was used for the same purpose.

Dr. Lee, in his "Glossary of Liturgical and Ecclesiastical Terms" (1877, 268), defines "parvis" as a church porch over which is erected a chamber; and hence the term, " keeping school in the parvise." But there has been some difference of opinion on this point, and Mr. J. A. Picton writes : * " It seems to be admitted on all hands that there is not the slightest evidence that a church porch, or the room over it, was ever called a *parvise* in mediæval times,

* *Notes and Queries,* 5th series, xii. 49.

and that the derivation of the word, 'parvis pueris ibi edoctis,' is utterly untenable. There is no record to be found of any school having been kept in the *parvise*, wherever and whatever that may be." He would regard the term parvis as a survival of the "paradisus" of mediæval cathedrals—an enclosure in front of the sacred building. And he adds, "it was used for various public purposes. The sacred relics were occasionally exhibited there while the chapter intoned the *Gloria* from the exterior arcades of the church. Here also was erected the scaffold or pillory for the punishment of delinquent clerics. There is evidence that a *parvis* formerly existed at the west end of St. Paul's, and it is no doubt to this that Fortescue (De laudibus Legum. Angl., iii. 124) alludes when he describes the students from the Inns of Court after dinner, " Se devertunt ad *pervisum* et alibi consulentes cum servientibus ad legem et aliis consiliariis suis." The law students attended there to consult the serjeants who frequented the parvis as a place of general resort to see there clients, and bring themselves before the public. It is in this sense that the hackneyed quotation from Chaucer's prologue is to be understood—

> " A serjeant at law, ware and wise,
> That had often been at the parvise."

In the absence of any real *parvis* in the English churches, the church porch and the room over it, where there happened to be one, might occasionally be called by the name. Cotgrave, writing in the early part of the seventeenth century, interprets Fr. *parvis* as " the porch of a church," but adds, "more properly, the utter part of a palace." But that schools were often held in some part of the church is clear from " Twelfth Night " (act. iii. sc. 2), where Maria speaks of " a pedant that keeps a school i' the church."

Many of these chambered porches are of special interest. The north porch of St. Mary's, Redcliffe, is hexagonal, and has perhaps no equal for beauty in England. There are two chambers, an upper and a lower. The small upper room has been made famous as the place where the unfortunate Chatterton professed to have discovered in an old chest, which went by the name of " Canynges' Cofre," manuscripts attributed by him to Rowley, a monk. The fragments of the coffer are still preserved in their original place in the attic of the porch.

Fine specimens of Early English chambered porches exist at Norwich, at Christ Church, Hampshire, where the chamber is lighted by two pairs of couplets on each side, the access being by a circular stone staircase leading from the north aisle, and at St. Cross, near Winchester. At Bishop's Cleeve, Gloucestershire, the lower part of the porch is Norman, but the chamber is later, with a pointed window.

Perpendicular examples are to be met with at Gloucester, where the chamber is over the south porch; and at Hereford, where it covers the north porch, and is lighted by three large windows with rich tracery. At Berkeley, the porch is Decorated, but the chamber Perpendicular. A late instance occurs at St. Peter in the East, Oxford; and in the small but fine Perpendicular example at St. Mary, Bridport, there is a beautiful little oriel of two lights, filled in with modern stained glass. The chamber here is approached from the south aisle of the church, as in St. George's, Doncaster, which was destroyed by fire in 1883.

Until the time of Edward VI., marriages were performed in the church porch, when it was discountenanced, the ecclesiastical reformers ordaining that the ceremony should be solemnized in the body of the church. In the Anglo-Saxon ritual, the parties to be married came to the porch of

the church with their attendants, **where they were met by**
the priest, **who** first blessed the **ring, and then gave it to**
the bridegroom, who placed it **on** the middle finger **of the**
bride's left hand. **Then** the priest recited a form of **blessing
over the parties,** after which he led them into the chancel,
where they remained during the Mass.

The mode of procedure, as directed by the Sarum Missal,
was thus. The parties standing at the church door, **the**
priest published the banns thrice. The woman was **given**
by her father, or friends, having her hand **uncovered, if**
single; if a widow, covered. The man said, **"I N, take**
thee N to my wedded wife, **to** have and **to** hold from this
day forward, for better for worse, for richer for poorer, in
sickness **and in** health, till death us depart, if holy Church
will **it** ordain, **and thereto I** plight thee **my** troth." **The
woman said as above, "to be** boner and buxom in bed and
at board till **death us** depart," **etc.** The man then gave the
ring to the priest, who, having blessed it, and sprinkled it
with holy **water,** returned it to him to put on with his three
fingers and thumb, repeating at each, " In the name of the
Father, Son, and Holy Ghost. Amen." After saying some
prayers, they went into the church to the steps of the **altar,**
the priest saying other prayers as now.[*]

It was at the church porch that Chaucer's **wife of Bath
was** wedded to the five husbands she **survived—**

> **" She was** a worthy woman all her live,
> Husbands at the church dore had she **five."**

In September, 1299, the primate **solemnized the** marriage
of Edward and Margaret at the church door of Canterbury,
towards the cloister, near the door of St. Thomas the
Martyr. The practice was **not** confined to this country,
and that it prevailed **in** France much later than in England

---

[*] See Gough's " British Topography " (1780), ii. 321. See i. 412.

is shown by Charles I.'s marriage (by proxy) with Henrietta Maria at the door of Nôtre Dame.

At St. Oswald's Church, Gruseley, the old customs of "porch marriages" and "horse marriages," writes Mr. W. H. Hatton, in his "Churches of Yorkshire," p. 32, were formerly observed. "One reason for performing the ceremony at the church porch may have been through the custom of the wedding-party going to church on horseback. At Gruseley, the bride and bridegroom, on horseback, preceded by the village pipers and fiddlers, went in procession along the lanes. There was a long strap fastened to the bride, which the bridegroom held fast in order to prevent her from falling off the horse. If there was not a sufficient number of animals in the village to accommodate the whole of the guests, then two would ride on the back of one horse. The custom, somewhat modified, was occasionally carried out at Gruseley at the commencement of the present century."

It was formerly, also, customary to pay a bride's dower, or to deliver the deed by which land or money was secured to her, at the church porch—a practice which continued as late as the seventeenth century. In Bridge's "History of Northamptonshire" (i. 135), we read how "Robert Fitz-Roger, in the 6 Edward I., entered into an engagement with Robert de Tybetot to marry, within a limited time, John, his son and heir, to Hawisia, the daughter of the said Robert de Tybetot, to endow her at the church door, on her wedding-day, with lands amounting to the value of one hundred pounds per annum."

It may be remembered, too, that in the early ages of the Christian Church, it was customary to bury persons of rank, or of eminent sanctity, in the church porch, none being allowed to be buried within the church itself.* St. Awdry,

---

* See Brand's "Popular Antiquities," ii. 245.

who was a victim of the pestilence in 669, and St. Chad, who died in 672, with others of reputed sanctity, were amongst the first to be buried within the church porch. Among the many legends told of St. Swithin, there is the well-known one which relates how his corpse, not being allowed to enter the church, was placed in the church porch, where it remained forty days, during which time it rained incessantly.

Coming down to a later period, John Crouche, Mayor of Rye in the years 1491 and 1495, gave the following directions in his will relating to his burial: "I leave my soul to God the Father, and Son, and Holy Ghost, and my body to be buried in the church burying-place, in the south porch of the parish church of Rye."

Further instances of this mode of burial occur in the churchwardens' accounts of Banwell, Somersetshire, where we find these two entries: "1521. Recd. Robert Cabzu, for lyying of his wyffe in the porch, 3*s.* 4*d.* Recd. of Robert Blundon, for lying of his wyffe in the church, 6*s.* 8*d.*"

In Yorkshire it was long customary for young people to sit and watch in the church porch on St. Mark's Eve from eleven at night until one o'clock in the morning. In the third year—for this ceremony must be gone through three times—it was supposed the ghosts of all those about to die in the course of the ensuing year would pass into the church. When any one was taken ill who was thought to have been seen in this manner, it was quickly whispered he would not recover, "for that such a one, who has watched St. Mark's Eve, says so." James Montgomery, in his "Vigil of St. Mark," has thus described this curious piece of folk-lore—

> " 'Tis now,' replied the village belle,
>   ' St. Mark's mysterious eve ;
> And all that old traditions tell
>   I tremblingly believe.

> " ' How, when the midnight signal tolls
>   Along the churchyard green,
>   A mournful train of sentenced souls,
>   In winding-sheets are seen.
>
> " ' The ghosts of all whom death shall doom
>   Within the coming year,
>   In pale procession walk the gloom,
>   Amid the silence drear.' "

Such are some of the principal uses to which the church porch has been applied in times past. But, at the present day, little of interest attaches to this once important spot. Old customs have ceased to be observed, and with their disuse the church porch has lost most of its romance of bygone years.

CHAPTER V.

MANY curious and instructive instances of the various ways whereby the discipline of the Church was enforced, in bygone times, are to be found in our old parish books and registers. Thus persons convicted of "grievous and notorious crimes" were required to make an open confession of the same, and to make satisfaction for the scandal caused by their evil example by doing penance in their parish church. Attired in a white sheet, and carrying a faggot, the offender was placed in some conspicuous place in the sacred edifice until, in the presence of the parishioners, a public acknowledgment of the wrong committed was made in a prescribed form of words.

Among the early instances of this practice may be quoted that of Agnes Black, in the church of Fen Ditton, Cambridgeshire : "Sexto die mensæ Januarii, anno 1593. Parte of penance injoyned unto Agnes Black, of Fen Ditton. The saied penitent shall uppon Sunday, beinge the eighte daie of February next cominge, clothed in a white sheete downe to the grounde, and havinge a white wande in her hand, resort unto the parish churche porche of Fen Ditton aforesaid, and there shall stande from the second peele to morninge prayers untill the readinge of the seconde lesson, desiringe the people that passe into the cherche to praie to

God for her, and to forgive her; at which time the minister there shall come down to this penitent and fetche her into the churche, reading the psalm of Miserere in Englishe, and place her in the middle alley, aparte from all other people, where she shall penitently kneel until the readinge of the ten commandments, at which time the minister there shall come to this penitent and cause her to saie and confesse as followethe, viz. : 'Good people, I acknowledge and confesse that I have offended Almightie God, and by my evill example you all, for that I have broken His divine laws and commandments, in committinge the most shameful and abominable sinne of adulterie, or fornicacion, for which I am most hartily sorry, and I ask God and you most hartily forgiveness for the same, promisinge by God's helpe never to offend hereafter in the like againe.' And at the end of this confession, the first daie, the minister to rede the homely against adultrie or fornicacion, and the third daie to reade the homely of repentance, the penitent standinge by all the while; and in like manner and form in every point and condicion as above is prescribed, she shall doe two other Sundaies or holy daies next ensueinge after the first. And if the penitent doeing this uppon all the saied three severall Sundaies or holy daies, she shall under the hands of the minister and churchwardens there personallie certifie together with those present the xxvii daie of February, at Greate St. Maries church in Cambridge, and then and there receave such further order herein as shall be appointed.—Bennet Thorowgood.

"This penitent hath donne hir pennance three several Sundaies or holy daies in the parish church of Fen Ditton, according to the premis. Ita est ut testatum. Thomas Godbed, Cur. ibid. church.—By me, Edward Warden Brady."

The register of Croydon, Surrey, under 1597, records how "Margaret Sherioux was buried 23rd June. She was enjoyned to stand iij. market days in the town and iij. Saboathe daies in the church, in a white sheete, with a paper on her back and bosom showing her sinne, . . . She stood one Saturday and one Sunday, and died the nexte." The offence of which she pleaded guilty having been one of terrible immorality.

Archbishop Grindal ordered the guilty person to be "set directly over against the pulpit during the sermon or homily, and there stand bareheaded with the sheet, or other accustomed note of difference, and that upon some board raised a foot and a half at least above the church floor." Penance of this kind was commonly performed after a judicial sentence, the mode of procedure being given by Godolphin in his 'Repertorium Canonicum" (1680, Append., p. 18): "Besides these greater censures, ecclesiastical penance is used in the discipline of the Church, which doth affect the body of the penitent, by which he is obliged to give a public satisfaction to the Church for the scandal he hath given by his evil example."

In the visitation articles for Peculiars of Canterbury, 1637, an order is made "for you, the Churchwardens at the charge of your parish, to provide a convenient large sheet and a white wand, to be had and kept within your Church or Vestry, to be used at such time as offenders are censured for their grievous and notorious crimes."

Paul's Cross was sometimes appointed as the place of penance; and, occasionally, it was enjoined that the sinner should do a public penance in the cathedral or in some public market, bare-legged and bare-headed, in a white sheet, and to make an open confession of his crime "according to the quality of the fault and the direction of the judge." In "Hierurgia Anglicana" (1848, p. 198) is a "form of penance and reconciliation of a renegado" of the date of 1635, quoted from Wilkins' "Concilia" (1737, iv.

522); and further on (p. 333) we find a note of one Richard Appleby, who did penance at Whorlton, Northumberland, in 1626; and at (p. 343) is noticed the penance imposed upon certain parishioners of Hulme Chapel, in 1689.

Constant reference is made to this practice of public penance in parish documents, some of which are of comparatively recent date. In the eighteenth century such notices are of frequent occurrence, and afford interesting examples of church discipline. On November 25, 1717, at Sutton Vallence, Kent, the register tells how "Eliz. Stace did public penance for yᵉ foul sin of adultery committed with Thos. Hutchins, junʳ., in Sutton Vallence Church, as did Anne Hynds for ýᵉ foul sin of fornication committed with Tho. Daws. Sa. Prat., Vicar." At Uxbridge Church, Middlesex, this entry occurs: "1728. N.B. On July 7, Unity Winch did penance at morning service for 26 May." In the parish register of North Aston, Oxfordshire, we find this entry: "Memorandum. That Mr. Cooper sent in a form of penance by Mr. Wakefield, of Deddington, that Catherine King should do penance in yᵉ Parish Church of North Ashton, yᵉ sixth day of March, 1740, and accordingly she did. Witness, William Vaughan, Vicar. Charles May, John Baillis, Churchwardens." The sin of the penitent seems to have been unchastity. The following is from the parish register of Roxby, Lincolnshire: "Memorandum. Michⁱ. Kirby and Dixon Wid had two bastard children, one in 1725, yᵉ other in 1727, for which they did publik Penance in our P'ish Church, Feb. yᵉ 25th, 1727, for adultery." In the churchwardens' accounts of Little Glemham, Suffolk, these items occur under December 10, 1764: "Pᵈ. the 'Paritor when the Widow Chrisp did penance, 5s.; for yᵉ use of a sheet and washing it, 6d."

In the latter half of the last century, a young woman who

had been seduced **did penance in Poulton Church, Lanca**-shire, and "barefoot, clothed in white, with a lighted candle in each hand, **she had** to pass along the aisles, **a** spectacle of mirth **and** jeering to an unfeeling crowd." **Jane** Breckul **was the** last **to** undergo this painful exhibition at Poulton, **for the** cries of this unfortunate girl, melting the hearts of the well-disposed, raised a clamour against it, which led **to** its discontinuance. In the belfry of Bispham parish church was formerly to be seen "a simple-looking wooden frame, formed of four pieces of wood with cross-bars, etc. This was said to have been used as **a** penance stool; the offending parties having been fastened to **it** by means **of** cross-pieces of wood." **A** woman who died in 1836, it **is** said, was **the last offender who** performed penance **in** Bispham Church and stood **upon** this stool.*

Coming **down to the** present **century, an** early case is **recorded in the** "Annual Register" for 1838 : "**A** woman **did penance** in public at Walton Church, by order of the Ecclesiastical Courts, for defaming the character of her neighbour. The white sheet, however, was not enforced." The following incident also occurred somewhere about **the** same time : "A poor female, one Elizabeth Ripley, **of** Skirethorns, **in** the parish of Linton, in Craven," **writes a** correspondent of *Notes and* **Queries** (5th series, iii. 154), " did penance in the Parish Church of Linton, and was wrapped in **a** white sheet; **she** had **a** lighted candle **in one hand.** **Her** offence was having an illegitimate child."

A remarkable case of penance occurred **in** 1840, the details **of** which were published **in a** chap-sheet, "Par-ticulars of a most Singular Penance, performed in St. Peter's Church, Liverpool, this (Wednesday) morning (February 19, 1840)." "For some time past the Fish Market in Liverpool has been in **a** state of **the greatest**

* Harland's " Lancashire Legends," 170, 174.

confusion and uproar, owing to a dispute between two well-known characters in the fish line. We are told that the parties, some time since, had a regular row, in the course of which Mrs. Hutton had the unwarrantable audacity to call Mrs. Newton the very impertinent and opprobrious name ——, for which offence Mrs. Newton instituted proceedings against her in the Ecclesiastical Court. These proceedings were last week brought to a trial, and Mrs. Hutton was found guilty of scandal, and adjudged to pay all expenses, and afterwards to stand in a sheet in St. Peter's Church, and make a public declaration of her assertion being false. Accordingly this day, Wednesday [February 19, 1840], was appointed for the ceremony to take place. For some time before the appointed time a vast number of persons of all grades had assembled in the neighbourhood of the church, and when the doors were opened an immense number entered the church in order to have a glimpse of the degrading ceremony. All was suspense for a time, but at length the woman made her appearance, attired in a white sheet, walked up the aisle, and after some ceremony being performed by the officers of the court, she made a public recantation of the expressions she had made use of, and declared that she was sorry for what she had said."

Penance was done in St. Bridget's Church, Chester, about 1851. The sentence was that the individual convicted should stand for about an hour in a white sheet within the church, but the church doors were ordered to be locked, that the penance might be private. As lately as 1882 a case occurred at East Clevedon, and was thus noticed in the local press : "An extraordinary scene was witnessed on Sunday evening, July 30th, at All Saints' Church, when a man named Llewellyn Hartree did public penance for the seduction of a servant-girl, who now awaits her trial for manslaughter. The church was crowded, and the vicar having delivered an address on church discipline, Hartree confessed his sin, and promised to take his place in the Assize Court, next to the unfortunate girl, upon her trial at Wells."

But that offenders were not always willing to comply with this mode of penance may be gathered from the following extract from Middleham Register, which runs thus: "Burials, October 29th, 1792. I enter under the head of burials, as spiritually dead, the names of John Sadler, Clerk to Mr. John Breare, Attorney-at-Law, of this place, and Christopher Felton, Clerk to Mr. Luke Yarker, Attorney-at-Law, of this place : first, for irrelevant behaviour in church a second time after public reproof on a former occasion of the same sort ; and secondly, when mildly admonished by me not to repeat the same, they both made use of the most scandalous and insolent words concerning myself, for which I thought proper to pass a public censure upon them after sermon (though they were wilfully absent) in the face of the congregation, and enter the mention of the same in this book that the names of those insolent young men may go down to posterity as void of all reverence to God and his ministers.—Witness my hand, ROBERT B. NICKOLLS, Dean."

Cases of this kind were probably not uncommon ; and even occasionally when the required form of penance had been fulfilled it was an empty show. About the middle of the present century a female did penance at St. Mary's Church, Islington, for defamation of female character. "I saw the virago," writes a correspondent of *Notes and Queries*,* "leave the church, and when clear of consecrated ground, she acted in a most indecorous manner, which proved that she was not either 'sadder' or 'wiser' for what

---

* 5th series, iii. 154.

she had undergone." We may also quote the following entry from the register of Scotter, Lincolnshire : " 1667–8 Jan. 19. Mem. That on Septuagesima Sunday one Francis Drury, an excommunicate person, came into the church in time of divine service in yᵉ morning, and being admonisht by me to be gon, hee obstinately refused, whereupon yᵉ whole congregation departed ; and after the same manner in the afternoon the same day he came againe, and refusing againe to goe out, the whole congregation again went home, soe yᵗ little or noe service p'formed yᵗ day. I prevented his further coming in yᵗ manner, as he threatened, by order from the justice upon the statute of Q. Elizabeth concerning the molestation and disturbance of public preachers. —" Wᴍ. Caʀɪɴɢᴛoɴ, Rector. *O tempora ! O mores !* "

The vigorous exercise of discipline in olden times is further shown by the excommunication of persons for trivial rather than grave offences. Thus, in 1667–8, one " Matthew Whalley of Scawthorp was excommunicated March 24, "*p̃ non solvendo taxat eccl'iæ ;*" and in the register of Quorndon, Leicestershire, it is recorded that " an excommunication against Anne Turlington, the wife of Thomas Turlington, in not sending an inventory by order of the Ecclesiastical Court in Leicester was published this 4th day of Feb. 1749–50 by me, Moor Scribo."

Even churchwardens did not always escape, for it appears that at All Saints, Northampton, they were excommunicated on Jan. 12, 1637–8, for disobeying the archbishop's monition respecting the railing in of the communion-table.

The homily on keeping clean of churches, speaks of " minstrelsy dogs and hawks profaning them." To prevent any breach of church discipline by the intrusion of dogs in the sacred edifice during divine worship, an official, known as the " dog-whipper," was paid an annual stipend to keep watch. Numerous entries illustrative of this practice occur

in many of the parish registers and **churchwardens' accounts.**
It has been said that the custom of **introducing dogs in the**
church was **due to the** Puritan faction, to show **their con-**
tempt for consecrated places. **In** 1571, **as appears from**
the **church** books of St. Mary's, Reading, **John Marshall**
was chosen clerk and sexton, and for **the sum of** 13*s.* 4*d.*
he was "to see the church kept clean from time to time,
the seats swept, the mats beaten, the dogs driven **out of**
the church, the windows made clean, and all other things
done that shall be necessary for the good and cleanly
keeping of the church, and the quiet of divine service."

At Worksop, in 1597, the sum of ninepence was "**paid**
to old Verde for whipping of dogs," and "for whipping
dogges out **of** y* church one whole year," **the** sum of
twelve pence was given in **1616. In** the churchwardens'
accounts of Smarden, Kent, this entry occurs under 1576:
"**Pd. to John Quested,** for whipping dogs out **of** the
churche xij*d.* ;" **and** in the parish accounts of Ogbourn St.
George, near Marlborough, similar instances of such payments are given—

"1632. To Looker for whippinge the doggs out **of the**
church for one quarter, xij*d.*

"1633. To Looker for keepinge out doggs **a whole**
year, iiij*s.*

"1639. To Looker for keepinge the dogs, **etc., ij*s.*"**

The "dog-noper," an official appointed for **this** purpose,
still holds office at Ecclesfield; **and in the records** of
Goosnargh, Lancashire, it was ordered (April **10,** 1704)
that the sexton, "so long as he demean himself dutifully,
do sweep **the** church, and whip **the dogs out of** it every
Lord's day. . . ."

The churchwardens of Trysull, Staffordshire, still receive
an annuity of one pound a year under the will **of John**
Rudge, dated April 17, **1725. He** charged his **lands for**

ever with the payment of five shillings a quarter to a poor man, who was to walk up and down the parish church during divine service, for the double purpose of driving stray dogs out of the church, and of waking up any of the congregation who went to sleep during the sermon. A similar rent-charge of eight shillings a year is paid at Claverley, in Shropshire, under a deed dated August 23, 1659. According to Edwards's "Remarkable Charities" (222), "ten shillings a year is paid by the tenant of Sir John Bridges, as a charge on lands called "Dog-whipper's marsh, containing about two acres, to a person for keeping order in the church during divine service." In the churchwardens' accounts of the parish of Bradeston Church, Norfolk, under 1544 occurs this entry: "It. paid for a hesppe of twynne for yᵉ nette at yᵉ church dore, ij ob," which, it has been suggested, was placed in the church doorway during service to keep dogs out.

It would seem that in 1644 Canterbury Cathedral either had no dog-whipper among its officers, or that he performed his work but negligently. Richard Culmer, in his "Cathedral Newes from Canterbury," relates how "one of the Great Canons, or prebends [there], in the very act of his low congying towards the Altar, as he went up to it, in prayertime, was (not long since) resaluted by a huge mastiffe dog, which leapt upright on him once and againe, and pawed him in his ducking saluting progresse and posture to the Altar, so that he was fain to call out aloud, ' Take away the dog, take away the dog.'" At Chichester, the duty of the verger, who has charge of the cloister, was formerly to "purge the churchyard of hogs and dogs and lewd persons that play or do noise therein." At St. David's and Durham the dog-whipper is a statutable servant; and in 1632 it is recorded how dogs ran into the choir of the latter and disturbed the service. In the life-size portrait of old

Scarlett, the **sexton, hung in** the **nave of** Peterborough Cathedral, his dog-whip **is seen** thrust **through his waist-**belt. **In the** register **of St.** Mary-le-Bow, Durham, **this** entry **occurs:** " **Brian Pearson, the** Abbey dog-whipper, bur. **6 April.**"

Dogs, however, **were** probably not **the only intruders.** The following entry, **for** instance, taken **from a church-**warden's private book, is preserved in the " History **of the** Church of Chester-le-Street : " " Aug. 10, 1834. **In the** middle of the morning service Joseph Lewin's ass passed through the church, and in the afternoon **a hen and** chickens. Both occurred in time of divine service."

Irregularities of good behaviour, and **order, during service-**time in church, **were formerly** regulated **by** rules **for en-**forcing **discipline which** nowadays **are** practically obsolete. **Reverence in the** house **of** God apparently **was** often lax. **According to a** popular rhyme—numerous variations of **which occur in** different parts of the country—the abuse of church-going which much prevailed in bygone years, and which, alas ! no doubt still exists to a large extent, is thus summed up in the West of England—

> " Some go to church to fetch a walk,
> Some **go** to church to have a talk,
> Some go to church to meet a friend,
> Some go there an hour to spend,
> **Some go** there to hear the news,
> **Some go** there to sleep in pews,
> **And yet,** 'tis very strange and odd
> How few go there to worship God."

A Suffolk **version is** slightly different—

> " **Some** go to church just for a walk,
> **Some** go there to scoff and talk,
> **Some go there** to meet a friend,
> **Some go there** their **time** to spend,

> Some go there to see a lover,
> Some go there their faults to cover,
> Some go there to doze and nod,
> But few go there to worship God."

In 1736 the churchwardens of Prestwich, near Manchester, resolved that " thirteen shillings a year be given to George Grimshaw, of Rooden Lane, for yᵉ time being ; and a new coat (not exceeding twenty shillings) every other year, for his trouble and pains in wakening sleepers in yᵉ church, whipping out dogs, keeping children quiet and orderly, and keeping yᵉ pulpit and church walks clean." Later 'on, these entries occur—

" Pᵈ for a coat for George Grimshaw, yᵉ new bobber, £1.

" Pᵈ George Grimshaw's yearly wages for bobbing, etc. 13/s."

What the term " bobbing " denoted may be briefly explained by the following note :* " My mother, who was born at Warrington in the last century, can remember Betty Finch, a very masculine sort of woman, being the bobber at Holy Trinity Church in the year 1810. She walked very majestically along the aisles during divine service, armed with a great long stick like a fishing-rod, which had a bob fastened to the end of it ; and when she caught any sleeping or talking, they got a " nudge." Her son was engaged in the belfry, and often truthfully sang—

> " My father's the clerk,
> My sister's a singer ;
> My mother's the bobber,
> And I'm a ringer."

This custom, whilst varying in different localities, gave rise to many amusing incidents. On Midlent Sunday, in 1795, when the Vice-Chancellor, Dr. Yates, Master of St. Catherine's Hall, Cambridge, went over to Burwell, which

---

* *Notes and Queries*, 3rd series, iv. 71.

is four miles from Newmarket, to preach the annual sermon, a somewhat exciting scene took place, which is thus described in Gunning's " Reminiscences of the University and town. of Cambridge" (ii. 12) : " The excellence of the tenant's ale was apparent, not only in the red face of the vicar, the clerk, and the sexton ; but also in the vigour with which two or three officials, furnished with white staves, exercised them whenever they found any of the children inattentive. Not contented with showing their authority over the younger part of the congregation, one of them inflicted so heavy a blow on the head of a young man who was sleeping, that it resounded through the church. The person thus distinguished started up, and, rubbing his head, had the mortification to find all his neighbours laughing at his expense ; to use a fancy phrase, " he showed fight," and I believe he was only restrained by the presence of the Vice-Chancellor (who rose to see what was the matter) from giving the peace-officer a hearty drubbing."

At Handsworth Church, near Birmingham, the beadle, attired in his official costume, used to make the rounds of the church during service, carrying a stout wand, surmounted with a gilt knob. This instrument, we are told, " he used in waking up sleepy boys and girls ; the unruly ones he admonished by a sharp tap on the head, which could be distinctly heard all over the church." At Fleet parish church, Lincolnshire, this practice having some years ago fallen into disuse, a former rector expressed to the sexton his wish that it might be revived, and provided him with a new instrument for the purpose. The sexton seemed reluctant to resume his old duties, remarking—

" Well, but, sir, be I to waken *all* of 'em ? Be I to nope Mr. M—— on the head if I catches him asleep ?" (alluding to one of the principal farmers in the parish).

"Well, Mike," said the rector, "perhaps not **Mr. M——**, nor **Mr. W——**, nor **Mr. ——**" (naming some three or four others); "but if you see any one else sleeping, rouse him up."

In Bishop Thirlwall's "Letters" (p. 185), there is an amusing account of a custom observed at Kerry, in the county of Montgomery, for awakening sleepers in church: "As I returned through the churchyard I was greeted very respectfully by a person whose dress seemed to indicate that he was a functionary of the church. I learnt that he was the sexton, but that he also discharged another very useful office, which, as far as I know, is peculiar to Kerry. It appears that it is by ancient custom a part of his duty to perambulate the church during service-time with a bell in his hand, to look carefully into every pew, and wherever he finds any one dozing to ring the bell. He discharges this duty, it is said, with great vigilance, intrepidity, and im-partiality, and consequently with the happiest effect on the congregation ; for, as everybody is certain, that if he or she gives way to drowsiness, the fact will be forthwith made known through the whole church by a peal which will direct all eyes to the sleeper, the fear of such a visitation is almost always sufficient to keep every one on the alert." The *Sporting Magazine* for July, 1818, quoted from a local paper a somewhat unique method of rousing sleepers. The clergyman of a Welsh church, it stated, had a tame goat that attended service, and if it saw a drowsy Cambrian nodding, accepted it as a challenge, and made so effectual a butt at its supposed antagonist, that he slept no more while the service lasted.

CHAPTER VI.

CHURCH PIGEON-HOUSES.

SCATTERED throughout the **country, there** may still **be** seen in many churches the remains of the pigeon-house which **would seem to** have been an established usage as **far** back **as the** thirteenth century. **In** an interesting paper on the subject **read before** the Royal Archæological Institute (**Aug. 11,** 1888), at Leamington, **by** Mr. **J. T.** Micklethwaite, **and** published in the journal **of** the society,* some curious examples are given, which we quote below.

In the north-west tower of Selby Church, a chamber exists "which has in its walls a number of holes an inch **or** so in diameter, and arranged in rows. In some of the holes there remain, or did remain, the ends of wooden **pegs** which had been broken off short at the surface of the **wall.''** As these pegs appear to " have been intended to carry some rough shelving, which could easily be divided by upright partitions," **it** is probable that this chamber **was once upon** a time originally fitted up for a pigeon-house.

From the accounts of Denis Hyndolweston, *Custos*, of the cell at Yarmouth, we gather there **was a** pigeon-house in the church roof at Yarmouth. Making up his accounts for the year 1484-5, this **Denis** enters, " About three dozen pigeons from the pigeon-house above the chapel **vault**

* 1888, xlv. **374-378.**

bred in the household." This extract showing that the pigeons were kept in the space between the vaulted ceiling of the chapel and the wood roof.

The parish church of SS. Peter and Paul, Marlborough, had a vaulted chancel of the fifteenth century, and in the loft above it pigeons were, in olden days, kept. But in 1863, when the church was restored, "the east gable was rebuilt, and a new window put in to light the loft over the chancel, taking the place of the narrow slit through which the pigeons entered, and which was fitted with alighting boards or flat louvres." In a print of the church in Neale's "Views of Collegiate and Parochial Churches," * both the pigeons and the entrance to their house are *plainly depicted.* A similar arrangement existed at Elkstone, in Gloucestershire, and in the "Ecclesiologist" for 1865, p. 313, it is noted of Overbury Church, Worcestershire, that "some twenty years ago the space above the vaulting of the chancel was used as a pigeon-house."

Professor J. H. Middleton, in a paper on Stanley St. Leonard's Church, in the fifth volume of the "Transactions of the Bristol and Gloucestershire Archæological Society," informs us that above the flat ceiling of the north transept of that church "there is a boarded floor, and the space above the roof has been used as a *columbarium.* The walls are full of pigeon holes all around, and these have evidently been built with the walls, and are not additions. Access to this chamber was gained by a round-arched Norman door in the north wall of the tower, leading from the ringing chamber."

As in the case of Selby, the pigeon-house was sometimes located in the tower. Thus, at Birlingham, near Pershore, is a church with a west tower, the middle story of which is arranged for a pigeon-house. And in the "Ecclesiologist" (xvii. p. 233), a further example is given at Collingham

* 1825, vol. ii.

PIGEON-HOUSES IN CHURCHES: BIRLINGHAM, NEAR PERSHORE.

Page 68.

Ducis, Wilts. "The tower of this church, oblong in plan, seems to have been originally constructed so that its middle stage might be used as a dove-cote. A window, or rather opening with a sill on which the birds might alight, is still preserved."

There were pigeons, too, as Mr. Micklethwaite writes, "at York Minster, in 1497, for the keeper of the fabric then bought a net to catch them with for three shillings and eightpence, and has duly entered it in his account. And to this day pigeons, which perhaps descend from monastic times, make their homes in the towers and roofs of Westminster Abbey."

CHAPTER VII.

ACOUSTIC JARS AND HORSES' SKULLS.

THE old jars found in various churches are supposed to have been used for the purpose of improving the resonance of the sacred edifice, after the manner of the brazen *Echeia* noticed by Vitruvius as used in some ancient Roman theatres. "It is certain," writes Sir E. Beckett,[*] "that the Ancients had devices for improving the acoustics of large buildings, besides their better knowledge of the requisite proportions, which we have lost altogether; for in the days of the vast ancient theatres, such as the Coliseum at Rome, ten times as many people could see and hear as in modern churches. And they had a peculiar contrivance of horizontal pots along the seats, which are understood to have augmented the sound in the same way as a short and wide tube presented to a hemispherical bell when struck augments its sound." Hence, the jars which have been occasionally discovered during the restoration of certain churches in different parts of the country, have generally been considered survivals of this old custom.

Mr. Gordon Hills[†] mentions two interesting finds— one was at East Harling Church, Norfolk, where four jars

[*] "Book on Building" (1880), 281.
[†] "Journal of Arch. Assoc.," xxxv. 95.

were brought to light during repairs of the roof, arranged at about equal spaces along the north side of the chancel, and resting upon the top of the wall above the wall-plate.

The other discovery was at the church of Leeds, near Maidstone, Kent, where forty-eight to fifty-two earthenware pots were found in August, 1878, embedded in the top of the nave wall on both sides of the church, immediately under the wall-plate. Below the jars in the north side was discovered a very remarkable arrangement consisting of two sound-holes, made apparently for the purpose of carrying the effect into the north aisle. These jars have been pronounced to be of Romano-British make.

Some years ago, during the restoration of St. Peter's Mancroft, Norwich, a singular arrangement was discovered beneath the floor of the chancel, in front of the place formerly occupied by stalls. A trough, about three feet deep, and the same wide, was found to extend from end to end of the chancel, on either side. In the walls of this trough, were placed horizontally, and at equal distance between the base and the surface, short pitchers, bedded in mortar, the mouth of each pitcher (of glazed pottery with fluted bands) being open to the trough. A similar arrangement has been found at All Saints, Norwich.*

In other parts of England, the archæologist has had brought under his notice specimens of the same practice. At Fairwell, Staffordshire—found while the church was being pulled down in 1747; at Denford Church, Northampton-shire, at St. Peter's Upton Church, near Newark, at St. Olave's, Chichester, and at St. Clement's Church, Sandwich, high up in the chancel.

Two cases were discovered in Devonshire, one at Luppitt Church, and the other at Ashburton, where the jars were

* See Eastern Counties Collectanea, 1872-3. *Notes and Queries,* 6th series, iii. 413, 147.

found on the inside of the chancel walls in 1838, when the old plaster in the course of repairs was removed. The jars lay on their sides, their mouths directed to the inside of the church, covered over with a piece of slate to each, and that hid behind the plaster.*

The *Norwich Mercury* of December 3, 1848, in an account of the restoration of St. Nicholas' Church, Ipswich, described certain "flictile vessels found beneath the roof," and adds how "on digging near the foundation of the wall which has been removed to enlarge the church, several earthen vessels were found carefully embedded in brickwork. One was removed entire. Beneath the roof were also found some vessels of red earth, and also some of half-baked bluish material." In the south aisle of Newington Church, Kent, there are or were three vessels in the east gable, and some years ago a large jar, supposed to have been put down for the same purpose, was discovered in the chancel of Slaugham Church, Sussex.

At Fountains Abbey, several earthenware vessels were discovered in removing the earth and stones from the floor in the basement of the now destroyed choir screen, at the entrance to the choir. These jars were laid in mortar on their sides, and then surrounded with the solid stonework, "their necks extending from the wall like cannons from the side of a ship." This was, in all probability, an acoustic contrivance similar to those already mentioned, but several explanations have been suggested for their existence. According to one conjecture, these jars were used to burn incense, but their mouths must have been hidden when the stalls were standing. Another solution is that they were intended to receive the ashes of the heart, or some other portion of the body, in case a canon attached to the

* "Jour. of Arch. Assoc.," xxxviii. 38, 219; see Transactions of Royal Institute of British Architects, May 29, 1854.

church should will that any part of his remains should be so deposited.[*]

Acoustic jars were also found some years ago in the walls of St. Mary's Church, Youghal, in the course of restoration. In the process of repairs the old plastering was hacked off the walls, and there was discovered at the western end of the north wall of the chancel, and at about twenty-five feet from the ground, a series of orifices, five in number, each formed in a piece of freestone, and varying from three to six inches in diameter, and which were found to be vents of an equal number of earthenware jars, placed immediately behind them, and imbedded in the masonry; the vessels were placed in irregular distances from each other. On examination, the jars were found to be lying on their sides, perfectly empty, some being well glazed, others unglazed. Subsequently, five similar jars, but of a smaller size, were discovered in the same position at the opposite side of the chancel.[†] "These orifices are now open," writes Mr. Richard Rolt Brash,[‡] "and the arrangement restored to its original purpose, and I can testify to the effect produced by these acoustic jars. I have frequently worshipped in the church, and have been many times struck with the fact that when kneeling at the extreme end of the north transept, I could hear most distinctly the Communion Service, though read by a person of very moderate power. The voice appeared to have a peculiarly sonorous and ringing tone. The hearing in other parts of the church was equally satisfactory."

Numerous instances of this practice have been found abroad, as in Strasburg Cathedral. In 1842, in the church

---

[*] See the "Yorkshire Archæological and Typographical Journal," (1875, 1–7).

[†] "Proceedings and Transactions of the Kilkenny and South East of Ireland Archæological Society" (1854–5), iii. 303.

[‡] *Gentleman's Magazine* (1863), xv. new series, 752.

of St. Blaise, at Arles, a number of horn-shaped earthenware jars and pots were discovered built into the walls,* and in the vaulting of St. Martin's, at Angers ; and in the walls of St. Jacques et les Innocents, at Paris, similar jars have been found.†

Occasionally the skulls of horses have been found in sacred buildings ; the popular idea being that, like earthenware jars, they were built in for acoustic purposes ; although it has been suggested that the remains of sheep and horses found under the floors of churches, indicate the traces of heathen sacrifices on the spot in earlier times. Some years ago, "a horse's head was placed under the organ in a parish church in Munster, to give increased effect to the music ; " "a superstition," writes a correspondent of *Notes and Queries* (4th S. iii. 564), " very prevalent in the county Clare. Near the old mansion of R——, where I spent some of the years of my childhood, was a field in which was a very fine echo. This was invariably attributed to the skull of a horse which had lived on the estate for thirty years, and which was buried in that field. I remember well finding the skull, and carrying it away from the field, with no injury to the powers of the echo." In the bell turret of Elsdon Church, Northumberland, there were found built into the masonry three skulls of horses. Horses' skulls, too, have frequently been put into the sounding boards over the heads of Presbyterian ministers in Scotland ; and when an old meeting-house in Bristo Street, Edinburgh, was taken down in the early part of the present century, to make room for the church, the old sounding-board above the pulpit was found filled with horses' skulls.‡

---

* " Annales Archeologiques," vol. xxii.

† See *Gentleman's Magazine*, Nov., 1863 ; and the *Builder* (1863), xxi. 820 ; (1864), 17.

‡ *Notes and Queries*, 4th series, iv. 66 ; 6th series, i. 424.

CHAPTER VIII.

BELLS AND BELFRIES.

For nearly fourteen centuries the bell has been employed by the church; and, consecrated to Christian purposes, its sound has penetrated to the most distant regions of the globe. From its airy height in the old church-tower, "it gives a tongue to time which would otherwise pass over our heads as silently as the clouds, and lends a warning to its perpetual flight. It is the voice of rejoicing at festivals, at christenings, at marriages, and of mourning at the departure of the soul." * Hence, it is fraught with memorial associations of every kind, and—

> "O, what a preacher is the time-worn tower,
> Reading great sermons with its iron tongue!"

An important ceremony, in early times, was the benediction or naming of the church bell; and in this, we are told, "the ecclesiastics followed all the ceremonies employed in the christening of children." It was carried to the font, it had godfathers and godmothers, was sprinkled with water, was anointed with oil, and was finally covered with the white garment, or chrisom, which in the Roman Catholic ritual was put upon infants at the conclusion of the rite, as an emblem of innocence. Nothing could exceed

* *Quarterly Review* (1854), xcv. 309.

the pomp and solemnity of the service. "Costly feasts were given, and even in poor villages a hundred gold crowns were sometimes spent on the ceremony." The custom continued in England down to the Reformation, and an instance occurs in the churchwardens' accounts of St. Lawrence, Reading, in 1499 : *

"Payed for halowing of the bell named Harry, vjs. viij*d.* And over that, Sir William Symes, Richard Clech, and Mistress Smyth, being godfaders and godmoder at the consecracyon of the same bell, and berying all other costs to the suffragan."

Superstition soon enlisted bells into her service, and it became customary at their benediction to pray that they might be endowed with power to drive away devils, and dissipate thunderstorms, hail, and tempests. It was supposed that evil spirits were the cause of foul weather, and being terrified at the saintly sound of the bells, they precipitately fled. This was one of the delusions which Latimer exposed at the Reformation. "Ye know," he said, "when there was a storm or fearful weather, then we rung the holy bells ; they were they that must make all things well ; they must drive away the devil ! But I tell you, if the holy bells would serve against the devil, or that he might be put away through their sound, no doubt we would soon banish him out of all England ; for I think, if all the bells in England should be rung together at a certain hour, there would be almost no place but some bells might be heard there, and so the devil should have no abiding place in England." Numerous allusions to the practice occur in old manuscripts, and in various churchwardens' accounts payments are to be found for "ringing the hallowed belle in grete tempestes and lightninges," for "ringing in the thundering ;" for the ringers' refreshments

---

* *Quarterly Review* (1854), xcv. 315, 316.

for "ringeing att the tyme of gret thunder," and the like. Aubrey, in his "Miscellanies," says that it was once customary, whenever it thundered and lightened, to ring St. Adhelm's Bell at Malmesbury Abbey; and Wynkin de Worde tells us that bells were rung during thunderstorms, to the end that fiends and wicked spirits should be abashed, and flee and cease the moving of the tempest.

But that bells are no effectual charm against lightning, writes Dr. Fuller, "the frequent firing of abbey churches by lightning, confuteth the proud motto commonly written on the bells in their steeples, wherein each entitleth itself to a sixfold efficacy." The belief, however, was widespread, and allusions, like in the following lines formerly suspended in the belfry at Gulval, Cornwall, were frequent—

> "Good sirs! our meaning is not small
> That God to praise assemblies call;
> And warn the sluggard when at home,
> That he may with devotion come
> Unto the church and joyn in prayer;
> Of absolution take his share.
> Who hears the bells, appears betime,
> And in his seat against we chime.
> Therefore I'd have you not to vapour,
> Nor blame ye lads that use the Clapper.
> By which are scar'd the fiends of hell,
> And all by virtue of a bell."

On the eve of the feast of Corpus Christi, the choristers of Durham Cathedral ascend the tower, and in their surplices sing the Te Deum. This ceremony is in commemoration of the miraculous extinguishing of a conflagration on that night, A.D. 1429. The monks were at midnight prayer when the belfry was struck by lightning and set on fire; but although the fire raged all that night, and until the middle of the next day, the tower escaped serious damage, and the bells remained uninjured; an escape that was attributed to the special influence of the incorruptible St. Cuthbert enshrined in the cathedral.* So late as 1852, the Bishop of Malta ordered all the church bells to be rung for an hour to allay a gale, and in many places when the superstition had ceased, "the practice was kept up from mere habit, there having grown up in lieu thereof a notion that the ringing of bells dispersed storms, or retained them at a distance by moving the air." †

The supposed potency of bells in terrifying spirits explains other virtues and supernatural tales associated with them. The bell of St. Fillan, which belonged to the old chapel at Killin, in Perthshire, was reputed to cure lunacy. After the patient had dipped in the well or pool of St. Fillan, and passed a night in the chapel, the bell, if he survived, was set on his head in the morning with great solemnity, and his wits returned. It was further believed that if this invaluable specific was stolen, it would extricate itself from the hands of the thief, and return from whence it was taken, ringing all the way. The same power was attributed to a bell in Leinster. A chieftain of Wicklow got possession of it, and he was obliged to tie it with a cord to prevent its escaping to its home, at St. Fillan's church, in Meath.

A similar story is told of the bell of St. Illtyd. The legend runs that a certain king had stolen it from the church, and carried it to England, tied about the neck of one of his horses. For this deed, "the king was destroyed, but, repenting before his death, he ordered the bell to be restored to its place in Wales. Without waiting to be driven, the horse with the bell about his neck set out for Wales, followed by a whole drove of horses, drawn by the melodious sound of the bell. The horse was even able to cross the river Severn, and make its entry into Wales, the other horses following. Then, hastening

* "Book of Days," ii. 49.
† *Quarterly Review,* xcv. 329.

along the shore, and over the mountains, and through the woods, it finally reached the banks of the river Taf, when a clergyman, hearing the sweet sound of the bell, went out to meet the horse, and helped in carrying the bell to the gate of St. Illtyd's Church." Then the horse bent down and loosed his precious burden from his neck, and "it fell on a stone, from which fall a part of it was broken." *

Another story tells how Clothaire II. carried off a bell from Soissons, in Burgundy, which resented its removal in an effectual manner. It became dumb on the road, and when it arrived at Paris its voice was gone. On being sent back to its old quarters, it no sooner approached the town than it recovered its tone, and rang so loudly that it was heard while yet seven miles distant.

Speaking of stolen bells, about 1830, the treble bell at Cherington, Gloucestershire, was stolen and set up in Avening Tower to make a ring of six. The culprits were discovered, convicted, and punished. A vulgar error prevailed in the locality that if a bell could be taken from one tower and put up in another without the offender being caught in the act, there was no redress. The following song used to be sung in the village in memory of this event—

> " Those Cherington bells, those Cherington bells,
> What a sad tale their jingling tells !
> Alas ! their now imperfect chime
> Proclaims our folly and our crime.

> " Our hours of sport have passed away,
> Our hearts now droop that once were gay,
> For we are confined in these dreary cells,
> For taking one of the Cherington bells.

---

* Wirt Sikes, " British Goblins," 342, 343.

> " Little was it supposed by us,
>   The matter would have ended thus,
>   And doubtless all would have been well
>   Had we restored the furtive bell.
>
> " But we, alas ! fools as we were,
>   Carried the silly joke too far ;
>   And this famed bell, tradition says,
>   Belonged to us in former days.
>
> " And was purloined from Avening Tower
>   A century ago or more,
>   And thence convey'd to Cotswold Hills,
>   And placed among the Cherington bells.
>
> " This absurd story we believed,
>   But we're egregiously deceived,
>   For its inscription plainly tells
>   'Twas always one of the Cherington bells.
>
> " Sorry we are for what we've done,
>   We're paying dearly for our fun ;
>   Oh, that we were out of the cells,
>   We'd ne'er again take Cherington bells."

In October, 1844, a bell was stolen from the church steeple of Glyssop, Derbyshire; and, in December, 1856, the fifth bell at Church Brampton, Northamptonshire, disappeared. It was unhung at the time, and lay on the tower floor. Some men broke open the door, rolled the bell down the churchyard into a cart, and took it away, nothing having been heard of it since. In May, 1803, a bell was stolen from the Abbey Church of Pershore, Worcestershire, and, on May 24, 1863, it was discovered that the second bell, weighing about five cwt., was missing from the tower of Worcester Cathedral.*

In Spelman's " History of Sacrilege " will be found some curious stories relating to the sacrilege of bells. " When I

---

* H. T. Ellacombe, " The Church Bells of Gloucestershire " (1881), 144.

was a child," he writes, "I heard much talk **of the** pulling down of bells in every part of my country, the county of Norfolk, then common in memory; and the sum of the speech **usually** was, that in sending them over sea, some were drowned in one haven, some in another, as at Lynn, **Wells,** or Yarmouth. I dare not venture upon particulars, for that, I then hearing it as a child, regarded it as a child. **But the** truth of it was lately discovered by God himself, for that in the year . . . . He sending such a dead neap (as they call it) as no man living was known to have seen the like, the sea fell so far back from the land at Hunstanton, that the people going much further to gather oysters than they had done at any time before, they there found a bell with the mouth upward, sunk into the ground to the very **brim. They** carried the news thereof to Sir **Hamon L'Estrange, lord of the town,** and of wreck and sea-right there, who shortly after sought to have weighed up **and** gained the bell; but the sea never since going so far back, they hitherto could not find the place again."

"In the reign of King Henry VIII., there was a clockier, or bell-house, adjoining to St. Paul's Church, in London, with four very great bells in it, called Jesus bells. Sir Miles Partridge, a courtier, once played at dice with the king **for** these bells, staking £100 against them, and won them, and then melted and sold them **to a** very great gain. But in the fifth year **of** King Edward **VI.** this gamester had worse fortune, when he lost his life, being executed on **Tower** Hill, for matters concerning the Duke of Somerset.

"**In** the year **of** our Lord **1541,** Arthur Bulkley, Bishop **of** Bangor, sacrilegiously sold the **first** five bells belonging to the cathedral, **and** went to the seaside to see them shipped away, but at that instance he was stricken blind, and so continued to the day of his death."

Spelman further relates his discourse when dining **with**

"my lord of Canterbury," who told him how, when he was in Scotland, he visited certain churches, but found the bells had disappeared from them. "In Edinburgh," he added, "there was no bell in that city, save only in the Church of St. Andrew. And inquiring what had become of the rest, it was told him that they were shipped to be carried into the low countries, but were drowned in Leith haven."

But returning to the mystic powers belonging to bells, it would seem that they strongly resent any sacrilegious or profane act. "To this day the tower of Forrabury Church, Cornwall, or, as it has been called by Mr. Hawker, "the silent tower of Bottreaux," remains without bells. It appears that many years ago the inhabitants of Forrabury parish determined to have a peal of bells which should rival those of the neighbouring church of Tintagel. The bells were cast, blessed, and shipped for Forrabury; and as the ship, after a favourable voyage, glided along the northern shores of Cornwall, the pilot, on hearing the vesper bells at Tintagel, thanked God for the safe and quick journey they had made. The captain laughed at his superstition, and swearing that all was due to himself and his men, laughed to scorn the pilot's prayer. But while yet the captain's oaths were heard, a huge swelling of the ocean was seen, and as it rolled in towards the shore, overwhelming everything by its weight and force, the ship sunk in an instant close to land, beneath its fury. As the vessel sank, the bells were heard tolling with a muffled peal; and ever since, when storms are at hand, their sound is still audible from beneath the waves. *

A similar legend is told of Jersey. Many years ago "the twelve parish churches in that island possessed each a valuable peal of bells, but during a long civil war, the bells

* Hunt's "Popular Romances of the West of England," 438, 439.

were sold to defray the expenses of the troops. The bells were sent to France, but on the passage the ship foundered, and everything was lost, to show the wrath of Heaven at such a sacrilege. Since then, during a storm, these bells always ring from the deep ; and to this day the fishermen of St. Ouen's Bay always go to the edge of the water before embarking, to listen if they can hear the bells, for, if so, nothing will induce them to leave the shore." In the same way, too, where churches have been swallowed up, their bells are still said to send out their wonted music on certain occasions from the depths of the earth, or from beneath the waters. According to a tradition at Tunstall, in Norfolk, the parson and churchwardens disputed for the possession of some bells, which had become useless because the tower was burnt. During their altercation, the arch-fiend walked off with the bells, but being pursued by the parson, who begun to exorcise in Latin, he dived into the earth with his ponderous burden, and the place where he disappeared is a boggy pool of water, called Hell Hole. Notwithstanding " the aversion of the powers of darkness to such sounds, even these bells are sometimes permitted to favour their native place with a ghostly peal."

Near Blackpool, about two miles out at sea, tradition tells us, once stood the church and cemetery of Kilgrimol, long ago submerged. Even now, the melancholy chimes of the bells sounding over the restless waters may oftentimes, the sailors say, be heard, especially in rough and tempestuous weather.

At Echingham, Sussex, there is a singular tradition. The church was originally closed by a moat, a remarkable appendage to a sanctuary, but turning to the rude old times when in seasons of war and civil commotion men turned the house of God into a fortress. At the bottom of this moat there lies, says the legend, a great bell. How it came there is not known, nor will it ever be seen **by mortal eyes** till six yoke of oxen shall be brought to the spot to bring it again to daylight.[*]

At a place known as Fisherty Brow, near Kirby Lonsdale, **there is a sort of natural** hollow scooped out, where, as the **legend runs, a** church, parson, and congregation, **were** swallowed up, and here the bells may be heard ringing on a Sunday morning **by any one** who puts his ear to **the ground.** A similar **fate is said** to have befallen the village of Raleigh, in Nottinghamshire, **and it was formerly customary** for the inhabitants on Christmas **morning** to go out into the valley, and listen to the mysterious **chimes of their lost parish** church.

Whitby Abbey was suppressed in the year 1539, **and shortly** afterwards dismantled.   **The** bells were sold, **and** were **to be conveyed by ship to** London. They were **duly placed on board, and,** amid the lamentation of the **people, the sails were unfurled,** and the anchor weighed. **But lo ! the vessel refused to bear away its** sacred burden. **A short distance it moved out into the bay,** and then sank **quietly beneath the waves ; and there** under the waters, **at a spot** within sight **of the abbey ruins,** the bells still **remain, and are still** heard **occasionally to ring** by invisible hands.   This legend **has been poetically described by Mr.** Phillips †—

> " Up from the heart of **the ocean**
>   The mellow **music peals,**
>   Where the sunlight makes its golden path,
>   And the seamew flits and wheels.
>
> " For many a chequered century,
>   Untired by flying **time,**
>   The bells no human fingers touch,
>   Have rung their hidden chime."

---

* " Sussex Archæological Society," xiv. 227.
† Rev. Thomas Parkinson, " Legend and Traditions of Yorkshire."

A pretty legend is told of the cathedral bells of Limerick. It is said that the bells were cast by an Italian founder for a monastery near his home, which was destroyed when his three sons fell together on the fatal field of Pavia. Years after, he came an exile to Ireland; on his reaching the Shannon, the evening was closing in, when from the square tower of St. Mary rang out a rich peal of melody. One note was enough; the aged stranger, with arms folded on his beating heart, leaned forward to catch the magical music of the chime; it was the well-remembered sound of his own dear bells, with their thousand agonizing memories of Florence, that had arrested his ear.

The subjoined rhyme relating to the tower and bells of Mevagissey, Cornwall, is current in the neighbourhood—

> " Ye men of Porthilly,
>   Why were ye so silly ?
>   In having so little power ;
>   Ye sold every bell
>   As Govan men tell,
> For money to pull down your tower."

The bell is hung above the lower stage of the tower, which is the only part remaining. At Berwick, Sussex, out of four bells in 1724, only one remains. In 1811 three were sold, one to Alfreston, and two as old metal. Hence it is said—

> " The parson was poor and so were the people,
>   So they sold the bell to repair the steeple."

At Crosmere, near Ellesmere, Shropshire, a chapel is said to have stood on the banks of the lake, and according to the *superstitio loci*, whenever the waters were ruffled by the wind, the chapel bells were formerly supposed to be heard ringing beneath the surface. Many more such traditions, slightly varied, might be mentioned, as, for instance, one at Romford, Essex. The old church of St.

Andrew's, pulled down nearly four centuries and a half ago, stood about half a mile from the town on a site in some meadows, still called "Old Church." The legend went, that every year, on St. Andrew's Day, at noon, the bells were still heard pealing merrily from Old Church.* To quote another instance recorded by Mr. Hunt,† it appears that once there stood on the northern shores of Cornwall, a city called Langarrow, which in its best days possessed seven churches, each of which was famous for its size and beauty. The inhabitants were wealthy, deriving their riches from the fertility of the land, which yielded them an abundance of tin and lead, and from the sea, which was overflowing with fish. To this city criminals were sent from various parts of the country, and made to work in the mines. Unhappily their proximity had a bad effect upon the people, who gave way to sinful pursuits and pleasures. Accordingly the wrath of God eventually descended upon them, and one night a violent tempest arose, raging with unabated fury for three days and nights : at the end of this time the city had entirely disappeared, being buried beneath the sandhills which the wind had heaped together on that ill-fated spot.

Legends of this kind show how widely bells were regarded with superstitious fear in olden times ; their occult powers having suggested most of the tales of wonder related of them. A legend of Trefethin tells how in the Church of St. Cadoc was a remarkable bell. "A little child who had climbed to the belfry was struck by the bell and killed—not through the wickedness of the bell itself—but through a spell which had been put upon it by an evil spirit. But though innocent of murderous intent, the wretched bell became forfeit to the demons on account of its fatal deed. They seized it, and

---

* *Notes and Queries*, 2nd series, xi. 421.
† "Popular Romances of the West of England."

bore it down through the earth to the shadowy realm of Annism, and ever since that day, when a child is accidentally slain at Trefethin, the bell of St. Cadoc is heard mournfully tolling underneath the ground where it disappeared ages ago." *

A Ledbury legend relates that St. Katharine had a revelation that she was to travel about, and not rest at any place till she heard the bells ringing of their own accord. This was done by the Ledbury bells on her approaching the town. At Abbot's Morton there is a tradition that the silver bells belonging to the abbot are buried in the site of his old residence there.

It was, it has been suggested, its reputed power in scaring away evil spirits that caused the bell to be employed in all the matters in which fiends were supposed to interfere. It was the weapon with which St. Anthony fought the legion of demons who tormented him during his long eremitical life, and, in the figures drawn of him during the Middle Ages, he is generally represented with a bell in his hand, or with one suspended from his staff. Hence, too, the passing-bell, which was formerly tolled for those who were dying, or passing out of the world, as well as the peal which was rung after their death, " grew out of the belief that devils troubled the expiring patient, and lay in wait to afflict the soul at the moment when it escape from the body." †
Douce considers that the passing-bell was originally intended to drive away any demon that might seek to take possession of the soul of the deceased ; and Grose says it " was anciently rung for two purposes : one to bespeak the prayers of all good christians for a soul just departing ; the other to drive away the evil spirits who stood at the bed's foot and about the house, ready to seize their prey, or at

---

* Wirt Sikes, "British Goblins," 339, 340.
† *Quarterly Review*, xcv. 331, 332.

least to molest and terrify the soul in its passage ; but by the ringing of that bell they were kept aloof, and the soul, like a hunted hare, gained the start." This would seem to explain a Huntingdonshire superstition recorded in *Notes and Queries* (1st series, **v.** 364): "An unbaptized child was buried, a neighbour expressed great sorrow for the mother because 'no bell had been rung over the corpse.' The reason she gave was 'because when any one died, the soul never left the body until the church bell was rung.'"

Prior to the Reformation, it was customary to toll the passing-bell at all hours of the night as well as by day, as the subjoined extract from the churchwardens' accounts for the parish of Walchurch proves : "Item, the clerke to have for tollynge of the passynge-belle, for manne, womanne, or childe, if it be in the day, iiij*d.* Item, if it be in the night, for the same, viij*d.*" At one time the sound of the passing-bell was heard in every parish, and in most of the visitation articles the custom was enjoined. The practice was retained at the Reformation, "and the people were instructed that its use was to admonish the living, and incite them to pray for the dying. To discourage the fancy that demons could assault the liberated soul, or that the jingling of bells would deter them from their purpose, only a single short peal was to be rung after death. In the articles of inquiry in different dioceses at various periods, inquisition is made both as to keeping up the practice of tolling the passing-bell, and the discontinuance of the former superstitious ringing. The injunction began to be neglected towards the close of the seventeenth century, and by the beginning of the eighteenth the passing-bell, in the proper sense of the term, had almost ceased to be heard. The tolling, indeed, continued in the old fashion, but it took place after the death instead of before. The short peal that was once the peculiar signal to announce that some mortal had put on immortality, is still rung in many places as **the prelude,** or the conclusion, to the tolling, though it has no **longer any** meaning." *

A **melancholy instance** of this custom was St. Sepulchre's bell. In 1605, Mr. R. Dowe left £50 to this parish, **on** condition that a person should go to Newgate in the still of **the night** before every execution-day, and, standing as near as possible to the cells of the condemned, should, **with a** hand-bell (which he also left), give twelve solemn **tolls,** with double strokes, and then deliver this exhortation—

> " All you that in the condemned hole **do lie,**
> Prepare you, for to-morrow you shall die ;
> Watch, all, and pray, the hour is drawing near
> That you before the Almighty must appear ;
> Examine well yourselves, in time repent,
> That you may not to eternal flames be sent,
> And when St. Sepulchre's bell to-morrow tolls,
> **The Lord** have mercy **on your** souls !
>
> Past twelve o'clock."

Dowe likewise ordered that the great bell of the church should toll on the morning, and that as the criminals passed the wall to Tyburn, the bellman or sexton should look over and say, " All good people pray heartily unto God for these poor sinners, **who are now** going to their death," for **which** service he was to receive £1 6s. 8d.†

The importance attached to the church bell from **its** sacred **use, and** superstitious veneration, may be gathered **from** the directions for the bell-ringers to be found in most belfries. Most of these, set to rhyme, are much the same, **varying in** phraseology rather than in detail, a few speci-mens of which **we quote** below. **On** the south side of the belfry of Hornsey church these lines are written—

---

* *Quarterly Review,* xcv. 331, 332.
† Mr. John Dowe according to Stow.

> "If that to ring you do come here,
>   You must ring well with hand and ear ;
>   If that you ring in spur or hat,
>   A quart of ale must pay for that.
>   And if a bell you overthrow,
>   Sixpence is due before you go.
>   And if you curse or swear, I say,
>   A shilling's due without delay ;
>   And if you quarill (*sic*) in this place,
>   You shall not ring in any case."

On the wall of the tower of Landulph Church, Cornwall, these rhymes occur—

> "Let awful silence first proclaimed be,
>   And praise unto the Holy Trinity ;
>   Then honour give unto our noble king.
>   So with a blessing let us raise this ring—
>   And Covering Tom comes rowling in the rear.
>   And now the bells are up, come, let us see
>   What laws are best to keep sobriety.
>   Who swears, or curses, or in a choleric mood,
>   Quarrels, or strikes, although he draw no blood ;
>   Who wears his hat or spur, or overturns a bell,
>   Or by unskilful handling mars a peal ;
>   Let him pay sixpence for each single crime,
>   'Twill make him cautious 'gainst another time.
>   But if the Sexton's fault an hindrance be,
>   We call from him a double penalty.
>   If any should our Parson disrespect,
>   Or Warden's orders any time neglect,
>   Let him be always held in full disgrace,
>   And evermore be banished this place.
>   So when the bells are ceased, then let us sing—
>   God bless the Church—God save the King."

At All Saints, Hastings, the rules are dated 1756, and supply another version—

> "This is the belfry that is free
>   To all those that civil be ;
>   And if you please to chime or ring,
>   It is a very pleasant thing.

> " **There** is no musick, play'd or sung,
>   **Like unto** bells when they're well rung ;
>   Then ring your bells well if you can—
>   Silence is best for every man.
>
> " But if you ring in spur or hat,
>   Sixpence you pay, be sure of **that** ;
>   And if a bell you overthrow,
>   Pray pay a groat before you go."

The following were the bell-ringing regulations at Hathersage Church, *circa* 1650—

> " You gentlemen that here wish to ring,
>   See that these laws you keep **in** everything ;
>   Or else be sure you must without delay,
>   The penalty thereof to **the** ringers pay.
>
> " First, when you do **into the bell** house **come**,
>   **Look if** the ringers have convenient room ;
>   For if **you be** an hindrance unto them,
>   Fourpence you forfeit unto these gentlemen.
>
> " Next, if you do here intend to ring,
>   With hat or spur, do not touch a string ;
>   For if you do, your forfeit is for that
>   Just fourpence down to pay, or lose your hat.
>
> " If you a bell turn over, without delay
>   Fourpence unto the ringers you must pay ;
>   Or if you strike, miscall, or do abuse,
>   You must pay fourpence for the ringers' use.
>
> " For every oath here sworn, ere you go hence,
>   Unto the poor then you must pay twelvepence ;
>   And if that you desire to be enrolled
>   **A ringer here, these orders keep and hold.**
>
> " But **whoso doth these orders disobey**,
>   Unto the stocks we will take him straightway ;
>   **There to** remain until he be willing
>   **To pay his** forfeit and the Clerk a shilling."

In the belfry of St. Michael's, Gloucester, there are **ten** panels, **with an** ornamentally painted **frame, on** which are written some doggerel verses in praise of ringing. From internal evidence of the spelling, etc., the composition is probably two hundred years old. They conclude thus—

> "Ring up, ringers! make your Numbers,
> Why so Clammes we say he slumbers,
> For his rope-mates he much cumbers—
> > Nicholas.

> "He that plyes his Rope aright,
> And guides his Bell by ear, not sight,
> He is (be it by day or night)
> > A ringer.

> "Come, Boyes, cleanely in and out,
> Keepe true Stroke at every Bout,
> And then I'll say y'are out of doubt
> > True changers." *

Whatever the origin of the Curfew, or *Couvre-feu*, which was in olden times rung at eight o'clock as a signal for the inhabitants to put out their fires and go to bed, its object, as far as can be traced, was exclusively social or political, and not religious. The most plausible conjecture as to the origin of the introduction of the practice into England, is that it was to diminish the risk of extensive conflagrations, at a period when houses were principally of wood. Milton, it has been remarked, has described it in a couplet sonorous and musical as the bell itself—

> "On a plat of rising ground,
> I hear the far-off curfew sound,
> Over some wide, watered shore,
> Swinging slow, with solemn roar."

It is an instance, too, of the tenacity with which we cling to a practice once established, that, though for centuries its only use has been "to toll the knell of parting day," it

* H. T. Ellacombe, "The Church Bells of Gloucestershire" (1881), 144.

continues to **be rung wherever there are funds to pay the** ringer, for which purpose we find many curious bequests. Thus, at Barton, Lincolnshire, the tradition goes that an **old lady,** being accidentally benighted on the Wolds, was **directed** in her course by the sound of the evening **bell of St.** Peter's church, when, after much alarm, she found **herself** in safety. Out of gratitude she gave a certain piece of land to the parish clerk, on condition that he should ring one of the church bells from seven to eight every evening, except Sundays, commencing on the day of the carrying of the first load of barley in every year, till Shrove Tuesday next ensuing inclusive. At Ringwould, **Kent,** half an acre of land, known as "Curfew Land," has always been held, says Edwards, in his "Remarkable Charities" (226), by the **parish clerk,** as a remuneration for ringing the curfew bell **every evening from the 2nd of** November to the 2nd of **February.** In the parish of St. Margaret's, **in** the same county, **the** story goes that, in 1696, an order was passed to ensure the proper application of the proceeds of five roods **of** pasture land, which had been given by a shepherd, who fell over the cliff, for ringing a curfew bell at eight o'clock every night for the winter half-year, and which ringing had fallen greatly into neglect. Many similar bequests **occur** in different parts of the country, and, here and there, the old custom still lingers on.

Then there was the Sanctus Bell. According **to Dr.** Rock in the "Church of our Fathers," **at** the celebration of the Mass, "as the priest said the Sanctus, etc., the custom was to toll three strokes on **a** bell, which was hung in a bell cote between the chancel and the nave, that the rope might fall **at a** short distance from the spot where knelt the youth, or person, who served at Mass. From the **first** part of its **use, this bell got the** name of the 'Saints,' 'Sanctys,' **or 'Sanctus' Bell, and** many notices **about it** are to be met with in old accounts." It is very likely, he adds, "in most places there were two distinct bells, one for the 'Sanctus,' the other for the 'Elevation.' Sometimes it was made of silver, and was called the 'Sacring' bell. On hearing the Sacring bell's first tinkle, those in church who were not already on their knees knelt down, and with upraised hands worshipped their Maker in the holy housel lifted on high before them."

"In the Church of Brokenborough, Wilts," writes Aubrey, "an old man told me that his father, who died twenty-four years since, was one hundred and ten at his death, and remembered in the time of the old law eighteen little bells that hung in the middle of the church, which the pulling of one wheel made them all ring, which was done at the Elevation of the Host." At Yaxley, Suffolk, and at Long Stratton, Norfolk, there are in pairs ornamental iron discs of mediæval character, supposed to be the remains of such wheels. In the neighbourhood of Canterbury the Sanctus bell was popularly known as the "Wakerell" or "Wagerell" bell, in inventories of 1552. In the churchwardens' accounts of St. Andrew's are these entries—

"1510. Paid for a cord for the wakrell.

"1517. For the makyng of a whylle to the wakrell."

In some parishes a bell is rung at noon, in others at one o'clock, or on the close of morning service, respecting the origin of which custom there is some uncertainty. Dr. Rock * says, "The bell which is still rung in some parishes in the morning, at noon, and in the evening—though its origin is forgotten, and it now only serves to summon the labourers to and from their work—is in reality a relic of the Angelus. The length of the ringing was regulated by the time it took the ringer to repeat the *Ave* and *Pater Noster*. The Angelus, or midday bell, came into use early

* "Church of our Fathers," iii. 340.

in the sixteenth century." In Barker's "Wensleydale" (42), the bell is spoken of as the "Gabriel Bell," and we are informed that "the sexton used to ring it morning, noon, and evening every day, as a bidding to the people, to the sick in bed, and to the healthy, to those at home and to those abroad, that they should, as the sound floated through the villages—the maiden in her cottage and the labourer in the field—reverently kneel and recite the allotted prayers, in remembrance of Christ's Incarnation for us, viz. *Angelus Domini*, etc. (hence it was called the Angelus Bell), and *Ave Maria*, etc. (hence called the Ave Bell)."

Another name for it was the "Pardon Bell," and, according to Burnet, in his "Reformation" (iii. 147, fol. edit.), it was silenced by Shaxton, Bishop of Sarum, in 1538: "That the bell called the *Pardon*, or Ave Bell, which of long time hath been used to be tolled three tymes after and before Divine service, be not hereafter in any part of my diocese any more tollyd." Mr. H. T. Ellacombe, alluding to the custom, says : "I think it will be found to have had its origin in early times, and for holy purposes, well understood by the faithful of those days ; for very early in the thirteenth century a bell entitled 'Ave Maria' was to be sounded *mane, meridie, et vespere.* These, from ancient custom, might have been continued after the Reformation, though the purpose was changed."

One of the popular explanations for sounding of the church bell, on the completion of Sunday morning service, is that it was to inform the parishioners who had not been able to attend that divine service would be celebrated in the afternoon. In scattered villages, or where a single clergyman had to perform the duties of more than one church, this arrangement, it is said, was formerly requisite. A correspondent of *Notes and Queries* (2nd series, ix. 567), writing from Normanton-upon-Soar, Notts, says, "This bell, which a very respectable **old man,** who was parish clerk **here for** fifty-four years, called the 'Sermon Bell,' is never tolled unless there is a second service. If at any time the morning service is not performed, the bell is tolled at twelve o'clock at noon, to inform the parishioners that an evening service will be held." * In some Lancashire parishes **it is** nick-named the "pudding-bell," under an impression that its use is to warn those at home to get ready the dinner. Another reason was assigned by the late Prebendary Mackenzie Walcott, who thus **wrote : "When I** was lecturer at St. Andrew's, **Enfield, the** bells rang out a short **peal** after Sunday morning prayers. I always thought it was probably **designed** to give notice to approaching funeral processions that the church service was over, as in the country **burials** —which are usually on a Sunday—immediately follow **the celebration** of morning service."

A bell used to **be** rung every Saturday in Newbury at three **o'clock, a** custom which is said to have originated through **the celebrated** cloth-worker, "Jack of Newbury," who built, or partly built, the Church of St. Nicholas in the same town, **and who died in** 1519. It was supposed **to be** rung as a summons for the weavers to **receive** their **weekly wages, but** this is **not** the true explanation. It is simply a survival **of the old custom of** ringing the bell **on each Saturday, which was known as the** "Morrow Mass bell." †

The gleaners' bell was once a familiar sound in harvest

* In the "Royal Injunctions" of 1547, we find **this** allusion to the Sermon-bell : "In the time of the **Litany,** of the Mass, of the Sermon, **and** when the priest readeth **the Scripture** to the parishioners, no manner of persons, **without a just** and urgent cause, shall **depart out of the Church ;** and all ringing and knolling of bells shall **be utterly** forborne at that time, except one bell **in** convenient time **to be rung and knolled before** the sermon."

† *The Archæological Journal,* xlviii. 54.

time. A correspondent of *Notes and Queries* (6th series, xii. 186) mentions the custom during the time of harvest in Rutland for each parish church bell, called the gleaning bell, to be rung at eight or nine o'clock a.m., when the women and children go into the fields to glean. The bell is again rung at five or six o'clock p.m., when they return to their homes, after which no gleaning is allowed until the time at which the gleaning bell rings on the following morning. At Goddington, Oxfordshire, it has been customary to ring one of the church bells after a coroner's inquest.

A small bell, about nine inches high, called the "Dag-tale Bell," was formerly hung outside the tower of Frodsham Church, Cheshire, about the height of the belfry. On Sundays, and other holidays, after the bells had ceased ringing, a man used to look outside the tower, and when he saw the vicar coming instantly ring the little bell.* In some places, writes Mr. H. T. Ellacombe, "it is not at all uncommon to ring a little bell, called the 'ting-tang,' or parson's bell, immediately after the chiming for service until the minister begins." Such bells have existed at Long Compton, Warwickshire, St. Mary Over, Cambridge, Milverton and Wells, Somersetshire, and at Barton, Lincolnshire.

When Spur-money was originally demanded has been matter of conjecture. It can be traced back to 1228, when it was decided that the priors of Binham and Wymondham might attend the synod at Norwich in copes and with spurs, without changing their travelling garb. That it was a custom extensively practised in the sixteenth century is evident from the following passage, of the date of 1598: "Wee think it very necessary that every quirister sholde bring with him to Churche a Testament in Englishe, and turn to everie Chapter as it is daily read, or some other good and

* See *Notes and Queries*, 4th series, v. 90, 238, 327, 437.

H

godly prayer-book, rather than spende their **tyme in** talk
and hunting after spur-money, whereon they set their whole
mindes, and do often abuse dyvers if they doe not bestowe
somewhat on them." In our cathedrals, it **was a fine for**
entering the choir with spurs on, as their jingling interrupted
the service; if, however, the youngest chorister **being**
summoned failed to repeat his gamut, the fine could not be
levied. In the memorials of John Ray occurs this passage:
" July the 26th, **1661, We** began our journey northwards
from Cambridge, and that day, passing through Huntingdon
and Stilton, we rode as far **as** Peterborough, **twenty-five**
miles. There I first heard the Cathedral Service. **The**
choristers made us **pay** money for coming into the choir
with **our spurs on."** In the ancient cheque-book **of the
Chapel Royal is an order** made **by** the dean of the
Chapel Royal in 1622, to this effect: " That if anie
knight or other **person** entituled **to weare** spurs enter the
Chappell in that guise, he shall pay to y⁰ quiristers the
accustomed fine **; but, if** he command yᵉ youngest quirister
to repeate **his** gamut, **and he faile** in **yᵉ so** doing, the said
knight, or other, shall not **pay yᵉ** fine." It is stated that the
Duke of Wellington once entered the Chapel **Royal** booted
and spurred, and was called upon for the **fine; but, he calling**
upon the youngest chorister to repeat his gamut, **and the**
boy failing to do so, the impost was not persisted **in.** One
reason, it has been said, for the introduction of **this custom,**
was the interruption of divine **service, occasioned by** the
ringing of **spurs** worn **by persons walking, and** transacting
business in cathedrals, **and especially in St.** Paul's, where,
it is reported, " they threatened imprisonment in the choir
for a whole night **to** all who refused them money. Bishop
Finch paid eighteen pence as an offender, but the Duke of
Cumberland pleaded successfully that it was **hard if he**
could not **wear** his spurs where **they** had **first been buckled**

on. At the installation of the Knights of the Bath, the Cook of Westminster stands with a cleaver at the door, threatening to strike off the spurs of any unworthy of their honour. He receives a fee for his speech." * In most of the rules for ringers found in belfries is the well-known one already alluded to relating to the time-honoured prohibition—

> "If you ring in spur or hat,
> Sixpence you pay, be sure of that."

There are many amusing doggerels on the tone and quality of church bells. According to a Nottinghamshire rhyme—

> "Colston's cracked pancheons, Screveton egg-shells,
> Bingham's 'tro-rollers,' and Whatton merry bells."

Another version of which is current in Derbyshire—

> "Barrow's big-boulders, Repton merry bells,
> Foremark's cracked pancheons, and Newton egg-shells."

At Tolpuddle Church, Dorset, there were formerly only three bells, which were supposed to ring, "My turf's out, my turf's done,"—turf being the principal fuel of the peasants ; when their firing was done, they repaired to the belfry to keep themselves warm by ringing.†

A Lincolnshire doggerel runs thus—

> "Brentingly pancheons,
> And Wyfordby pans,
> Stapleford organs,
> And Burton ting-tangs."

The Bridgnorth bells are supposed to say—

> "Up Severn and down Morfe,
> Says the bells of Bridgnorth."

Shipton-on-Cherwell and Hampton Gay, Oxfordshire, are

* "Traditions and Customs of Cathedrals," **91**.
† *Notes and Queries*, 6th series, iii. **457**.

very near together, although in different rural deaneries and in different patronage. The metal in the two campaniles, less than a quarter of a mile asunder, resounds, says the local legend, after a wedding in this wise—

> " Hampton bell and Shipton two,
> Proclaim the joys of Tom and Sue."

And readers of "Tom Brown at Oxford" (ch. xlvii.) will recollect how at Englebourn the church bells sounded forth, "One more poor man undone."

At Rockingham, co. Rutland, we find this doggerel—

> " Rockingham ! poor people,
> Nasty town, castle down !
> One bell, wooden steeple."

The low square tower of Hornsea Church, Yorkshire, once had a tall spire, which fell in a gale in 1773. An absurd superstition says that a stone was found when the spire fell with this inscription—

> " Hornsea broch, I built thee,
> Thou wast ten miles from Beverley,
> Ten miles from Bridlington,
> And ten miles from the sea."

To quote a further curious doggerel, current at Kinkell, Strathearn, of which there are several versions, the story goes that " the minister had been hanged, the precentor drowned in attempting to cross the Earn from the adjoining parish of Trinity Gask, the steeple had been taken down, and the bell had been sold to the parish of Cockpen, near Edinburgh." Hence it was said—

> " Was there e'er sic a parish, a parish, a parish,
> Was there e'er sic a parish as that o' Kinkell ?
> They've hangit the minister, drowned the precentor,
> Drucken the bell, and dang down the steeple."

Occasionally the local witticism takes the form of question and answer. For instance, the first we hear of the nightly ringing of Bow bell, Cheapside, is in 1315. It was the go-to-bed bell of those days; and two old couplets still exist, supposed to be the complaint of the sleepy 'prentices of Chepe, and the obsequious reply of the Bow Church clerk. The rhymes are—

> "Clarke of the Bow bell, with the yellow lockes,
> For thy late ringing, thy head shall have knockes."

To this the clerk replies—

> "Children of Chepe, hold you all still,
> For you shall have Bow-bell rung at your will."

The three bells at Bulwell, Notts, are supposed to say, "Who rings best? Who rings best?"

Whereupon the two at Radford reply, "We do! We do!" which, however, is denied by the solitary bell of Hyson Green, ringing out, "No! No!"

Similarly, the three bells at Burton Stather, on the brow of the hill, overlooking the Trent, in N.W. Lincolnshire, were supposed to ask, "Who ring best? Who ring best?" to which the two at Luddington, on the other side of the river, replied, "We two! we two!"

On the arrival at Derby, writes a correspondent of *Notes and Queries* (6th series, iii. 175), of the London coach, bringing fish, the news, it is said, was announced by the church bells, each peal, as the coach passed, taking up the tale. Thus St. Peter's, six bells, stood near the entrance of the town, and was the first to cry, "Here's fresh fish come to town; here's fresh fish come to town." Next came All Saints' with its peal of ten, "Here's fine fresh fish just come into the town; here's fine fresh fish just come into the town." Close by All Saints' stood St. Michael's, with but three bells, and one of them cracked, enviously suggesting, "They stink'n; they stink'n," but quickly answered, a furlong further on, by the six of St Alkmund's, with, "Put more salt on 'em, then; put more salt on 'em, then."

Among the many old customs connected with the calendar may be noticed the "Pancake bell"—originally the Shriving bell—which was rung in many parishes in the forenoon of Shrove Tuesday, to call the faithful to confession before the Season of Lent. In recent times the "Pancake-bell" has been rung in numerous places; and at Daventry, Northamptonshire, the bell was muffled on one side with leather, or "buffed," and was locally known as the "Panburn-bell." Jingling rhymes commemorative of this day are still repeated by the peasantry, the bells of the town being represented as sounding the following jingle—

> "Pancakes and fritters,
> Says the bells of St. Peter's.
> Where must we fry 'em?
> Says the bells of Cold Higham.
> In yonder land thurrow (furrow),
> Says the bells of Wellingborough.
> You owe me a shilling,
> Says the bells of Great Billing.
> When will you pay me?
> Says the bells of Middleton Cheney.
> When I am able,
> Says the bells at Dunstable.
> That will never be,
> Says the bells at Coventry.
> Oh, yes it will,
> Says Northampton Great bell.
> White bread and sop,
> Says the bells of Kingsthrop.
> Trundle a lantern,
> Says the bells at Northampton."

That the bells of the Northampton churches were rung

on Shrove Tuesday may be inferred from the following similar bell-doggerel—

> " Roast beef and marsh mallows,
> Says the bells of All Hallows.
> Pancakes and fritters,
> Says the bells at St. Peter's.
> Roast beef and boil'd,
> Says the bells of St. Giles's.
> Poker and tongs,
> Says the bells of St. John's.*
> Shovel, tongs, and poker,
> Says the bells of St. Pulchre's." †

Formerly, too, on Shrove Tuesday, the inhabitants of Derby had a football match between the parishes of All Saints and St. Peter's. The bells of the different parishes rang their merry peals on the morning, a practice which gave rise to the following jingle on the five parishes of All Saints, St. Peter's, St. Werburgh's, St. Alkmund's, and St. Michael's—

> " Pancakes and fritters,
> Say All Saints and St. Peter's ;
> When will the ball come,
> Say the bells of St. Alkmum ;
> At two they will throw,
> Says Saint Werabo' ;
> Oh, very well,
> Says little Michael."

Whilst alluding to customs of this kind, it may be mentioned that in some parishes it has been customary to ring a muffled peal on Holy Innocents' Day, as at Wells Cathedral, and at Leigh-upon-Mendip, Somersetshire.

At Norton, near Evesham, it has been usual to ring first a muffled peal for the slaughter of the Innocents, and then

---

* St. John's Hospital.

† Miss Baker's " Northamptonshire Words and Phrases," ii. 92.

an unmuffled peal of joy for the deliverance of the Infant Christ.

There are the so-called "Sweet Bells" at Dewsbury, Yorkshire. In "Collectanea Topographica et Genealogica" (i. 168), we read of these bells: "One is known by the name of 'Black Tom of Sothill,' and the tradition is that it was an expiatory gift for a murder. One of the bells is tolled at Christmas Eve, as at a funeral, or in the manner of a passing-bell; and any one asking whose bell it was, would be told that it was the Devil's knell. The moral of it is that the devil died when Christ was born. The custom was discontinued for some years, but at Christmas, 1828, it was revived by order of the vicar."

Among further bells may be noticed the "Virgin Chimes;" the peal rung on Christmas Eve, or Christmas morning, having been so called. The "Judas Bell" was probably used in the Easter Eve ceremonies, in connection with which we find "Judas Candles" mentioned. And there were the "Easter Bells," which could not be rung before the bells of the cathedral, or mother churches, were sounded.

Once more, the church bell is the appointed voice of public rejoicing, and sound for every festive event. It rings in the new year, the new sovereign, the new mayor, the new squire, and the new rector. But in the last generation, it was sometimes employed on shameful occasions, such as to celebrate the winning of a "long main" at cock-fighting. The church bells were occasionally rung for successful race horses. In the accounts of St. Edmund's, Salisbury, is this item—"1646. Ringing the race day, that the Earl of Pembroke his horse winne the cuppe, v^s."

One of the most popular applications is to proclaim that two lovers have just been made happy; but, as a writer in the *Quarterly Review* (xcv. 333), has remarked, "there have been sequels to such a beginning with which the knell had been more in unison!" So thought one, Thomas Nash, who, in 1813, bequeathed £50 a year to the ringers of the Abbey Church, Bath, "on condition of their ringing on the whole peal of bells, with clappers muffled, various solemn and doleful changes on the 14th May in every year, being the anniversary of my wedding-day ; and also the anniversary of my decease, to ring a grand bob major, and merry mirthful peals unmuffled, in joyful commemoration of my happy release from domestic tyranny and wretchedness." In the village of Horningsham, Wilts, it was customary when a young person died unmarried, to ring the "wedding-peals" on muffled bells, immediately on the interment of the corpse, the effect of which, it is said, was singularly impressive.

At the induction of a new vicar, it is customary for him to ring himself in, by formally ringing the bell two or three times. Some time ago, writes a correspondent of *Notes and Queries* (6th series, iv. 307), "having to induct a newly made vicar, when he had locked himself in the church and gone up into the tower, as the custom is, to ring the bell, a gentleman standing by said to me, ' Let us see how many strokes he will give, because there is an old saying that the number of strokes a new incumbent gives will indicate the number of years he will remain in the parish.' "

Many curious jugs or pitchers, the property of ringers, are preserved in different parishes. At Hadleigh, in Suffolk, a pitcher of brown glazed earthenware is kept, which holds sixteen quarts, and bears this inscription—

"We Thomas Windle, Isaac Bunn, John Mann, Adam Sage, Georg Bond, Thomas Goldsborough, Robert Smith, Henry West," and below the names are these lines—

> " If you love me doe not lend me,
> Euse me often and keep me clenly,
> Fill me full, or not at all,
> If it be strovng, and not with small "

According to Mr. Glyde, in the *Suffolk Garland* (1866, 295), "it is still occasionally used by the ringers on the occasion of any profitable wedding, and it has been introduced into the belfry." It is said to be filled every Christmas, when the ringers assemble for a "frolic," with strong beer.

At Hinderclay, a ringers' pitcher is still preserved in the church tower, with an inscription which tells how—

"By Samuel Moss, this pitcher was given to the Noble Society of Ringers at Hinderclay, in Suffolk," etc. And afterwards are added these lines—

> "From London I was sent,
> As plainly doth appear :
> It was with this intent,
> To be filled with strong beer.
> Pray remember the pitcher when empty."

At Clare, Suffolk, there is also a jug of a similar kind, which holds more than seventeen quarts; and also one at Beccles, holding six gallons, less one pint, with inscription.

A correspondent of the *East Anglian* mentions a similar pitcher, called the "Ringers' Pot," which was formerly carried from house to house by the ringers of Ixworth, in Suffolk, to receive whatever beer the parishioners might be disposed to bestow. It has these lines inscribed on it—

> "Here you may see what
> I reqvst of Hanst [honest] gentlmen
> My Baly [belly] Filed Of The Bast I com
> Bvt now And Then." 1716.*

In a closet in the steeple of St. Peter's Mancroft, Norwich, a ringers' jug has been kept, belonging to the "Norwich Scholars." It holds thirty-five pints, is of brown earth, glazed.

---

* See *East Anglian*, i. 61. 273, 280.

An inscription on a jug in the Norwich Museum, dated 1676, is—

> "John W.
> J. F.
> Come brother, shall we join?
> Give me your twopence—here is mine."

The ringers' jug at Swansea has this couplet—

> "Come fill me full with liquor sweet, for that is good
> When friends do meet. When I am full then, drink about :
> I ne'er will fail till all is out."

Occasionally fines were levied for the omission of bell-ringing on special occasions. In the churchwarden's accounts of Bray, in Berkshire, for 1601–2, we find this entry : " It. payd for not ringing when the Queen dyned at Folly John, iii^s. iiii^d."

And in the accounts of St. Lawrence, Reading, for the year ending Michaelmas, 1529: " It. to the queen's armersmt for that the bells were not rong at her comyng into the town, viij^d."

And in the accounts of St. Mary, Lambeth, 1517–18, it is recorded: " Itm. paid to yem a amyner for defawtts off the rynginge off the bells at the kynge's comynge, ij^s. iiij^d."

CHAPTER IX.

CONSECRATION CROSSES.

ONE of the old ceremonies, connected with the consecration of a church, both in this country and on the continent, consisted in the officiating bishop marking upon the wall with oil of chrisms twenty-four crosses; three on the north, south, east, and west walls respectively, both inside and out.[*] It would appear that these crosses were made beforehand—sometimes being carved in stone, modelled in wax or plaster, painted, or by metal crosses affixed to the wall—ready for the bishop to put the chrism on. Very many of these interesting old crosses have disappeared through age, and owing to the scraping of the walls in the process of restoration. An important paper on these consecration crosses was laid before the Society of Antiquaries by Mr. John Henry Middleton (February 23, 1882), to which I am indebted for the following facts.

A very early specimen is at Bishop's Cleeve, Gloucestershire, date about 1190–1200, where it is very deeply cut into a respond of the nave arcade. There is a consecration cross of later date on each side of the west door, for the church was re-consecrated in the beginning of the fourteenth century, when the choir was lengthened, and the high altar moved eastwards. Occasionally, as in this case, "a conse-

[*] " The Archæologia " (1885), xlviii. 456–464.

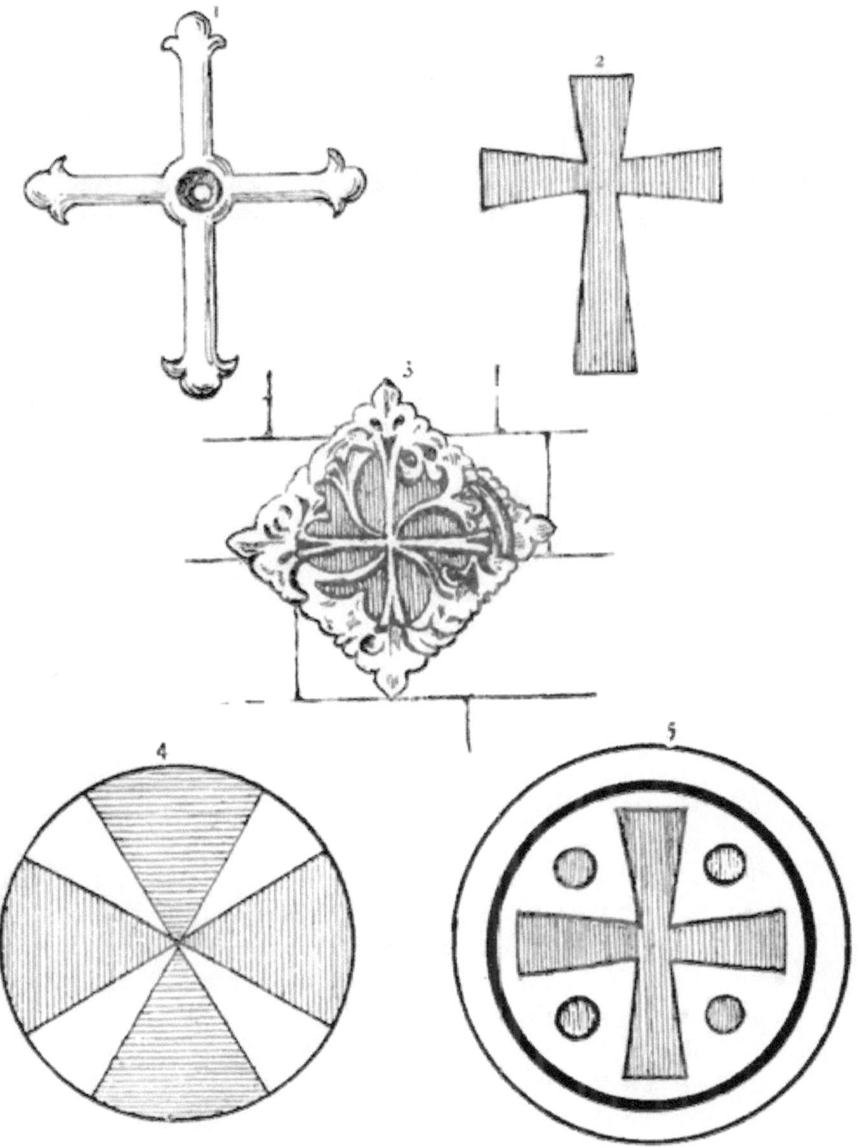

CONSECRATION CROSSES.

1. Badgeworth, Gloucestershire. 2. Chichester Cathedral. 3. Salisbury Cathedral.
4. Shurdington, Gloucestershire. 5. Brooke, Kent.

cration is often made later than the walls it is on, owing to the re-consecration of the *whole* building, when only a part was new."

When an addition to a church was a chapel complete in itself, the new part was, in some cases, only consecrated, and had all the twenty-four crosses, examples of which may be seen at Henry VII.'s Chapel, Westminster, where there are three small crosses in each side of the aisles, and three large ones at the west end above the doorways; and at Arundel Church there still remain five large crosses painted red, and, from their arrangement, it would seem that the nave and its aisles had the full number of crosses without counting any in the choir.

Salisbury Cathedral has a fine set of consecration crosses, eight inside and eight outside being still visible, the rest having been hidden by monuments, or destroyed by the hand of the restorer. But, as Mr. Middleton remarks, " unfortunately, at Salisbury, the 'restorer' has not been content with destruction, but has committed forgery as well. Outside, at the west end, two sham consecration crosses have been put up in the gables of the aisle door-ways, which was not the position of the original crosses." At Chichester Cathedral, we find another instance of recon-secration, where at the east end of the aisles "there are plain sunk crosses cut deep into the stone, possibly once filled up with metal. Above these there are a number of iron pins, as if for the attachment of another metal cross, added probably on the occasion of the second consecration."

An elaborate specimen of these consecration crosses is at St. Mary Ottery, Devon, these being carved in high relief on shields borne by angels within moulded panels, a quatre-foil in a square. Sometimes, too, the central cross at the east end was made more magnificent than the other for the sake of architectural effect. Among instances of this kind may be mentioned a medallion at Chisledon, Wilts, within which is carved a crucifix with St. Mary and St. John, similar crucifixes existing at Coggeshall, Essex, and at Purton, Wilts.

Of the many other consecration crosses mentioned by Mr. Middleton, may be noticed those at Berkeley, Wolston, Cheltenham, Swindon, Badgeworth, Oddington, and Shurdington Chapelry, in Gloucestershire ; Brooke, Kent ; one at Iffley, Oxfordshire ; remains of two crosses at the old chapel, now the library, Pembroke College, Cambridge ; several crosses at Uffington, Berks ;* one at Blofield, Norfolk ; three at Barfreston, Wilts ; and one at South Ferriby, Lincolnshire.   But unfortunately, many of these interesting consecration crosses have passed away with the work of church restoration.

* "The Archæologia," 463.

CHAPTER X.

APART from the sacred rite of baptism, the naming **of the** child has always been **an** important event, in connection with **which we** find many curious customs **in** our Church history. **Thus Strype** tells **us** how **when** the son of **Sir** Thomas **Chamberlayne** was baptized **at St.** Benet's Church, **Paul's Wharf, "the** church was hung with cloth **of** Arras, **and after** the christening were brought wafers, comfits, and **divers** banqueting dishes, **and** Hypocras and Muscadine wine, to entertain the guests." There was the sermon, and in Shipman's "Gossip," 1666, the customs connected with the ceremony of baptism are then summed **up—**

> " Especially since gossips now,
> Eat more at christenings than bestow ;
> Formerly when they us'd to troul
> Gilt bowls of sack, they gave the bowl ;
> Two spoons at least ; an use ill kept ;
> 'Tis well now if our own be left."

Previously to the Reformation, it **was** usual to baptize the child on the day of its birth if possible ; and in order to give facility to the astrologer in "casting the nativity," or telling the fortune of a child, should it be desired. Great precision was often observed in the entry of the birth in the parish register, as, for instance, in that of St. Edmund's,

Dudley: "1539.   Samuell, son of Sir William Smithe Clarke, vicare of Duddly, was born on Friday morninge, at 4 of the clocke, being the xxviij. day of February, the signe of that day was the middle of Aquarius ♌; the signe of the monthe ♓; the plenet of that day ♀; plenet of the same owre ☿ ; and the morrow day, whose name hath continued in Duddly from the Conqueste."

In the register of Hawstead, Suffolk, we find a further allusion to this practice: "M⁴.   That Mr. Robert Drury, the first sonne of Mr. William Drury, Esquire, was born 30 Jan. betwixt 4 and 5 of the clock in the morning, the sunne in Libra, anno 1574, at Durham House, within the parish of Westminster."

If there was any danger of the child dying before a priest could be fetched, the midwife was bound to baptize it. Indeed, before a midwife could obtain a licence, she was solemnly sworn to the due performance of her office, and in 1759 she was to use "pure and clear water only, and not any rose or damask water, or water made of any confection."   In the Archbishop of York's injunctions to his clergy, curates were enjoined "to instruct midwives openly in the church in the very words and form of baptism, to the intent that they may use them perfectly, and none other."   But the register of Hanwell records an awkward mistake, which happened at a baptism of this kind: "Thomas, son of Thomas Messenger and Elizabeth his wife, was born and baptized Oct. 24, 1731, by the midwife at the Font, called a boy, and named by the godfather, Thomas; but proved a girl!" *

In the sixteenth century, such names as "Creature," "Creatura Christi," or "Children of God," were applied to infants baptized by the midwife.   The register of Staplehurst, Kent, under 1547, tells us: "Ther was baptized by

* Burn's "History of Parish Registers in England" (1862), 89.

the midwyffe, and so buryed, the childe of Thomas Gold-ham, called Creature.;" but occasionally such children lived to be married, as the subjoined entry from the same register proves: "1579, July 19. Marryed John Haffynden, and *Creature* Cheseman, young folke." * The term "Crea-tura Christ" occurs in the register of St. Peters-in-the-East, Oxford, as below—

"1563. July 17. Baptizata fuit in ædibus Mrs. Hum-frey, filia euis, quæ nominata fuit Creatura Christi."

"1563. July. Creatura Christi, filia Laurentii Hum-fredi, sepulta fuit eodem die."

According to Mr. Brayley, in his "Beauties of England and Wales" (149), the phrase, "Children of God," was sometimes applied to illegitimate children, who seem to have been designated in various ways. Thus the Twicken-ham register (1590) speaks of the burial of "a scape begotten child," and that of Lambeth contains such entries as these—

"George Speedwell, a merry begott, bapt. Nov. 1, 1685.

"Anne, a byeblow in Lambeth marsh, bapt. Feb. 22, 1688-

"Joseph the base born Son of Ann Funny, bapt. Oct. 15, 1699."

Croydon register records the baptism of "William, filius terræ, May, 1582." And at All Saints, Newcastle, "Crad-dock Bowe, 'love-begot,' was baptized, 22 Feb. 1683."

During the troubles of the seventeenth century, lay baptism sometimes took place, and it is recorded that at Maresfield, Sussex, "the wife of Edward Watmouth appears to have been a very active and useful person in the parish, as she is often mentioned in the registers as sponsor to children baptized; and once or twice as privately baptizing infants herself." †

* R. E. C. Waters, "Parish Registers" (1887), 36.
† Sussex Arch. Soc. Collect., xiv. 161.

In many of our parish registers are entered similar christening by the laity, about 1643.

In many parishes it was customary to name foundlings from the parishes in which they were found, as in St. Lawrence, Old Jewry, where the surname of Lawrence has been invariably given. In "St. Clement Danes," such children are invariably called Clement, and from Diprose's "History of St. Clement Danes" (194), we learn that the justices of Middlesex reported in 1686, that this parish was charged in 1679 with sixteen foundlings, who are all named Clements; and that within the next six years fifty children had been found in the streets, who had all been baptized Clement. By the Temple register, it appears that from 1728 to 1755 no less than one hundred and four foundlings were christened there, all of whom were surnamed Temple or Templer.

Foundlings, again, were occasionally named by the caprice of the vestry; and most readers have heard of Sir Richard Monday, who died at Monday Place, in Crabbe's amusing poem of "The Parish Register"—

> "To name an Infant, met our village Sires
> Assembled all, as such event requires.
> Frequent and full, the rural sages sate,
> And speakers many urged the long bebate—
> Some harden'd knave, who rov'd the country round,
> Had left a Babe within the Parish bound.
> First, of the *fact* they questioned, ' Was it true?'
> The child was brought—' What then remained to do?
> ' Was't dead or living?'   This was fairly prov'd,
> 'Twas pinched—it roar'd—and every doubt remov'd.
> Then by what name th' unwelcome guest to call
> Was long a question, and it pos'd them all:
> For he who lent a name to Babe unknown,
> Censorious men might take it for his own.
> They look'd about, they ask'd the name of all,
> And not one *Richard* answer'd to the call.

> Next they inquir'd the day, when passing by,
> Th' unlucky peasant heard the stranger's cry ;
> This known—how food and raiment they might give
> Was next debated, for the rogue would live ;
> At last with all their words and work content
> Back to their homes, the prudent Vestry went,
> And *Richard Monday* to the Workhouse sent.
>
>   *   *   *   *
>
> Long lost to us, at last our Man we trace,
> Sir Richard Monday died at Monday Place."

In some country parishes, it has been usual to name the child after the saint on whose day he may happen to have been born. A correspondent of *Notes and Queries* baptized a child Benjamin Simon Jude. On expressing some surprise at the strange conjunction, he was informed that the child was born on the festival of St. Simon and St. Jude, and that it was always considered very unlucky to take the day from the child.

Many curious superstitions connected with baptism still linger on. "In Yorkshire," says Mr. Baring Gould, "it is said the first child baptized in a new font is sure to die—a reminiscence of the sacrifice which was used for the consecration of every dwelling and temple in heathen times, and of the pig or sheep killed and laid at the foundation of churches. When I was incumbent of Dalton a new church was built. A blacksmith in the village had seven daughters, after which a son was born, and he came to me a few days before the consecration of the new church to ask me to baptize his boy in the old temporary church and font. 'Why, Joseph,' said I, 'if you only wait till Thursday the boy can be baptized in the new font, on the opening of the new church.' 'Thank you, sir,' said the blacksmith, with a wriggle, 'but, you see, it's a lad, and we shu'd be sorry if he were to die ; ha' if t'had been a lass instead, why then, you were welcome, for 'twouldn't ha' mattered a ha'penny. Lasses are ower money, and lads ower few wi' us.'"

Occasionally in old churches, as in that of Wellcombe, a hamlet bordering on Morwenstowe, over against the font, and in the northern wall there is an entrance named the " Devil's Door." This was thrown open at every baptism for the escape, as it was commonly said, of the fiend, while at other times it was carefully shut.

The old practice of baptizing a boy before a girl is still kept up in some parishes. Although this rule is invariably the result of superstition, it is in accordance with ecclesiastical usage. Maskell, in his " Monumenta Ritualia Ecc. Angl." (i. 24, note 31), quotes the following rubric from the Leofric Missal : " Et accipiet presbyter eos a parentibus eorum, et baptizantur primi masculi deinde feminæ, sub trina mersione, Sanctam Trinitatem semel invocando," etc. A correspondent of *Notes and Queries,* writing from Darlington in 1867, says, " While standing at the font, and preparing to baptize two children, the nurse attending on one of the parties abruptly demanded of the other nurse if the child she presented was a boy. The reply seemed to satisfy her. I took an early opportunity to question her on the subject, and she replied that ' she wondered at my not knowing that a boy was always christened before a girl.' On my assuring her that such was not the custom here, she said, ' In Scarborough, where I came from, it is always the custom to baptize there a boy before a girl.' A Scotch reason for baptizing a boy before a girl is, that to reverse the order would make the girl of a masculine nature and have a beard, while the boy would become effeminate."

But Cuthbert Bede quoted an amusing case in *Notes and Queries* (2nd series, i. 226), showing that in a Worcestershire parish a prejudice existed against baptizing a boy before a girl. On the occasion in question there were three baptisms, two boys and a girl. When the first child was about to be baptized, the woman who carried the little girl elbowed her way up to the parson, in order that the child she carried might be the first to be baptized. As she did so, she said to one of the sponsors, by way of apology, " It's a girl, so it must be christened first," and christened first it was. On the next day, an opportunity was taken to discover her motive. This was her explanation : " You see, sir, the parson bain't a married man, and consequentially is disfamiliar with children, or he'd a never put the little girl to be christen'd after the boys. And though it sadly fluster'd me, sir, to put myself afore my betters in the way which I was fosed to do ; yet, sir, it was the doing of a kindness to them two little boys, in me a setting of my little girl afore 'em." " Why? " " Well, sir, I har astonished as you don't know. Why, sir, if them little boys had been christen'd afore the little girl, they'd have her soft chin, and she'd have had their hairy beards—the poor little innocent ! But, thank goodness, I've kept her from that misfortune."

CHAPTER XI.

THE MARRIAGE CEREMONY.

By the early discipline of the Church, marriages were prohibited during the seasons of Advent, Lent, and Whitsuntide, and in an old vellum register of the parish of
Cottenham, Cambridgeshire, this regulation is thus given in
doggerel Latin—

> " Conjugium Adventus prohibet, Hilarique relaxat
>   Septuagena vetat, sed paschæ octava remittit,
>   Rogamen vetitat, concedit Trina potestas,"

the well-known English version of which is given in the
register of Everton, Notts—

> " Advent marriage doth deny,
>   But Hilary gives thee liberty ;
>   Septuagesima says thee nay,
>   Eight days from Easter says you may.
>   Rogation bids thee to contain,
>   But Trinity sets thee free again."

The canons of the Anglican Church forbid marriages
to be celebrated between Rogation Sunday and Trinity
Sunday, though such prohibitions have practically ceased
to be regarded in England.* Thus in the parish register
of Twickenham, it is recorded, under 1665, that " Christopher Mitchell and Anne Colcot, married 4th June, by

* R. E. Chester Waters, " Parish Registers," 33.

permission of Sir Richard Chaworth, it being within the octave of Pentecost."

In the course of past years many changes have taken place in the customs connected with the marriage ceremony. A practice which seems to have shocked the saints of the Commonwealth was the **kiss, in** which the officiating priest joined.

> " **A** contract of eternal Bond of Love,
>   Confirmed by mutual joinder of your hands,
>   Attested by the Holy Close of lips,
>   Strengthen'd by interchangement of your rings." *

But from the first the Protestants evidently did **not relish** kissing **the priest,** for it is **one of the articles of visitation** in diocese **of London in 1554:** " Whether there be any **that** refuseth **to kysse the** Prieste **at the** solempnisation **of Matrimony, or use any** such lyke ceremonies heretofore writes **used and observed in the** Churche." Brand in his " Popular **Antiquities "** (ii. 140), writes, " It is still customary amongst persons of middling rank, as well as the vulgar, in most parts **of** England, for the young men present at the marriage ceremony to salute the bride, one by **one,** the moment it is concluded." **In** an old song the bridegroom thus addresses the parson—

> " It's **no very decent for** you to be kissing,
>   It does not look weel with the black coat ava,
>   'Twould hae set you far better tae hae **gi'en us your blessing,**
>   **Than thus** by such tricks **to be breaking the law.**
>
>   **Dear** Wattie, quo' Robin, it's just **an** old custom,
>   **An the** thing that is common should **ne'er** be ill ta 'en,
>   **For where** ye are **wrong,** if ye **had na a** wished him,
>   **You should ha'** been **first. It's yoursel'** is to blame."

Mr. Henderson † tells how a parson—a stranger **in the**

---

* " Twelfth Night," act **v. sc. 1.**
† " Folklore of Northern **Counties,"** 39, 40.

neighbourhood—after performing a marriage in a Yorkshire village, was surprised to see the party keep together, as it expecting something more. "What are you waiting for?" he at last asked. "Please, sir," was the bridegroom's answer, "ye've no kissed Molly." "Some years ago," adds Mr. Henderson, "I am informed that in Ireland it was customary for the clergyman to conclude the ceremony with the words 'kiss your wife,' and occasionally the bridegroom was hard put to prevent one, or other, of his companions from intercepting the salute designed for himself."

In the sixteenth century, it was usual to preach a wedding-sermon at the marriage of almost every person of consequence. By the Rubrics of the 2nd and the 5th, Edward VI., it was enacted that "after the Gospel was to be a sermon, wherein ordinarily the office of a man and wife should be declared according to Holy Scripture, or if there was no sermon, then the minister was to read several sentences out of Scripture, setting forth the said duties." In the *Monthly Magazine* for 1798, the custom is noticed of the singers in country churches chanting, on the following Sunday after a couple had been married, a particular psalm, called the Wedding Psalm."

Drinking wine in the church at the marriage ceremony was enjoined by the Hereford Missal; the Sarum Missal directing that the wine as well as the cakes or wafers, called sops, which were soaked therein, and the cup that contained it, should be blessed by the priest. The wine was drunk, and the sops were eaten by the bride and bridegroom, and the company present. In an old inventory of the goods and ornaments belonging to Wilsdon parish, Middlesex, mention is made of "two masers that were appoynted to remayne in the church for to drynk in at bride-ales." The churchwardens' accounts for Tallaton, in Devonshire, under 1595, contain an item of "Paid for bread and wine for three weddings,

6*d.* ;" and under **1601**, " Paid for bread and wine against a wedding, **2*d.***"   Shakespeare, in the " Taming of the Shrew " (iii. **2**), alludes to the practice where Gremio relates how—

> " Stamp'd and swore,
> As if the vicar meant to cozen him.
> But after many ceremonies done,
> He calls for wine :—' A health,' quoth he, as if
> He had been aboard, carousing to his mates
> After a storm :—quaff'd off the muscadel,
> And threw the sops all in the sexton's face ;
> Having no other reason,
> But that his beard grew thin and hungerly,
> And seem'd to ask him sops as he was drinking."

By an Act of Parliament passed on 24th August, 1653, it was enacted that marriages should be solemnized before a Justice of the Peace.   In the register of the parish of Elvetham, Hampshire, we find this entry : " 1654.   I, A B, do here in the presence of God, the searcher of all hearts, take thee, C D, for my wedded wife, and doe, also in the presence of God, promise unto thee to be a loving and a faithful husband.   Thomas Patrick, of Hartley Witney, and Lucie Watts, of Elvetham, were married before Robert Reynolds, Esqr, in the presence of Ambrose Iver and Thomas Townsend, March **16**, 1654.—Robert Reynolds, Justice of the Peace."

For several years after 1653 this order was complied with, but many marriages, says Burn in his " Parish Registers " (**162**), at Northampton, about the same period, were solemnized before the mayor and the minister of the parish. In Flecknoe's " Diarium " (1656) is the following *jeu d'esprit*, entitled, " On the Justice of Peace's making marriages, and the crying them in the market—

> " Now just as 'twas in Saturn's Reign,
> The Golden Age is returned again ;
> And Astrea again from heaven is come,
> When all on earth by Justice is done.

"Amongst the rest, we have cause to be glad
  Now Marriages are in markets made ;
  Since Justice, we hope, will take order there,
  We may not be cousened no more in our ware.

"Besides, each thing would fall out right,
  And that old próverb be verified by 't— -
  That Marriage and Hanging both go together,
  When Justice shall have disposing of either.

"Let Parson and Vicar, then, say what they will,
  The custome is good (God continue it still) ;
  For marriage being now Trafique and Trade,
  Pray where but in Markets should it be made.

" 'Twas well ordain'd they should be no more
  In Churches nor Chappels, then as before ;
  Since for it in Scripture we have example,
  How buyers and sellers were drov'n out o' th' Temple.

"Mean time, God bless the Parliament,
  In making this Act so honestly meant.
  Of these good marriages God bless the breed,
  And God blesse us all, for was never more need."

The marriages in the parish of Dale Abbey were, till a few years previous to the Marriage Act, solemnized by the clerk of the parish, at one shilling each, there being no minister.

At an early date it was customary to make offerings at marriages. In the privy purse expenses of Henry VII. these entries occur—

" 1492. May 20. For offring at Master Scrops marriage, 6s. 8d."

" — June 2. For offering at Sir Charles Somerset's marriage, 6s. 8d."

" 1494. May 26. For offering at the four marriages, £1 6s. 8d."

From numerous entries, too, in churchwardens' accounts

during the seventeenth century, it seems to have been a common practice to distribute money among the needy at marriages. The "Pleasures of Memory," a chap-book of the last century, describing a contemporary wedding, says, "They go from the church again, and first receive the joy of the beggars ; the bridegroom, for the grandeur of the wedding, throwing amongst them a handful of small money, which sets them scrambling." The accounts of All Hallows, Barking, contains the following entries—

"22nd Sept., 1654. Distributed at a marriage to the poore, 3 pounds.

"Febry., 1660. Gave six shillings to the poor, given by a gent. who was married on Easter Tuesday."

From the parish accounts of Hackney for 1663, we learn that it was customary to make collections at the church door upon the marriage of paupers, and that they were so considerable that the collection gave security that the couple for whom such collection was made should not become burdensome to the parish.

At Northwich, Cheshire, a curious privilege is ascribed by the charter of that church to the senior scholar of the Grammar School, viz. that he is to receive marriage fees to the same amount as the clerk, or, in lieu thereof, the bride's garters.* Similarly, at Burnley, Lancashire, an old custom prevails, by which all persons married at St. Peter's church are fined by the boys at the Grammar School. The money thus obtained is sufficient to maintain the school library.

At one time the banns of marriage were published on market days, and in the Act of Parliament of 24th August, 1653, it was enacted that the banns of marriage should be published three times on three separate Sundays in the church or chapel, or in the market-place, on three market

---

* Burn's " Parish Registers," 164.

days, between the hours of eleven and twelve o'clock. As
the Act, however, did not prescribe who was to publish the
banns in the market-place, it would, no doubt, often occur,
writes a correspondent of *Notes and Queries*, that the bellman of the town would be the most eligible person to
perform that duty, both on account of his bell and his
voice. This appears to have been a favourite mode of
proclaiming the banns, and in the parish register of Boston,
Lincolnshire, we find that the banns proclaimed in that
town during the years 1656, 1657, and 1658, were 102, 104,
and 108 respectively; those proclaimed in the church during
those years being 48, 51, and 52.

If, after the publication of banns, the marriage does not
come off, the deserted one is said in Worcestershire to be
"hung in the bell ropes," evidently meaning that the ringers
are waiting for the marriage ceremony to be performed, so
that they may aid in celebrating the event. In Cumberland
a couple are said to be "hinging i' t' bell-rope" during the
period which transpires between the first publication of
banns and marriage.

In some of the northern and midland counties it has
long been customary, on the evening of the Sunday when
the banns of marriage are published for the first time, to
announce the fact with a merry peal from the church bells.
This peal is called the "Spur Peal," and the Sunday "Spur
Sunday." To put in "the spurrings" is to give notice to
the parson to publish the banns, and to be "spurred up"
is to have had the banns published for three Sundays.
Formerly at Barnbydum, and also at Kirk Bramwith, Yorkshire, immediately after the publication of the banns, the
parish clerk responded, "God speed 'em well." A similar
custom prevailed at Hope church, Derbyshire, where the
clerk called out while the couple stood at the altar, "God
speed the couple well." At Wellow, in Nottinghamshire, it

has been customary from time immemorial, when the banns are published, for some person selected by the clerk to rise and say, "God speed them well," the clerk and congregation responding, "Amen." In the *Notts Guardian* of April 28th, 1853, we read, "Owing to the recent death of the person who officiated in this ceremony, last Sunday, after the banns of marriage were read, a perfect silence prevailed, the person chosen, either from want of courage or loss of memory, not performing his part until an intimation from the clerk, and then in so faint a tone as scarcely to be audible. His whispered good-wishes were, however, followed by a hearty Amen, mingled with some laughter in different parts of the church."

An old custom prevails at Belford, in Northumberland, of making the bridal pair, with their attendants, leap over a stone, known as the "louping" or "petting stone," placed in their path outside the church porch; on which spot, it is said, the bride must leave all her pets and humours behind her when she crosses it. At the neighbouring village of Embleton, writes Mr. Henderson, in his "Folk-lore of the Northern Counties" (38), "the stout young lads place a wooden bench across the door of the church porch, assist the bride and bridegroom and their friends to surmount the obstacle, and then look out for a donation from the bridegroom." In the year 1868, adds Mr. Henderson, at a wedding in a High-Coquetdale family, "it was proposed to have a petted stone. A stick was therefore held by two groomsmen at the church door for the bride to jump over. Had she stumbled or fallen, the worst auguries as to her temper would have been drawn." On June 5th, 1873, at Bamburgh church, on the conclusion of the wedding ceremony, on leaving the church, a three-legged stool, about a foot high, was placed at the churchyard gate, and covered with about two yards of carpet. The whole of the bridal party had separately to hop or jump over this stool (locally known as the "parting stool"), assisted on either side by a stalwart villager.

There has long been a vulgar error that a man is not liable for his wife's debts if he marries her in her shift only, and instances of this having actually taken place are recorded in register books. Thus at Chiltern All Saints, Wiltshire, "John Bridmore and Anne Selwood were married, Oct. 17, 1714. The aforesaid Anne Selwood was married in her smock, without any clothes or headgear on." At Ulcomb, Kent, in 1725, a woman was married in her shift, and in 1766 a similar case occurred at Whitehaven. Some years ago the parson, finding nothing in the rubric about the woman's dress, thought he could not refuse to marry her in her chemise only.

In the registers of Haworth church, Yorkshire, under 1733, occurs an entry of "Marriages at Bradford, and by clog and shoe in Lancashire, but paid the minister of Haworth," to which are subjoined certain fees. At Hilton, Dorsetshire, celibacy was apparently punished in the last century. Thus the register of that parish, under 1739, records the following mandate: "Ordered, that all young unmarried persons above seventeen years of age do forthwith go to service, or be proceeded against according to law."

One of the most interesting antiquities of Jarrow Church, Northumberland, is the chair of the venerable Bede. It is preserved in the vestry of the church, whither all brides repair directly the marriage service is over, to seat themselves upon it. According to the general belief, this act will make them the joyful mother of children, and the expectant mothers would not consider the ceremony complete until they had been enthroned in the venerable Bede's chair.*

---

* See *Antiquarian Repertory* (1817), i. 107.

Similarly, in years gone by, on the lower declivity of Warton Crag, in the parish of Warton, Lancashire, a seat called the " Bride's Chair," was resorted to on the day of their marriage by the brides of the village, and in this seat they were enthroned by their friends with due solemnity.* In years past, special precaution was taken to prevent brides sitting down on the left seat at the gateway of the entrance to Yarmouth Church, popularly known as the " Devil's Seat," this being supposed to render any one who sat upon it especially liable to misfortune ever afterwards.†

* Harland and Wilkinson's " Lancashire Folklore " (1867), 265.
† Hone's " Year Book," 254.

CHAPTER XII.

BURIAL CUSTOMS.

MARKED changes have taken place within the last few centuries in our burial customs. Many of our cathedrals and old parish churches have silently witnessed strange sights in the modes of interment occasionally practised by our forefathers, records of which have been preserved in local documents. An important disuse of an old practice is that of burying in the sacred edifice, as to the propriety of which many great and good men have entertained strong scruples. Archbishop Sancroft thought it "improper the House of God should be made the repository of sinful man." Sir Matthew Hale was wont to say that "churches were for the living, and churchyards for the dead;" and Joseph Hall, Bishop of Norwich, "did not hold God's house a meet repository for the greatest saint." Lanfranc, Archbishop of Canterbury, it is said, was the first who made vaults under the chancel, and even under the altar, when he rebuilt the choir of Canterbury, about 1075.

In the register of Great and Little Abingdon this entry occurs, which is a curious combination of business and sentiment: "Burial without a coffin, 1*s.*; for a grave in the church, 6*s.* 8*d.*; in the chancel, 13*s.* 4*d.* But the most honourable grave of any man whatsoever is in the church-yard, because that shows most honour to God's house. The great first Christian Emperor Constantine, and many of his successors, were buryed in the churchyard." In the last fifty years, however, a great alteration has taken place in England as far as interments in churches are concerned. In London the churchyards have been closed, and burials in any church or churchyard absolutely forbidden, except with the authority of the Secretary of State, which is rarely obtained.

But, going back to past times, the right of a church to have a mortuary when a person of consequence was interred within it led, writes the late Prebendary Mackenzie Walcott,* to some remarkable scenes. "Bishop Hatfield's body," he writes, "was carried to the door of Durham on a chariot drawn by five horses, which became the mortuary due to the abbey. The body of Lord Neville, in 1355, was removed from the funeral car at the cemetery gates, and carried into the church on the shoulders of his armed relatives. On the morrow, at Mass, four men-at-arms and eight horses—four of them apparelled for battle and four for peace—were offered. The horses were usually redeemed or exchanged for sheep—the rich hearse cloths used for church ornaments, and the huge torches converted into tapers. Four stately horses drew the hearse of Bishop Langley into the nave; and possibly owing to these cumbrous solemnities, the wall of the Nine Altars was broken through to permit the admission of the body of Bishop Bek in 1310. The obsequies of Henry V. were observed at St. Paul's and Westminster, and his three chargers, with their riders, were led up to the altar amidst the blaze of one thousand tapers. At Henry VII.'s funeral a knight rode into the rails of the hearse on a goodly courser trapped, which became the perquisite of the abbey." Instances of this kind, which might be easily enumerated,

---

* "Traditions and Customs of Cathedrals," 204–206.

show on how imposing a scale the funeral obsequies of the great were conducted in olden days. " The hearse, a grand erection of sumptuous woodwork, was often set up before the altar over the bier of royal personages. On that of Queen Mary at Westminster there were held lights to the number of a thousand and more."

The popular superstition, too, that the body of the murdered bled afresh if approached by the guilty persons, led to its exposure in public, in order to suppress any suspicion of foul play. For three or four days the naked bodies of the lords Warwick and Montacute lay in St. Paul's in Easter week, 1471, " that all men might see them." On May 22, 1471, attended by a number of armed men, the body of Henry VI. was silently exposed in an open coffin for two days before the high altar of St. Paul's, " where he bled ;" and that of Richard II., after his murder at Pontefract, was exposed for three days.*

The custom of taking out the heart of the deceased, and depositing it apart from the body, has obtained up to recent times. Westminster Abbey contains the hearts of several royal personages. It is said that the heart of Queen Mary was interred in the chapel at St. James's previous to her funeral in Westminster Abbey ; but when the royal vault was opened in 1670, the urns containing the hearts of Queen Mary and her sister Elizabeth were found within niches with their names inscribed upon them. A curious entry occurs in the Cotton Manuscript relative to the interment of the heart of Queen Mary—

" A box covered with black velvet.

" Robert Horwood, for half a yard of velvet, black, for covering a box for the Queen's heart ; of the Queen's store one quarter of sarsenet, red, for to wrap the Queen's heart in.

* " Traditions and Customs of Cathedrals," 204.

"John Grene for a box, and covering the same, 3*s.* 4*d.*

"Mary Wilkinson, four yards of passamayne lace to garnish the same.

"Canopy of blue velvet.

"Hatchments and mantellets.

"The coat and banner of arms."

Prince Henry of Wales, son of King James I., who died at the early age of eighteen, was buried in Westminster Abbey, his heart being enclosed in lead and placed upon his breast. Among further royal personages whose hearts were buried in a similar manner in Westminster Abbey, were Charles II., William and Mary, George, Prince of Denmark, and Queen Anne.

The heart of Edward Lord Bruce was enclosed in a silver case, and deposited in the Abbey Church of Culross, near the family seat. In 1808 this sad relic was discovered by Sir Robert Preston, the lid of the silver case bearing on the exterior the name of the unfortunate duellist, and after drawings had been taken of it, the whole was carefully replaced in the vault.* In St. Nicholas' Chapel, Westminster Abbey, was enshrined the heart of Esme Stuart, Duke of Richmond, where a monument to his memory is still to be seen, and an inscription, the first part of which runs thus—

"S.M.

Hâc in Urnâ

Includitur cor

Infra

Requiescit corpus

Illustrissimi Ducis

Esme Stuart," etc. †

---

* The urn which contained the heart is thirteen inches in height. It is now empty.

† Emily Sophia Hartshorne, "Enshrined Hearts of Warriors and Illustrious People" (1861), 310.

Many interesting instances are to be found in some of our parish churches. In the church at East Horndon, Essex, about sixteen miles from New Hall, which was once the seat of Sir Thomas Boleyn, a nameless black marble monument is pointed out as that of Anne Boleyn, "It is within a narrow window seat, and may have contained her head or her heart, for it is too short to contain a body. The oldest people in the neighbourhood all declare that they have heard the tradition in their youth from a previous generation of aged persons, who all affirm it to be Anne Boleyn's monument." * By her testament, Eleanor, Duchess of Buckingham, wife of Edward, Duke of Buckingham, who was beheaded on May 17, 1521, appointed her heart to be buried in the church of the Grey Friars, within the City of London. In the Sackville vault, in the church of Withyam, Sussex, is a leaden box in the shape of a heart, on a brass plate which is inscribed :—

"The heart of Isabella, Countess of
Northampton,
Died the 14th October, 1661."

The heart of Robert Vaughan, of Merionethshire, was buried in the church at Ludlow, 1642, and it is said that Henry Spencer, Earl of Sunderland, who received his death wound|at the fatal battle of Newbery, "was buried in the church at Brington, which is the parish of Althorp, the family seat. This, however, does not appear to be at all certain, as there is no entry in the register recording the fact; but a leaden drum deposited in vault in the church is supposed to contain his heart. This case has no inscription, or even date upon it." † At Catterick, Yorkshire, was buried the

* See Miss Strickland's "Lives of the Queens of England," ii. 702.
† "Enshrined Hearts," 292.

heart of John, son of Sir John Lawson, as the following inscription shows—

"Hic jacent Reliquiæ Johannis Lawson de Burgh **Baronetti et** Catharinæ charissimæ ejus conjugis filiæ Gulielmi **Howard de** Narworth Castello in comitatu Cumberlandiæ Equitis Aurati.

Obit { Ille, 26 October, 1698.
{ Hæc, 4 July, 1668.

Ibidem hic   reponitur
Cor Johannis   filii natu Maximi.

Supradicti Johannis Lawson, Baronetti.

Requiescant **in pace**."

Lord Byron's heart was enclosed in **a silver** urn, and placed **at Newstead** Abbey, in the family vault, while that of Percy **Bysshe** Shelley was placed in an urn, and deposited in the English burying-ground at Rome. His body, it may be remembered, was washed on shore on the coast of the Gulf of Spezia, and, according to Italian custom after drowning, the body was burnt to ashes. But the heart would not consume; hence its burial.

In some cases, buried hearts have been accidentally discovered, little or **no** trace being left to identify them with **any certainty**. At Waverley Abbey, Surrey, in 1731, there were found in a stone oculus, two leaden dishes soldered together, containing a human heart, well preserved **in** pickle, and supposed to have been that of Bishop Peter de Rupibis, **who** gave directions that it should be preserved **at** this religious **house**. **During** the rebuilding of Chatham Church, Kent, **in** 1788, **a** leaden pot was found in one of the vaults, containing, according to an inscription, the heart of **a woman, named** Hester Harris. When the chancel at Landbeach was repaired in 1759, a heart was found, variously supposed to be that of the founder of the church, of a Crusader, or to have belonged to a Chamberlayn, or a Bray, lords of the manor.* On a stone in Chichester Cathedral is a trefoiled panel, within which is the figure of a heart upheld by two hands, and in Lombardic characters the legend : " Ici gist le couer mand de." And at Yaxley, near Peterborough, there was found some years ago, in the north transept wall, a box containing some dust, doubtless that of a heart, a figure of which, upheld by two hands, was placed before it.

A singular deposit of a heart, encased in clay, was found some years ago in a church in Kent, near East Peckham. And not far from a curious niche, destined for a double heart deposit, was discovered at Leybourne Church, Kent, a leaden box conjectured to hold the heart of Sir Roger de Leybourne.† At Wells Cathedral, enclosed in a box of copper, a heart was found, supposed to be that of one of the bishops, and in the crypt was shown an urn, and the shrivelled remains of a heart, represented to be that of king Ina, from whose coffin it was said to have been taken.‡ A few years ago, at the church of Little Hereford, Shropshire, a heart was discovered in a mural sepulchre ; and in the family vault of the Hungerfords, at Farely Castle, a heart was accidentally found in a glazed earthenware pot covered with white leather. In 1773, a heart was unearthed at Edinburgh, in the foundations of St. Cuthbert's Kirk. It was enclosed in a leaden box in the shape of a heart, and had been embalmed with spices.

A very remarkable instance of a heart-interment was

* See Gough's " Sepulchral Monuments."
† See Rev. L. Larking in " Archæological Cantiana," v. 136.
‡ Miss Hartshorne's " Enshrined Hearts," 400.   See also Pettigrew's " Chronicles of the Tombs," for instances of heart-burial.

some years ago discovered in the church of Ewyas Harold, an adjoining parish to Dore, in Herefordshire, where there is an effigy of a lady, nearly life size, holding between her hands, which rest on the breast, such a vessel as might be supposed to contain a heart. Its date appears to be about 1300, or a little later. On opening this tomb "in October, 1861, in the presence of the vicar, the Rev. W. C. Fowle, and others, there was found under the hands and only a few inches below the effigy, a flat stone covered by an intervening flat stone of larger size, on which lay some rubble, and then the effigy ; and in the lower of these two stones was a hemispherical cavity, about five inches in diameter, in which were fragments of a metal vessel that seemed to have been lined with a woven fabric, and probably had contained a heart. Immediately over this cavity, on the under side of the stone that covered it, was painted in white the form of a vessel suitable for enclosing a heart, and such as might have been, and probably was, deposited in the cavity. No trace was discovered of the body, that, most likely, was interred elsewhere. It is not known who the lady was, but there is some reason to suppose that she was Clarice, the elder daughter of John de Tregoz, who held by barony the castle at Ewyas Harold, and died about 1300." *

Many notices of burial in erect posture occur in the literature of the past, and Hearne, in his "Collection of Antiquarian Discourses" (i. 212), says this custom was formerly adopted in the case of captains in the army : "For them above the grounde buryed, I have by tradition heard, that when anye notable captaine dyed in battel or campe, the souldyers used to take the bodye and to sette him on his feet uprighte, and put his launce into his hand ; and then his fellowe souldyers did by travell everye man bringe so muche earthe, and laye aboute him as should

* "Journal of Archæological Association," xxi. 142, 143.

cover him, and mount up to cover the top of his pike." Wordsworth, in his "White Doe of Rylstone," alludes to this practice—

> "Pass, pass who will yon chantry door,
> And through the chink in the fractured floor,
> Look down, and see a grisly sight,
> A vault where the bodies are buried upright ;
> There face by face, and hand by hand,
> The Claphams and Mauleverers stand."

In Whitaker's "Craven," we are told that "at the east end of the north aisle of Bolton Priory Church is a chantry belonging to Bethmesley Hall, and a vault where, according to tradition, the Claphams were buried upright."

The church of East Meon, Hants, has on its walls a stone with this inscription, "Amens Plenty," and there is a tradition that three armed men are buried upright beneath.

At Box Hill, Dorking, a Major Labelliere is buried in a curious position, the grave being at the summit of the eminence, in a recess cut out of the grove of box trees. By his desire he was buried head downwards, it having been a constant remark of his that the world was turned topsey-turvey, and that at the last day he would then be placed right.

A curious story of Ben Jonson has often been related to the effect that he is interred upright in his grave at Westminster Abbey. Knight, in his "Old England" (i. 290), gives the tale thus—

"The Dean of Westminster rallied the poet one day about his burial in the Abbey vaults. 'I am too poor for that,' said Jonson, 'and no one will lay out funeral charges upon me. No, sir ; six foot long by two wide is too much for me—two foot by two will do for what I want.' 'You shall have it,' replied the dean, and so the conversation ended. On the poet's death, continues the story, a demand was made for the space promised, a hole made in it eight feet deep, and the coffin deposited therein upright." In the "Ingoldsby Legends," this anecdote is mentioned—

> " Besides in the place,
>   They say there's not space,
>   To bury what wet nurses called a ' Babby.'
>   Even ' Rare Ben Jonson,' that famous wight,
>   I am told is interr'd there bolt upright,
>   In just such a posture, beneath his bust,
>   As Tray used to sit in to beg for a crust."

In 1858, the vault of the Powletts, Barons Bolton, in Wensley Church, Yorkshire, being opened for a burial, a correspondent of *Notes and Queries* (5th series, ii. 347) tells us he "entered in, and saw the leaden coffin of the Marchioness of Winchester in an erect position."

It was not unusual, when persons of distinction died, to have the funeral service performed with a *Corpus fictum*, or effigy of the deceased, in all the different churches with which they were connected, and such funerals were entered in the parish registers as if they were actual burials, although the body was buried elsewhere. Queen Elizabeth was buried in this way in all the London churches; and the register of Selborne, Hants, records in 1594 the burial of Thomas Cowper, Bishop of Winchester, although he was actually interred in his own cathedral church.[*]

When persons of rank, too, died in one parish and were buried in another, the burial was usually recorded in the registers of both parishes.

Notices of "solemn burials" occur in many registers, the preparation for which necessarily took up much time, so that the funeral was often postponed for several weeks after the interment. The following entry, for instance, shows that Sir Edward Clere, who died on June 8, 1606, was buried on

[*] R. E. C. Waters, " Parish Registers in England " (1887), 47.

June 21, but the solemn funeral was not celebrated until August 14th : , "Blickling, Norfolk, 1606.　Dnus Edwardus Clere Miles, quondam Dnus de Blickling, obiit Londinii 8to die Junii, atque sepultus fuit apud Blickling 21° die mensis predicti, cujus funera summa *Cum Solemnitate* celebrata fuere 14° die Augusti A.D. 1606."　In the parish of Iselham, Cambridge, under 1590, this entry is given : "Mr. Robert Peyton, Esquier, died 19 Oct., and was solemnly buried 12 Nov. next following."　"Such solemn burials," writes Mr. Waters, "were directed and served up by the Heralds, who drew up funeral certificates which were subscribed by the executors of the deceased, and were recorded in the College of Arms.　The series of these certificates began in 1567, but have been discontinued since 1688, and the Heralds have ceased to attend, except at royal and public funerals, at which they still marshal the procession, and proclaim the style of the deceased."

Connected with the solemn funeral were the sermon and feast, for which wealthy persons generally made provisions in their wills.　Thus, William Methoulde, Citizen and Mercer of London, by his will dated April 25, 1580, gave 10*s.* to the vicar of St. Lawrence in the old Jewry, "for the sermon on the day of my funeral," and directed that "the people, poor and rich, dwelling in the alley of Milk Street, in our end of the parish of St. Lawrence, be feasted on the day of my funeral ; some at dinner and the rest at supper," and £40 was to be spent on their entertainment.　The burial feast went out of fashion in the seventeenth century, but there was always a funeral sermon, after which wine, wafers, gloves, and rosemary were distributed.　This custom was so universal among all funerals of the better sort, that Smyth *　thought it worth noting in his *Obituary* how Mr. Cornelius Bee, a bookseller in Little Britain, was buried on Jan. 4,

* R. E. C. Water's " Parish Registers," 48.

1671–2, at St. Bartholomew's the Great, "without a sermon, without wine or wafers ; only gloves and rosemary."

In days gone by, among some of the curious scenes witnessed within the walls of our churches, have been burials by torchlight. On the night of November the 11th, 1760, George II. was interred at Westminster Abbey in Henry VII.'s chapel ; and of those whose funerals took place at a similar time in the same sacred structure may be mentioned the poet Cowley, John Addison, Thomas Betterton, and Samuel Foote.

Occasionally nocturnal burials took place for the sake of secrecy. In the parish register of Weedon Beck, Northamptonshire, we are told how "William Radhouse, the elder, dying excom⁴, was buried by stealthe, in the night time, in yᵉ churchyard, yᵉ 29th day of January, 1615, whereupon yᵉ church was interdicted a fortnight." * Among further notices of this custom may be mentioned the following extract from the will of Frances Countess Dowager of Thanet, dated June 11th, 1646, which directs that "my bodie may bee buried at Raynham, where the body of my deare Lord Nicholas, late Earle of Thanett, deceased, doth lie, and that it may bee buried in the night season as his was." In the parish register of Bruton this entry is given : "1688, June 6. The Right Honorᵇˡᵉ Charles Lord Viscount FitzHarding, was between twelve and one of the clock in the night, after a sermon preached by Mr. John Randall, the minister of Brewton, buried in the vault in the chancell, in a coffin of lead." In the *Gentleman's Magazine* (1817, lxxxvii. pt. ii. 13) is an account of the funeral of the

---

* In the churchwardens' accounts of St. Mary's, Cambridge, is a charge of 8 ob. "for the new hallowing or reconcyling of our church, being interdicted at the buryall of Mr. Bucer, and the charge thereunto belonging, frankincens and sweet perfumes for the sacrament, and herbes," etc. (Harl. MSS., 7044, p. 184).

Duchess of Northumberland in 1782, which it is recorded "took place by torchlight at four in the morning, to avoid the mischief of too great a number of persons interrupting the same; which, however, was not the case, as the concourse of people was so numerous at the screens to the small chapels surrounding the south aisle of the choir (in the farther end of which is the Percy vault), that many had their legs and arms broken, and were otherwise much bruised. From this time no burials have been performed by torchlight except royal ones, a sufficient guard attending to keep order on the occasion." From time immemorial it has been the custom of the ancient family of Dyott, of Treeford, to bury its deceased members by torchlight.

Aldermen of London, who had filled the mayoralty, were, by ancient custom, buried with special solemnity, and usually by torchlight. But these funerals at night were so often scenes of disorder that they were at last prohibited by Charles I. A curious letter on the subject, written by the Earl Marshal to the Lord Mayor, July 16th, 1635, on the occasion of the death of Alderman Sir Richard Deane, who had served as Lord Mayor in 1628, has been preserved in the College of Arms :

"My very good Lord,

"Whereas I am informed that Sir Rich. Deane, Kt., Aldn and late Lo. Mayor of the Citty of London, is lately deceased, and to be buryed as I am given to understand, in a private manner, no way sutable with his degree and eminent quality of chief magistrate of the citty, not only contrary to the laudible custome of his predecessors, but allsoe to yor owne constitutions made amongst yor selves for the solempne and ceremonious entertment of such as have borne office in the place of Lo : Mayor, fforasmuch as his Mātie hath lately signefied his expresse pleasure and com̄and for the prohibitinge all nocturnall funeralls whatsoever for the suppression of which disorders as I am obliged by the place I hold to be carefull in the execution of his Māties **Royale** comãand, so am **I** likewise **as formerly** I have done in the like case ernestly **to** desyre your lo[p], **and** the Executors of **the defunct whom** it may concerne, **to see the** auncient and **reuerend** ceremonies **at the** enterm[t] both of this **gent :** deceased, and those of his qualety **in** the citty, **to be** decently celebrated and duly observed according **to the** accustomed solemnities, and with vsuall rights to the memory **of** the deceased. So, not doubting of yo[r] redinesse **herein** I rest,

> "Yo[r] lo[p] **very** loving friend,
>> "ARUNDELL & SURREY.

> " **Arundell House,** 16 July, **1635.**
>> " **To my** honorable friend,
>>> " **The Lo :** Mayor of the City of London."

Sir Walter Scott **in "The** Antiquary" (chap. **xxvi.),** **alludes to** the custom of **the** Glenallan family being buried by torchlight, and in the mouth of Elspeth Mucklebackit gives as the reason—

" They hae dune sae since the time the Great Earl fell **in the** sair battle o' the Harlaw, when they say the coronach was cried in ae day from the mouth o' the Tay to the **Buck of** the Cabrach, that ye **wad** hae heard nae other sound but **that** of lamentation for the great folks that had fa'en fighting **against** Donald of the Isles. But **the** great **Earl's** mither **wad** hae nae coronach cried for **her** son, but **had him** laid in the silence o' midnight in his place o' **rest,** without either drinking the dirge or **crying the lament, and sae** she **laid him in** his grave wi' **dry eyes, and** without a groan or a wail."

In the parish **register of Norton,** Derbyshire, **it is** stated, **under 1601, how** " Anthonius Blythe de Brychet p'œ de dranfield Armiger sepult' fuit in Capella Eccl'eæ p'oâli de Norton adjunct Tertio die Junii in nocte." And in the registers of Toddington, Bedfordshire, this entry is given: " Honoratissimus, D.D., Thomas Wentworth Comes cliniæ fidelissimus regis subditus patronus meus multis hominibus Colendus sepultus erat in Crypta circiter, Nov. 9, nocte April 4° (1667)."

A mid-Shropshire squire of long ago, who was credited with being very wicked, was buried, writes Miss Jackson in her "Shropshire Folklore" (119), "in an old-world fashion," after the following manner, as told by the narrator: " When I was a little wench it was, the old squire died. And he lied in state, and they buried him at midnight, and crowds of people come to see him. And there was men in black with torches in the church, and the vault was opened, and we all went down into it to look at the coffins. And my grand-mother took me, and I ketched out on her hand. And she asked me, was I frightened? But I wasn't frightened. And my grandmother said it was an old custom with some of the gentry to bury at midnight."

Interments in the actual walls of churches were not unfre-quent. At St. John's Priory Church, Clerkenwell, during some repairs in 1812, in the wall near the southernmost east window, the skeleton of a child was found in a cavity of the masonry; and during the restoration of Purton Church, Wilts, a skeleton was discovered in one of the walls. Blomefield mentions an instance of intra-mural burial at Foulden, Norfolk: " On the foundation of the south aisle, facing the churchyard, is an arched monument over a flat marble gravestone, partly covered by the arch, partly by the wall, and apparently about the time of Edward I." *

In the church of Preshute, near Marlborough, on pulling down one of the old walls during the restoration, a body

* See *Notes and Queries*, 1st series, iii. 37.

was discovered in the wall near the site of the pulpit, and Mr. T. J. Micklethwaite says: "The side walls of the extension eastward of the chapter-house of Kirkstall Abbey have built into them a considerable number of coffins. With the exception of one," he adds, "these coffins are empty; and it is probable that they were originally placed under the floor, but were disturbed when the place was altered, and both economy and decency suggested building them up in the new walls as the best way of disposing of them." [*]

At Brent Pelham Church, Herts, there is the tomb of one Piers Shonkes, the inscription on which has these words: "Hoc tamen in muro tutus." The story goes that the devil swore he would have Piers Shonkes, no matter whether buried within or without the church. So, to outwit his satanic majesty, he was built up in the wall of the sacred edifice. An amusing legend of a similar kind is told respecting the building of an ancient manor-house, locally known as Barn Hall, in the parish of Tolleshunt Knights, on the edge of the Essex marshes. In the middle of a field an enclosed uncultivated spot is still shown, where the legend says it was intended to erect the hall, had not the devil come by night and destroyed the work of the day. A knight, attended by two dogs, was set to watch for the intruder; a tussle ensued, and the Prince of Darkness, snatching up a beam from the building, hurled it to the site of the present hall, exclaiming—

> "Whereso'er this beam shall fall,
> There shall stand Barn Hall."

The devil, enraged at the knight's interference, vowed that he would have him at his death, whether he were buried in the church or out of it. But this doom was averted by

[*] *Notes and Queries*, 5th series, ii. 234.

burying him in the wall, half in and half out of the church.[*]

In the north wall of the church of Tremeirchion, near the banks of the Elwy, North Wales,[†] is the tomb of a former vicar, Daffydd Ddu, who was also celebrated as a necromancer, flourishing about 1340. It is said he proved himself more clever than the Wicked One himself. A bargain was made between them that the vicar should practice the black art with impunity during his life, but that the devil should possess his body after death, whether he were buried within, or without, the church. But the worthy vicar cheated his ally of his bargain by being buried within the church wall itself.

The practice of burying either inside or under the pillars of churches has excited considerable interest, instances of this peculiar custom having from time to time been discovered.

According to a correspondent of *Notes and Queries* (2nd series, x. 521), Clement Spelman of Narburgh, Recorder of Nottingham, who died 1679, is immured upright, enclosed in a pillar in Narburgh chancel ; and some years ago, when St. John's Church, Clareborough, Notts, was undergoing restoration, it was necessary to take down to the foundation one corner of the tower owing to its bad condition. On the removal of the stones and mortar, it was found that they had been built on a solid rock, which "had been hollowed out in the usual shape of a stone coffin, and the remains of a human skeleton were discovered within it. The buttress and corner of the tower were built over the corpse, the feet were towards the east."[‡] About sixty years ago, during some repairs of York Minster, it was found

---

[*] "The Antiquary," iv. 279.
[†] See Pennant, ii. 139 ; *Notes and Queries*, 1st series, ii. 513.
[‡] *Notes and Queries*, 4th series, xii. 149.

needful to lay bare part of the foundation, when it was discovered that under a pillar, prepared for the purpose, an interment had taken place. The body was that of a bishop in his robes. The Rev. W. Taylor, F.R.S., minor canon of York,* was present when the grave was opened, and it would appear that the place of interment in the foundation of the pillar had been properly prepared by the builder with the view of receiving a body; the cavity not being of sufficient size to impair the stability of the pillar itself.

In 1679, an Act was passed, termed "An Act for burying in Woollen," and was intended "for the lessening the importation of linen from beyond the seas, and the encouragement of the woollen and paper manufactures of this kingdom." By this Act the clergy were enjoined to state in the entry of burials that the law had been kept. The custom then arose for the parish clerk to ask at the conclusion of the burial service, "Who makes affidavit?" One of the relations of the deceased made the necessary oath, and the fact was noted in the register.† In the "Reliquary" lxvii. 93), a specimen of one of these affidavits is thus given—

"Dec. 20, 1718, recd. this affidavit.

"Com. Lan. Manchester, Dec. 20, 1718, which day Ann wife of Saml. Hampson of Stretford, in the parish of Manchester, Thatcher made oath y^t the body of Sarah wife of Tho. Tipping, of the township and parish aforesaid, Husbandman, lately deceased (December 14), was interr'd according to the Act of Parliament for burying in Wollen.

"Radley Ainscough, Cap. (Chaplain)

de Manchestr."

But the higher classes generally evaded the law, and in

* *Notes and Queries*, 4th series, xii. 311, 458.

A printed form of the affidavit will be found in the Sussex "Archæologia," xviii.

many of the parish registers this fact is notified.   Thus at
Burwash, Sussex, we find this entry—

" 1680. Mar. 26. Bur. Johanes Theobald   } Nulla affidavit
　　,,　　　,,　　31. Bur. Gualterus Theobald } mulcta secun-
                                                 } dum legem in-
                                               } flicta."

In the register of St. Mary-le-Bow, Durham, we are told
how " Christopher Bell, Gent. was lapped in linen, contrary
to the late act, Dec. 1678;" and in that of Gayton, Northamptonshire, this entry occurs: " 1708. Mrs. Dorothy Bel-
lingham was buried April 5, in *Linnen*, and the forfeiture of
the Act payd fifty shillings to y* informer, and fifty shillings to
y* poor of the parishe." * Pope wrote of Mrs. Oldfield, who
was buried in Westminster Abbey in a Brussels lace head-
dress, a holland shift with tucker, and double ruffles of the
same lace, and a pair of new kid gloves, these lines—

" 'Odious ! in woollen ! 'twould a Saint provoke '
  (Were the last words that poor Narcissa spoke) ;
  ' No, let a charming chintz and Brussels lace
  Wrap my cold limbs, and shade my lifeless face.'"

The following copy of a certificate, under the Act for
burying in Woollen, relates to Southwold parish, and is dated
April 26, 1690—

" These are to Certifie y* Anne Burnet, in Waldwick,
in the county forsd, came before mee y* day abovesd, and
made Affidavit upon oath, in p'nce of those whose names
are hereunto sett, y* Elizabeth, y* wife of Andrew Lillie, in
the above-named parish and county, lately deceased there,
was buried in the ordinarie Burying place thereof, being
wound, wrapt up, and layd foorth, in woollen only, and no
other material then what is made of sheeps wool only :

---

* Quoted in Burn's " History of Parish Registers " (1862), 117.

according to yᵉ Act of Parlia't, made for Burying in woollen only.

> "Jurat coram me
> > "Ja. Petre, Miʳ of So'wold.

"Witnesses { Barbara Petre.
Katrine Petre." *

With the uncoffined dead, it was easy to discover whether the enactment had been complied with. Up to 1694, it was customary at Melbourne, Derbyshire, "to bury the bodies without coffins, simply wrapped in woollen ; and in the case of Sir Robert and Lady Hardinge, no exception appears to have been made, so that their bodies had mingled with the common earth." †

Baptized infants, who died within the month after their baptism, were generally shrouded in the white cloth,—chrisom—put on the head at baptism, and were therefore called "chrisoms." The use of the chrisom is thus mentioned in the first Prayer-book of Edward VI. (1549): "Then the Godfathers and Godmothers shall take and lay their hands upon the child, and the minister shall put upon him his white vesture, commonly called the chrisom, and say, 'Take this white vesture for a token of the innocency which by God's grace in this holy sacrament of baptism is given unto thee ; and for a sign whereby thou art admonished, so long as thou livest, to give thyself to innocency of living, that, after this transitory life, thou mayest be partaker of the life everlasting.'"

The white garment thus presented to the child at baptism was then wrapped round it, and retained as part of the clothing till the churching of the mother, who, in the first Prayer-book of Edward VI., is directed to present it to the

---

* The *East Anglian*, ii. 92.
† "Reliquary," i. 19.

minister with her other accustomed offering.*   Infants
dying with this vesture upon them are commemorated on
various monumental crosses, as at Southfleet, Kent.†

A curious inscription exists in the Church of Chesham-
Bois, Bucks, illustrative of this practice.   It is on a small
stone in the chancel, underneath a brass figure of a chrisom
child, and runs thus—

> " Of Rog' Lee, gentilma' here,
>   lyeth the son Bendict Lee
>   Crysom, who' soule ih'u p'dō." ‡

Similar brasses remain at Rougham, 1505–1510; Kettering-
ham, Norfolk, 1530; Lavenham, Suffolk, 1631; and at
Aveley, Essex, 1583.   Specimens are engraved in Cotman's
" Norfolk Brasses," and a very good example is to be seen
at the Church of Stoke D'Abernon, Surrey.   It should be
noted that monumental brasses, when laid down to the
memory of chrisom children, have a distinctive feature
peculiar to themselves.   The figures are generally represented as bound up in folds of linen, ornamented with
vandyked edges, bound down with strips of vandyked linen
in such order that the intersection on the upper and lower
fourth of the body's length shall present the form of a cross.§
Numerous references occur in our old parish registers of
the burial of " chrisom " children.   And although the
chrisom was expunged from the Prayer-book of 1552, the
memory of it long lingered in the hearts of the people,
and down to the eighteenth century, babes dying in their
innocence were called chrisoms in the bills of mortality and

---

* Within recent years, it was customary at Horndon-on-the-Hill,
Essex, at the churching of woman, for her to give a white cambric
handkerchief to the priest as an offering.

† See " Reliquary," xxv. 29.

‡ Pardon.   See *East Anglian* (1886), ii. 93.

§ A full account of chrisom children will be found in the transactions
of the Exeter Diocesan Architectural Society.

in parish registers. In the register of Westminster Abbey, under 1687, this entry is given : "The Princess Ann's child, a chrisome, bur. 22 Oct."

In many registers we find the cause of death entered very carefully, a practice which was recommended by Dr. Burrows, in his "Strictures on the use and defects of Parish Registers," 1818. Entries of this kind are often very quaint, if not always refined. In the register of St. Alkmund's, Derby, under 1720, it is recorded how Jane Cressop was buried, "killed by the coloquintada, or bitter apple, which she took to procure an abortion. God give others better grace." The register of Staines, Middlesex, tells how, on March 25, 1791, was "buried a man, unknown, of some parish in Cambridge, whose death was occasioned and hastened by the improper treatment of William Seymour, farmer of the poor, for which a bill was found against him, and he confined in Newgate a year and a day."

In Teddington parish register, an entry informs us that one "James Parsons, who had eaten a shoulder of mutton or a peck of hasty pudding at a time, which caused his death," was buried March 7, 1743–44. Loughborough register, under 1579, relates how one "Roger Shepherd was slain by a lioness which was brought into the town to be seen of such as would give money to see her. He was sore wounded in sundry places, and was buried the 26 Aug^t." To quote a further instance, it is recorded in the register of Bowes, Yorkshire, how "Rodger Wrightson, jun., and Martha Railton, both of Bowes," were "buried in one grave on 15 March, 1714. He died in a fever, and upon tolling his passing-bell, she cryed out, 'My heart is broke,' and in a few hours expired, purely, as was supposed, from love, aged about twenty years each." The melancholy fate of these lovers is immortalized in Mallet's ballad of "Edwin and Emma "—

> " I feel, I feel, this breaking heart
>   Beat high against my side ;
> From her white arm down sunk her head,
>   She shivering, sighed and died." *

In the parish register of Tregaron, Cardiganshire, among the customary fees formerly paid by the inhabitants on various occasions, the following was due to the parish clerk in case of a funeral : " At the death of every marryed man and woman there is . . . to ye Clerk of y⁰ man's wearing apparel, his best hatt and his best shoes and stockings, and from every woman her head flannen or hood, and her best shoes and stockings, besides what is due for digging of their graves."

In olden times it was by no means unusual for the parish to provide a coffin for general use, which was popularly designated " the parish coffin." In some old churchwardens' books, such coffins appear as "chistes," as in the Louth accounts for 1521–22, where this entry occurs : " He [the bellman] shall bere and convey the chiste or chistes as nedys shall require to every place in the towne wher any corse is, or corses, as shall happen. He shall take for setting of herse every time he settes it 1*d.* and no more." A further reference to this custom occurs under 1593 : " Pade for y⁰ mendyng of bothe y⁰ coffins in y⁰ churche, xiiij*d.*"

In the churchwardens' accounts of St. Michael, Cornhill, this item is entered under 1554 : " Paide for mendynge of the coffen that carrys the corses to churche for bourde, neylles, and workemanshippe, xii*d.* ; " and we are told of a curious old-fashioned black-painted coffin preserved in the parish church of Easingwold, which, it is said, was formerly used for conveying the bodies of the departed to the churchyard for interment. In Wales, a little more than a century

---

* See Burn's " Parish Registers," 127–131.

ago, writes a correspondent of *Notes and Queries* (5th series, i. 166), "the poor were not buried in coffins; they were merely wrapped up in canvas, and carried away to be buried in a coffin, which was kept for common use in the church, just as a bier is now. There were two coffins kept, a large and a small one."

In the account-book of St. Mary Coslany, Norwich, we find the subjoined entries for the burial of a vagrant, 1681–82—

"Paid for winding for y* stranger that died at the Wool-pack, £0 3*s.* 0*d.*

"Paid the bearers that carried him, and y* women that did bind him, and the charges expended at the Woolpack for y* burying of y* stranger, £0 3*s.* 0*d.*

"Paid y* Clarke for bell ringing, and grave making, and chiming, £0 2*s.* 6*d.*"

At Oxford it is the custom for a bellman to precede the funeral procession of any member of the University, sound-ing a hand-bell at intervals till the corpse arrives at the place of interment. This custom prevailed at Caerleon, in Wales, a bell being carried about the streets and sounded just before the interment of a corpse. Such a bell is generally known as the "Lyche Bell," or "Corse Bell."

The following passage from "Anthony Wood" is inter-esting: "June 27 (1648). The visitors ordered that the bellman of the University should not go about in such manner as was heretofore used at the funeral of any member of the University. This was purposely to prevent the solemnity that was to be performed at the funeral of Dr. Radcliff, Principal of B.N.C., lately dead. For it must be known that it hath been the custom, time out of mind, that when the head of a house, doctor, or master of considerable degree, was to be buried, the university bellman was to put on the gown and the formalities of the person defunct,

and, with his bell, to go into every college and hall, and
there make open proclamation, after two rings with his
bell, that, forasmuch as God had been pleased to take
out of the world such a person, he was to give notice to
all persons of the University that on such a day, and at
such an hour, he was solemnly to be buried, etc.   But
the visitors not only forbid this, but the bellman's going
before the corpse from the house or college to the church
or chapel."

CHAPTER XIII.

THE lich-gate—the gate of the dead, or, as it is sometimes called, the corpse-gate—which frequently stands at the entrance of our country churchyards, is usually protected by a broad outspreading gable roof, in order that those who accompany the bodies of the departed to their last resting-place may find shelter while waiting for the priest to perform the introductory part of the burial service. In Herefordshire, lich-gates are * known as "scallage," or "scallenge-gates," and the approach to Ludlow church from the town, at its south entrance, is by a passage now crowded with houses, but still retaining the name of the "skallens," or "kalends," which Sir G. C. Lewis and other correspondents of *Notes and Queries* have identified with the ancient lich-gate. In some parts of Devon and Cornwall, where lich-gates mostly prevail, they have long been known as "trim-trams," a term which, it has been suggested,† may be a corruption of "trim-train," *i.e.* "the halting-place at the entrance of the churchyard where the train—that is, not only the pall, but the whole funeral party—might be trimmed, or duly

---

* G. G. Lewis, "Gloss. Herefordshire Words," 1839.

† *Notes and Queries*, 3rd series, iii. 29. Tram, as an old word, bore several meanings. It was a *train*. It was, and is, a car mounted on wheels.

adjusted, and brought into proper order, so as to be in a state of preparation for the officiating minister, on his coming forth to meet them there, and commence the burial service."

It has been suggested that these erections are all of the Post-Reformation period, but in Britton's "Antiquities" mention is made of a lich-gate which formerly stood near Gloucester Cathedral, in a lane called Lich Lane, where the corpse of King Edward II. rested on its way to interment. It would appear that the word "lic" was in common use in all the northern countries of Europe, with the same meaning—"place for the corpse;" and authorities are quoted in Bosworth's "Anglo-Saxon Dictionary," in the different northern tongues, to prove that *lic* was a compound with all funeral terms, *i.e.* "lic-rest," a body-rest; "lic-man," a man who provides for funerals, etc. Many of the lich-gates, too, have an early look; and although, as it has been pointed out at our archæological meetings, it is difficult to assign to them any precise date, there is little doubt that they existed prior to the Reformation.

An interesting facsimile of an illumination representing the funeral of a king of France, in which the procession is seen entering a churchyard through a lich-gate constructed partly of stone, partly of wood, may be seen in the illustrations to Froissart's "Chronicles."

Among some of the notable lich-gates in England may be mentioned that at Arundel, in Sussex. Many years ago it was removed from the entrance to the graveyard, and erected as a porch on the north side of the church. At Hartfield, in the same county, the lich-gate is built under a house; and, among further instances, may be mentioned those at Worth and Pulborough. At Troutbeck, Westmoreland, there are three stone lich-gates in one churchyard. Over the gate at Bray, Berkshire, there are two chambers,

LICH-GATES.   *Page* 155.

1. Burnsal.   2. Beckenham.

connected with an ancient charitable bequest, and over that at Barking, Essex, is a chamber called the Chapel of the Holy Rood.

In Devonshire many of the lich-gates are of stone. "A gabled wall," writes a correspondent of *Notes and Queries* (4th series, i. 445), "was built up on either side of the church path, and a roof built from one gable to the other on stout beams. Of such a fashion was the old 'bier-house'—this was the local name—at Tor-Mohun and Paignton, both now destroyed, and is the fashion in many other places. . . . There is another fashion of bier-house found at other places in Devon, *e.g.* Bickington and Throwleigh. Here the bier-house is associated with the 'church-house,' in the former case the church-house being built over the lich-gate, in the latter on one side. At Tawstock there is a small room on either side of the gate, and at Berry Harbor the lich-gate is in the form of a cross. In Cornwall we often find the stone-work without a gate, as at St. Winnow, but at St. Levan there is a gate with seats, cross, and stone."

The curious arrangement for opening and closing the gate at Burnsall, Yorkshire, is thus described: "The stone pier on the north side has a well-hole, in which the weight that closes the gate works up and down. An upright swivel-post, or 'heart-tree,' as the people there call it, stands in the centre, and through this pass the three rails of the gate; an iron bent lever is fixed to the top of this post, which is connected by a chain and guide-pulley to the weight, so that when any one passes through, both ends of the gate open in opposite directions." The gate at Rostherne churchyard, Cheshire, is on a similar plan.[*] Kent, in years past, has possessed several old lich-gates, as at Beckenham, Boughton, Monchelsea, and West Wickham. But, with the work of church restoration, many of these

---

[*] *Notes and Queries,* 4th series, i. 445.

curious relics of the past have from time to time disappeared, a modern iron gate only too frequently taking the place of these time-honoured, and picturesque, structures.

In days gone by, the lich-gate was often the scene of a curious superstition—one which still lingers on, here and there, in different places—the idea being that the spirit of the last person watches round the churchyard till another is buried, to whom he delivers his charge. Thus Crofton Croker, in his "South of Ireland" (p. 169), says that "It is a general opinion among the lower orders, that the last-buried corpse has to perform an office like that of 'fag' in our public schools by the junior boy, and that the attendance on his churchyard companions is duly relieved by the interment of some other person." Serious consequences have resulted from this notion, and terrific fights have taken place, at the entrance of the churchyard, to decide which corpse should be buried first. Similar scenes have been witnessed in Scotland in times past, and Sir John Sinclair, in his "Statistical Account of Scotland," says that in certain parts of the county of Argyll, when two burials were to take place in one churchyard on the same day, a singular sight occurred. "Both parties staggered forth as fast as possible to consign their respective friend in the first place to the dust; if they met at the gate, the dead were thrown down till the living decided by blows whose ghost should be condemned to porter it."

To more effectually prevent any chance of a wedding and a funeral party meeting, it is customary at Madeley, Shropshire, for them to approach the church by different ways. The churchyard has two gates—large double iron ones— about thirty yards apart, both opening into the same street. The right-hand entrance is used for weddings, the left-hand one for funerals. Both enter the church by the same door, but the provision of different pathways reduces the chance of an encounter to a *minimum*. A similar arrangement formerly prevailed at Barthomley, Cheshire, where it was believed that misfortune, if not death within the year, would befall a bridal pair who passed through the lich-gates.*

Similarly, there has long been a prejudice against being the first to bury one's dead in a new churchyard, from a belief that such a corpse is seized by the devil. The churchyard round St. John's Church, Bovey Tracey, South Devon, was for many years unused, the peasantry maintaining that the devil would seize the first body laid in it. At last a stranger was buried there—the servant of a visitor in the parish, after which interments began to take place.

From time immemorial there has been a popular antipathy among the inhabitants of rural parishes to "burial without the sanctuary." This does not imply in unconsecrated ground, but on the north side of the church, or in a remote corner of the churchyard. The origin of this repugnance is said to have been the notion that the northern part was that which was appropriated to the interment of unbaptized infants,† excommunicated persons, or such as had laid violent hands upon themselves. Hence it was generally known as the "wrong side of the church." In many parishes, therefore, the spot remained unoccupied, while the remaining portion of the churchyard was crowded. White, in his "History of Selborne," alluding to this superstition, says that as most persons wished to be buried on the south side of the churchyard, it became such a mass of mortality that no person could be interred "without disturbing or displacing the bones of his ancestors." A

---

* Miss Jackson's "Shropshire Folklore," 646.

† A correspondent of *Notes and Queries*, 3rd series, v. **34,** mentions the custom in an old **Scotch** parish of burying the still-born children of the parish all along the outside walls of the church, and as close to the walls as they could be laid.

clergyman of a rural parish in Norfolk says, "If I was on any occasion to urge a parishioner to inter a deceased relative on the north side of the church, he would answer me with an expression of surprise, if not of offence, at the proposal, 'No, sir; it is not in the sanctuary.'" In Epworth churchyard there is a tombstone, bearing date 1807, with a long poetical inscription, of which the concluding couplet runs thus—

> "That I might longer undisturbed abide,
> I choos'd to be laid on this northern side."

Sir John Cullum, in his "History of Hawstead" (1784, 38), says, "There is a great partiality here to burying on the south and east sides of the churchyard. When I first became rector, and observed how those sides—particularly the south—were crowded with graves, I prevailed upon a few persons to bury their friends on the north, which was entirely vacant; but the example was not followed, as I hoped it would be, and they continue to bury on the south." In the "Cambrian Register" (1796, 374) there is an amusing allusion to this piece of churchyard lore: "In country churchyards the relations of the deceased crowd them into that part which is south of the church, the north side, in their opinion, being unhallowed ground, fit only to be the dormitory of still-born infants and suicides. For an example to his neighbours, and as well to escape the barbarities of the sextons, the writer of the above account ordered himself to be buried 'on the north side of the churchyard.' But as he was accounted an infidel when alive, his neighbours could not think it creditable to associate with him when dead. His dust, therefore, is likely to pass a solitary retirement, and for ages to remain undisturbed by the hands of men."

A portion of many churchyards is said to have been left

unconsecrated for the burial of excommunicated persons, and that this was not always on the north side is evident from the following extract from the register of Hart, Durham: "December 17, 1596. Ellen Thompson, fornicatrix (and then excommunicated), was buried of yᵉ people in yᵉ chaer at the entrance unto yᵉ yeate or stile of yᵉ churchyard on the east thereof." But that the north side was more usual in such cases is clear from the numerous instances recorded of this practice. Thompson, in his "History of Swine" (1824), relates how "a man, who was executed at Lincoln, was brought to Swine, and buried on the north side of the church, as the proper place in which to bury a felon." In an appendix to the register of Pentrobin parish, Flintshire, this entry occurs, in which it has been suggested the term "backside" refers to the north side (*Notes and Queries*, 1st. iii. 125): "1750, October 23. One Mary Davies, of Pentrobin, single woman, though excommunicated, was on this day, within night, on account of some particular circumstances alleged by neighbours of credit in her favour (as to her resolving to come and reconcile herself, and do penance if she recovered), indulged by being interred on the *backside* the church, but no service or tolling allowed." In Southwark there was formerly a burial ground, called "The Single Woman's Churchyard," in which were buried the inmates of the licensed stews, who were generally excommunicated.* "At Newcastle," says Burn, "more burials take place in unconsecrated ground, called the Ballast Hills, than at the church and chapels altogether, and of these no register is kept."

It has long been a vulgar error that a road along which a corpse has been taken to the parish graveyard becomes thereby a public highway. A correspondence on the subject, in *Notes and Queries*, elicited the fact that this

---

* Burn's "History of Parish Registers in England" (1862), 107.

belief has prevailed in Cheshire, Derbyshire, Worcester-shire, Buckinghamshire, Glamorganshire, and Cornwall. On one occasion at a Welsh funeral, it being suggested that the body of an infant three months old should be carried by the way of an ancient footpath across some fields to the church, the grandfather of the child refused, although the journey to the graveyard would have been much shortened. * Speaking of the right-of-way, it appears there had always been a right-of-way through the churchyard of Walpole St. Peter, near Lynn Regis, and when the new church was built in the time of Henry VI., the edifice extended almost to the verge of the churchyard, thus obstructing the path. The parishioners being unwilling to give up their path, a vaulted way was constructed under the chancel, which caused the altar to be approached by ten steps. †

* *Notes and Queries*, 4th series, xi. 374.
† Ibid., 5th series, vii. 6.

CHAPTER XIV.

THE funeral garland which, in bygone years, was carried
before the corpse of an unmarried girl at her funeral, and
afterwards suspended over the seat she had occupied in the
parish church, was, writes the late Mackenzie Walcott,
undoubtedly an imitation " of the radiant coronet prepared
for virgin souls," the crown of victory to which Keble *
and Jeremy Taylor † allude.   In the legend of St. Cecilia,
an angel gives her a crown of roses and lilies from Paradise,
saying none but the pure can use them. ‡

This pretty and symbolical custom seems to have prevailed extensively in most parts of the country, although it
did not escape censure, for Wren, Bishop of Ely, in 1662,
inquired at his visitation, " Are any mean toys and childish
gewgaws, such as the fonder sort of people prepare at some
burials, suffered to be fastened up in your church at any
one's pleasure ? or any Garlands and other ordinary funeral
ensigns to hang where they hinder the prospect, or until
they grow foul and dusty, withered and rotten ? "

* " Christian Year : Wednesday before Easter."
† " Holy Living," c. xi. s. 3.
‡ *Notes and Queries*, 5th series, i. 12.

M

An early illustration of a virgin garland is contained in a black-letter broad-sheet ballad, "The Bride's Buriall," printed by Henry Gosson, *temp.* James I. The bride having, at the immediate close of the marriage ceremony, received "a chilling cold" that "struck every vitall part," fell down "in a swound," "as cold as any stone," and soon afterwards died, "a maiden and a wife." Her parting words as she lay dying are very touchingly expressed in the ballad, and are interesting as telling of the burial customs of the period—

> " Instead of musicke sweet,
>   Go toll my passing-bell,
> And with those flowers strow my grave
>   That in my chamber smell.
> Strip off my bride's array,
>   My corke-shooes from my feet ;
> And, gentle mother, be not coy
>   To bring my winding-sheet.
>
> " My wedding-dinner drest,
>   Bestow upon the poore,
> And on the hungry, needy, maim'd
>   That craveth at the door.
> Instead of Virgins young
>   My Bride-bed for to see,
> Go cause some cunning carpenter
>   To make a chest for me.
>
> " My bride laces of silke,
>   Bestow'd on maidens meete,
> May fitly serve, when I am dead,
>   To tie my hands and feet ; "
>
> * * * *

At her burial the ballad goes on to tell—

> " A garland, fresh and faire,
>   Of lilies there was made,
> In sign of her virginity,
>   And on her coffin laid.

FUNERAL WREATH, AND MAIDEN'S FUNERAL.

Page 162.

> Six maidens, all in white,
>   Did beare her to the ground ;
> The bells did ring in solemn sort,
>   And made a solemn sound.

> " In earth they laid her then,
>   For hungry worms a prey ;
> So shall the fairest face alive,
>   At length be brought to clay." *

The " funeral garlands," which some forty years ago still hung in Shrawardine Church, Shropshire, were believed by the villagers to be the work of giants. This is curious, writes Miss Jackson ("Shropshire Folklore," 6), "as the practice of carrying such garlands at funerals was still kept up in that part of Shropshire less than a hundred years before, so that the belief must have sprung up within two or three generations."

Many interesting accounts exist of these old funeral garlands. In a valuable paper on the subject, by the late Llewellynn Jewitt, in "The Reliquary" (i. 7), an account is given of five garlands in the north aisle of Ashford-in-the-Water Church, and of some which formerly existed at Matlock, but are now preserved in a local museum. "The garlands are each composed of two hoops of wood, with bands crossing each other at right angles, and attached to the hoops, thus forming a kind of open-arched crown. The hoops and bands are all of wood, wrapped round with white paper, and at the top is a loop for suspension. The hoops and bands of another are decorated with paper flowers and rosettes, and at the top is a flower formed of hearts, and having somewhat the appearance of that of the *Clarkia pulchella*. From between the rosettes of the upper hoop, a paper riband, gimped on the edges, and ornamented by diamonds cut out with scissors, hangs down to below the lower band, to which they are not attached.

* "Reliquary," xxi. 145.

In another example the hoops and bands are decorated with paper flowers or rosettes, intermixed with bunches of narrow slips or shreds of paper, and at the top is a bunch of the same over paper folded like a fan. Originally the flowers have been formed, some of plain, and others of folded or crimped paper, and others again of both; and in some parts the paper has been afterwards coloured red or blue, thus producing a somewhat gay appearance. From the centre of the top are suspended a pair of gloves cut out of white paper, and a kerchief or collar, also of paper, gimped in the edges, and carefully folded. In most instances, the name of the female, in whose honour these garlands were prepared, was written on the collar, gloves, or handkerchiefs.

The form of garland differed in various localities, although similar in general design. In some of the metropolitan churches, instead of consisting of real flowers, or of paper ones, it was often composed of wire formed into filagree work resembling flowers and leaves, ornaments of gum, wax, and other materials. In some districts the garlands were only allowed to remain suspended in the church for a year after the burial of the young woman. In others the garland was buried in the same grave with her. In Derbyshire, they appear to have remained hung up on the arches or beams of the roof, until they were removed or allowed to decay away.

In "Hamlet" (v. 1) the priest says, "Yet here she is allowed her virgin crants," and Gay thus speaks of the custom—

> "To her sweet mem'ry flow'ry garlands strung,
> On her now empty seat aloft were hung."

At Heanor, not many years ago, a number of these funeral relics, which had hung there for years, were removed at a general church-cleaning, which took place at the coming in of a new incumbent. At Llandovery, the garlands and gloves hang a year in the church, and are then taken down, and on each anniversary of the death of the virgin, the grave is decorated with flowers, and a pair of gloves is laid on it. These gloves are taken away by the nearest relative who visits the grave that day." [*]

Some deeply interesting relics of the dead are to be seen in the numerous specimens of " funeral armour," suspended over their tombs in many of our churches. The practice of thus hanging up the arms and accoutrements of persons of note prevailed at an early period, and is noticed by Laertes in " Hamlet " (iv. 5)—

> " His means of death, his obscure burial—
> No trophy, sword, nor hatchment o'er his bones,
> No noble rite, nor formal ostentation."

And in " 2 Henry VI." (iv. 10) Iden says—

> " Is't Cade that I have slain; that monstrous traitor ?
> Sword, I will hallow thee for this thy deed,
> And hang thee o'er my tomb, when I am dead."

The custom, as is well known, has not been confined to England, and, to quote an historic incident, it is recorded that when Napoleon I. entered Potsdam in 1806, after the battles of Jena and Auerstadt, he took the sword of Frederick the Great from the church where it hung, and sent it to the Invalides at Paris, remarking, as he drew it from its scabbard, " I am better pleased with these relics than if I had found a treasure of twenty millions of francs."

Many early instances of suspending funeral armour in churches are noticed in local histories, and Thomas Hearne says the custom came from Canute's placing his crown upon the head of the crucifix at Winchester, after he found that he could not make the waters obey him."

[*] Chambers's " Book of Days," i. 274.

In 1444, when a dispute arose between the two powerful Angus families of Lindsay and Ogilvy as to the justiciarship of the regality of the Abbey of Arbroath ; the parties came to blows, and on Sunday, January 23, 1445, was fought between the adherents of the Earl of Crawford and that of Sir Alexander Ogilvy of Inverquharity, what is known in local history as the battle of Arbroath. It resulted disastrously to the Ogilvy side, Sir Alexander being killed when taking flight. He was buried in the Ogilvy Aisle of the parish church of Kinnell, and over his tomb was suspended his boot with the spur attached. In process of time, the boot rotted away, but the spur remained suspended, and has been preserved. It is of great size, being nine inches in length, and four in width at the fork ; the rowel is as large as a crown piece, and has twenty-seven points.*

Sir David Owen, knight, by his will, dated Feb. 20, 1529, desires : "My body to be buried in the Priory of Esseborne, after the degree of a banneret, that is, with helmet and sword, my war armour, my banner, my standard, my pendant, and set over a banner of the Holy Trinity, one of Our Ladye, another of St. George," etc.† In Brickleigh Church, near Plymouth, there is suspended over the monument of Nicholas Slanning, his visored headpiece, gorget, and gauntlets. This ill-fated man was killed in a duel which he fought with Sir John Fitz, knight. An inscription informs us that his death took place "On the 8th day of Aprill in the yere of our Lorde God, 1582."

In Husborne Crawley Church, Bedfordshire, is an elaborate tomb to the memory of John Thomson, who died in 1597 ; and over, or attached to, this tomb were some pieces of funeral armour, since packed away in an ancient chest under the tower. A helmet hangs over the monument

---

* *Notes and Queries*, 5th series, xi. 73.
† "Testamenta Vetusta," 700.

of Paul Cleybroke, in St. John's Church, Margate. His death took place in 1622.

It would seem, however, that occasionally the armour suspended over tombs in our churches is nothing more than "undertakers' trappings," though often of considerable age. The practice of supplying imitative armour for funeral purposes is as old as the time of Sir William Dugdale, for in a manuscript at Merevale, dated 1667, he states the charges of various articles for the achievement of a knight: the helmet, gilt with silver and gold, £1; the crest, carved and coloured in "oyle," 13s.; the sword with velvet "scabard," 10s.; a gauntlet, 10s.; gilt spurs with velvet spur-bathers, 5s. But, despite this custom, there can be no doubt much of the armour preserved in our churches is genuine, although it may not have been actually worn by the person over whose tomb it hangs. Thus, as a correspondent of *Notes and Queries* observes (5th series, x. 129), "the helm of King Henry V., which hangs aloft over his grave in Westminister Abbey," is undoubtedly "a genuine tilting-helm of the first quarter of the fifteenth century, although it may be the identical one referred to in Rymer's 'Fœdera,' where the account of the price of a helm for the king's funeral is preserved."—"Item eidem Thomæ (Daunt) pro factura unius Crestæ et unius Helmæ pro Rege xxxiiis. ivd." Although this "may not have been the personal property of the king, it is a most undoubted genuine tilting-helm of the period. May it not be, that when a helm was wanted for a funeral achievement, if the knight's own helm was not available, his relations or executors went to the "heaul-mier's," and bought one—a real one—for the purpose." As regards "the deeply interesting and unique relics of the fourteenth century," adds the same correspondent, "which hang over the monument of the Black Prince in Canterbury Cathedral, the helm there, and the chapeau crest, and shield, may possibly have been made or bought for the funeral pageant of the prince, but I believe they were his own tilting accoutrements. With regard to the other relics—the gauntlet, heavily gilded, with gloves of leather stitched with silk, the surcoat of velvet, quilted with cotton stitched vertically and embroidered with the lilies of France and the lions of England in thread of pure gold ; and the sheath of the estoc, or short stabbing sword, of red leather adorned with gilt studs, I am quite convinced that these, at least, were the personal property of the prince, and used by him." From the latter half, however, of the seventeenth century, when armour was going out of date, that supplied by undertakers for funeral purposes was only too common, and there are several sham helmets, of comparatively modern date, stowed away in the triforium of Westminster Abbey.

In some cases funeral armour has met with somewhat rough usage ; an instance of which is mentioned by Mr. J. E. Cussans in his "County History of Hertfordshire," under the head of Baldock Church : "About twenty years ago the south porch was enlarged by removing the floor of the parvise above. This chamber had been closed for many years, and when it was broken into it was found to be nearly filled with armour, helmets, pikes, lances, and other weapons. The then rector, the Rev. John Smith, threw a large quantity down a well to get rid of it, after allowing the labourers to take as much as they liked, to sell for old iron." A correspondent of *Notes and Queries* (5th series, xi. 73), informs us that, about 1850, he was in Aldborough, Holderness, Yorkshire, and was there told of the existence of an old iron helmet in the church, which was employed habitually as a coal scuttle to replenish the church fires in winter.

The funeral armour of Admiral Sir Wm. Penn—the father of the founder of Pennsylvania—is in the Church of St. Mary Redcliffe, Bristol, where he was interred on October 3, 1670. It consists of the entire suit, with helmet, said to have been worn by the gallant knight—admiral and general—during his large expedition. At the east end of the parish church of Aldershot, there are two helmets with crests, belonging to members of the Tichborne family, which have the appearance of having been actually worn. In the Church of Broadwater, Sussex, is preserved the tilting-helmet of Lord de la Warre, with its remarkable ocularium. And in the Church of St. Michael Carhayes, Cornwall, there is, together with some helmets and other pieces, a sword which local antiquaries believe to have been borne at Bosworth by Sir Hugh Trevanion. The helmet of Sir John Fenwick, who was slain at the battle of Marston Moor, is preserved in Hexham Abbey Church; and a correspondent of *Notes and Queries* says, "When I was in the Church of Longbridge Deverill, Wilts, a few years ago, I saw hanging on the walls of the mortuary chapel belonging to the noble family of Thynne, of Longleat, several pieces of body armour, which I was informed belonged to Sir John Thynne, knight, and which were worn by him when he served under Lord Protector Somerset in the Scottish wars. There are two helmets, a sword, and a misericorde suspended above the fine monument to John Leigh in the chancel of Addington Church, Surrey; and the helmet of Sir William Harpur, founder of the Bedford Schools, formerly hung over his tomb in St. Paul's Church, Bedford, but it was lost during the restoration of the Church, about 1881.

There are two helmets in Brabourne Church, East Kent, one of which, a funeral trophy, belonged to Sir Thomas Scott of Scotshall, commander-in-chief of the Kentish forces at the time of the Spanish Armada, and Knight of the Shire for Kent.

With the old custom of suspending funeral armour in churches may be compared that of displaying and hanging up the trophies of war, historical instances of which are to be found in the chronicles of the past. Mackenzie Walcott, in his "Traditions and Customs of Cathedrals" (1872, 175, 176) relates how Edward IV., after leading Henry VI. a captive to the Tower, went in triumph to St. Paul's, where he offered at the altar the standard of the fallen king. In 1485, Henry VII. offered at St. Paul's three standards of St. George, the Red Fiery Dragon, and Dun Cow, in honour of his descent from Cadwallader and Guy, Earl of Warwick, with the Tudor colours, green and white, after the crowning battle of Bosworth Field. Banners were suspended round the shrine of St. Cuthbert, and the famous banner of the saint which was at the winning of Flodden Field and many other battles was carried in great processions. Archbishop Thurstan, in the famous "Battle of the Standard," led out to battle the sacred car crowned with a cross, and hung with the banners of York and Ripon, which the Scottish king addresses in the old ballad—

> "The Holy Cross
> That shines as bright as day ;
> Around it hung the sacred banners
> Of many a blessed saint,
> St. Peter, and John of Beverley,
> And St. Wilfrid there they paint."

At St. Paul's, in September, 1588, twelve standards, captured from the ships of the Spanish Armada, decorated the choir, and till within a recent period, when they were removed to Chelsea, flags taken in the wars from the capture of Louisburgh to the victories of Nelson were suspended round the dome. The flags of the old county regiments may now be seen at York, Canterbury, Chichester,

Exeter, Salisbury, Rochester, and other places. At an installation of the Knights of the Bath, the dean lays the swords upon the altar, and delivers them to their owners; the banners of the deceased are laid under it whilst the band plays the "Dead March in Saul." When the nine captured flags were received at St. Paul's in 1797, they were held in a circle and bowed before the king, who stood in the midst, and then the flag-officers, after the first legion, moving with solemn steps up to the altar, offered them there.

In White's "History of Essex" (1863, 457), under Ingatestone Church, we read: "In the chancel hang several pieces of ancient armour, and the banners used by the Ingatestone, Brentwood, and Billericay Volunteers, raised by the late Lord Petre for the defence of the nation about the close of the last century." The armour has since been removed, having been placed some years ago in the mortuary chapel on the north side of the chancel, which is used as a vestry.* It is stated in the *Mirror*, that the flags, etc., carried in procession at the funeral of Lord Chatham were hung up in the church near his seat at Hayes, in Kent.

According to the "New Statistical Account of Scotland" (vii. 323), among the honours bestowed by the kings of Scotland on Iona, was the dedication of the trophies of war. After the victory which Aidanus gained over the Picts and Scots, he sent the banner of his vanquished enemies to Columba to be preserved in his abbey. Kenneth Macalpine, also, after the final overthrow of the Picts, devoted the sword and armour of Dunstrenus, the Pictish monarch, to the Church of Iona.

At Derry, the staffs of the French flags captured by Dr. Walker, in a desperate sally of the garrison, and carried in

* *Notes and Queries*, 6th series, v. 58.

procession by the ladies of the city after the great siege was raised, are hung over the altar in the cathedral. At St. Patrick's the banners of the Knights of St. Patrick are suspended in the choir.[*]

* Mackenzie Walcott, "Traditions and Customs of Cathedrals," 238.

CHAPTER XV.

THE RIGHT OF SANCTUARY.

THE right of sanctuary, after having been allowed for
upwards of five hundred years, was forbidden in 21 James
I., when it was enacted that no sanctuary, or privilege of
sanctuary, should be admitted or allowed in any case. And
so ended a practice in this country which, while it had
saved the life of many a man, had frequently served as an
immunity to crime.

Among some of the churches which were formerly
privileged with the right of affording sanctuary, were St.
John's, Beverley, St. Martin's-le-Grand, London; St. Beurin's,
Cornwall; and Westminster; monasteries having shared the
same privilege. Originally, it appears, such churches, or
the churchyard connected therewith, were "termed sanctuaries, and the foundation of abjuration; for whoever was
not capable of taking sanctuary in either of these places,
could not have the benefit of abjuration. This abjuration
was, when a person had committed felony, and for safe-
guard of his life had fled to the sanctuary of a church or
churchyard; or if a person accused of any crime ('except
the treason, wherein the crown, and sacrilege, wherein the
church, were too nearly concerned') had fled for sanctuary,
and within forty days after went in sackcloth and confessed

himself guilty before the coroner, and declared all the particular circumstances of the offence; and therefore took the oath in that case provided, namely, that he abjured the realm, and would depart from thence forthwith at the port that should be assigned him, and would never depart without leave from the king; and if he observed strictly the conditions of the oath, by going with a cross in his hand, and with all convenient speed embarking, he by this means would save his life. If, during this forty days privilege of sanctuary, or on his road to the seaside, he was apprehended and arraigned in any court for this felony, he might plead the privilege of sanctuary, and had a right to be remanded, if taken out against his will. But by this abjuration his blood was attainted, and he forfeited all his goods and chattels." * Registers were kept of all persons availing themselves of this mode of refuge, with the nature of the offences, in respect of which they sought to escape the punishment of the law; great numbers having resorted to sanctuary for non-payment of debts.

The method of claiming sanctuary, and the ceremonies connected with it, varied in different parishes. At Durham, persons who took refuge fled to the north door and knocked for admission,† there being two chambers over it, in which men slept for the purpose of admitting such fugitives at any hour of the night. As soon as any one was so admitted, the sound of the great bell of the Galilee booming over the city told that some fugitive had fled to holy church.‡ The offender was required to declare before credible witnesses, the nature of his offence, and to toll the

* *The Antiquary* (1873), iii. 260. See Burn's "Eccl. Law," i. 365.

† The large knocker upon the north door of Durham Cathedral, is believed to have been the one actually used for the purpose of sanctuary.

‡ Traditions of a similar arrangement are preserved at Chichester and Norwich.

bell in token of his demanding the privilege of sanctuary. Every one who had the security of Durham was provided with a gown of black cloth, with a yellow cross upon the left shoulder, as the badge of St. Cuthbert, whose "peace" or "grith" he had claimed. They lay in a græte adjoining the Galilee, and were provided with meat and drink for thirty-seven days.* After this period had elapsed, if no pardon could be obtained, the malefactor, after certain ceremonies had been performed before the shrine, solemnly adjured his native land for ever, and was straightway, by the agency of the intervening parish constables, conveyed to the coast, bearing in his hand a white wooden cross, and was sent out of the kingdom by the first ship which sailed after his arrival.

The Durham notices of sanctuary recorded in the cathedral register, begin June 18, 1464. "Petitio immunitatis" is written on the margin, and occasionally the name of the fugitive. But the "Sanctuarium Dunelmense," a register of the persons who at different times found protection here, has been published—together with that of Beverley—by the Surtees Society. Some of the cases are recorded with the most minute detail. Thus, a man from Walsingham is committed to prison for a theft. He escapes and seeks refuge in the cathedral of Durham. He takes his stand before the shrine of St. Cuthbert, and begs for a coroner. A coroner attends, and hears his confession. The culprit, in the presence of the sacrist and sheriff, by a solemn oath renounces the kingdom. He strips to his shirt, and gives up his clothing to the sacrist as a fee. The sacrist restores the clothing. A white cross of wood is put into the culprit's hand. *Cruce signatus,* he is consigned to the under-sheriff, who commits him to the care of the nearest constable, who hands him over to

* See "Journ. of Brit. Arch. Assoc.," xiv. 103; "Archæologia," viii. 1–29.

the next in the direction of the coast. The last constable puts him into a ship, and he bids an eternal farewell to his country, "nunquam rediturus." Another entry tells us of two murderers who had escaped detection for eight or nine years, and a further one relates how a man killed a woman in self-defence, and afterwards resorted to the sanctuary of St. Cuthbert.

At Beverley, the oath imposed upon each person on admission to the sanctuary, is given in the "Sanctuarium Beverlacense" (p. 111). After answering what man he had killed, and wherewith, and both their names, "gar him lay his hand upon the boke, saying in this wise, 'Sir, take heed, on your oath you shall be faithful and trew to the lord archbishop; shall bere good herte to the bailis and governors; shall beare no pointed wepen or dagger against the peace; shall be ready, if there be debate, or strife, or sothern fire, to helpe to surcease it; shall do your dewte at ringing, and for to offer at the messe in the morn,'" etc. Food was supplied them in the refectory, and a lodging in the dormitory, for thirty days. At the end of that time they were conducted in safety to the borders of the county. They could claim the same security a second time; but for a third protection afforded the fugitive became permanently a servant of the Church.* The Beverley register begins about 1478. We are told how "Robert Beaumont, a person of education; and Elizabeth Beaumont, gentlewoman, of the Beaumonts of Yorkshire, charge themselves with the death of Thomas Alderley. This is the first lady who has been admitted to the sanctuary."

The area of the circuit in which a person could claim the privilege of sanctuary was not always the same. At Durham, for instance, it was confined to the church and churchyard. The liberties of St. John of Beverley

---

* "Journ. of Arch. Assoc.," xiv. 103.

extended, first, from the church for a mile every way; the second boundaries were designated by crosses of rich carving; the third commenced at the entrance of the church; the sixth included the high altar and the fridstol, a stone chair, near the altar, which conferred the greatest security.* The Welsh, it seems, were exceedingly strict in regard to this ordinance, and allowed, it is said, "all criminals, even murderers and traitors, to have security in churches, not only for themselves, but for their servants, and even for their cattle; to feed which last, considerable tracts of pasture land were assigned, in the whole compass whereof they were sacred and inviolable; nay, with relation to some of the principal churches, the right of sanctuary was extended so far as the cattle could range in a day and return at night." †

Before the north porch of Salisbury Cathedral, sentences of excommunication were published; and it has been suggested, though perhaps with no great probability, that it served as a " Galilee," or outer chapel for penitents.

At Hexham, there were four crosses set up at a certain distance from the church, " in the four ways leading thereunto; now if a malefactor flying for refuge to that church was taken or apprehended within the crosses, the party that took or laid hold of him there did forfeit *two hundredh;* if he took him within the town, then he forfeited four hundredh; if within the walls of the churchyard, then six hundredh; if within the church, then twelve hundredh; if within the doors of the choir, then eighteen hundredh; beside penance, as in case of sacrilege; but if he presumed to take him out of the stone chair near the altar, called

---

* This " Frith Stol " is rude and plain, and may perhaps be earlier than any part of the existing church.

† Lord Lyttelton, " Life of Henry II.," ii. 358. See " Archæologia," viii. 27.

' fridstol,' or from amongst the holy relics behind the altar, the offence was not redeemable with any sum, but was then become *sine emendatione, boteles,* and nothing but the utmost severity of the offended church was to be expected by a dreadful excommunication ; besides what the secular power would impose for the presumptuous misdemeanor."   As the *hundredh,* it is said, contained eight pounds, the last penalty was extremely heavy, nearly as much as the *weregild* for killing a crowned head in Wales.*

Turning to the principal sanctuaries in London, these were at the Hospital of St. John the Baptist, in the Savoy, in the purlieus (still bearing the name of the "Great" and the "Little Sanctuary") of Westminster Abbey, the precincts of the Mint, in Southwark, and of Whitefriars, in Fleet Street, and the Liberty of St. Martin's-le-Grand.

The privileges of St. Martin-le-Grand were very ancient, confirmed by Charters of William the Conqueror and Henry III.   But the enormities of the place had become so crying that, in the time of Henry VI., the legislature had to interfere.   Among the offenders enumerated are " subtil pickers of locks, counterfeitours of keys, contrivers of seales, forgers of false evidences, workers of counterfeit chaines, beades, broaches, ouches, etc.   And amongst the greater offenders, not only traitors and murderers were privileged, but felons were suffered to issue out of the bounds, and commit depredations at noonday, and then to return to shelter, and to riot in there ill-gotten gains."   Accordingly, by an ordinance of Henry VI., in 1457, the following rules were laid down for the regulation of sanctuary even here—

" 1. That every fugitive coming for sanctuary should come before the dean, and declare 'the cause of the fears moving him to come,' which shall be entered in the register.

" 2. That he shall give up any weapon or armour he may

---

* See " Archæologia," viii. 26.

possess, and shall not be allowed to carry any weapon while in sanctuary, ' except a reasonable knife to serve (carve) withall his meate, and that the said knife be pointless.'

" 3. That the doors and gates be closed from nine to six in the morning, and from nine till four during the remainder of the year."

The privilege of sanctuary attaching to the Savoy was derived from the Hospital of St. John the Baptist, which formerly stood on that site, and the precinct of Whitefriars inherited it from a convent of Carmelites, which were once located there. The latter sanctuary afterwards got the cant name of Alsatia. But some idea of the low degradation to which this so-called Alsatia had fallen, may be gathered from the graphic description given of it by Sir Walter Scott in " The Fortunes of Nigel." It seems that this privileged place was peopled by thieves of every grade, whores and their bullies, sots, gamblers, usurers, and ruffians of every sort. The wailing of children, the scolding of mothers, the miserable exhibition of ragged linen hung to dry from the windows of ruinous houses, all spoke the wants and distresses of the wretched inhabitants; while the sounds of complaint were overpowered by the riotous shouts, oaths, profane songs, and boisterous laughter that issued from every other house of deep potations (either ale house or gin palace).

Respecting the right of sanctuary at Westminster, which is called by Fabyan, "the seyntwary before the Abbey," Dean Stanley observes : * " The right was shared by the abbey with at least thirty other English monasteries, but probably in none did the building occupy so prominent a position, and in none did it occupy so great a part. The grim old Norman fortress, which was still standing in the seventeenth century, is itself a proof that the right reached back, if not to the time of the Confessor, at least to the period when

" Memorials of Westminster Abbey," 405.

additional sanctity was imparted to the whole abbey by his canonization in 1198. The right professed to be founded on charters of King Lucius." The sanctuary, which consisted of his chapels, an upper and a lower one—one being built over the other—we are further told " was a vast 'Cave of Adullam' for all the distressed and discontented of the metropolis, who desired, according to the phrase of the time, to 'take Westminster.' Sometimes, if they were of higher rank, they established their quarters in the great northern porch of the abbey, with tents pitched, and guards watching round, for days and nights together. Sometimes they darted away from their captors, to secure the momentary protection of the consecrated ground. 'Thieving,' or 'Thieven' Lane was the name long attached to the winding street at the back of the Sanctuary, along which 'thieves' were conducted to the prison in the Gatehouse, to avoid these untoward emancipations if they were taken straight across the actual precincts." The privilege of sanctuary at Westminster caused the houses within the precincts to be let for high rents, and one of the rules enjoined on "Sanctuary men" was that "they could not leave the precinct without the Dean's licence, or between sunset and sunrise."

In 1284, blood was shed, and the right of sanctuary violated, in old Bow Church, Cheapside. One Duckett, a goldsmith, having wounded in some fray a person named Ralph Crepin, took refuge in the church, and slept in the steeple. Whilst there, certain friends of Crepin entered during the night, and violating the sanctuary, first slew Duckett and then so placed the body as to induce the belief that he had committed suicide. A verdict to this effect was accordingly given at the inquisition, and the body was interred with the customary indignities. The real circumstances being discovered through the evidence of a boy, who, it appears, was with Duckett in his voluntary confinement, and had hid himself during the struggle, the murderers, among whom was a woman, were apprehended and executed. After this occurrence the church was interdicted for a time, and the doors and windows stopped with brambles.[*]

The sanctuary at Canterbury was granted by King Ethelbert, to the district, afterwards called Staple Gate, in the parish of St. Alphage, to mark it as the spot, where he received St. Augustine. Its state, in 1801, is thus described : " It has for many years been in a state of ruin and poverty, the houses in it being inhabited only by poor and unprincipled people, who fly hither as to a sanctuary and shelter from the liberty of the city."[†]

It should be added there was a sanctuary for all classes. Fallen from their high estate, the widowed queen, the orphan prince, and the discarded and deserted minister found there the same refuge with the poor and lowly. In 1441, the Duchess of Gloucester fled to the sanctuary, on a charge of witchcraft and high treason, but the wonted privilege was denied to her ; and, in 1456, the Protector (the Duke of York), the Earl of Warwick, and others, "were noted with an execrable offence of the Abbot of Westminster and his monks, for that they took out of sanctuarie at Westminster, John Holland, Duke of Excester, and conveyed him to the Castle of Pontfracte." Elizabeth Woodville, Queen of Edward IV., twice made the sanctuary her home. The first time was just before the birth of her eldest son. It is recorded how in 1470 she escaped from the Tower, and registered herself and her companions here as "sanctuary women," and how here, "in great penury, and forsaken of all her friends," she gave birth to Edward V., who was "born in sorrow and baptized like a poor man's

---

[*] "Old and New London," i. 336.
[†] Hasted's "History of Canterbury," i. 293.

child." In the sanctuary died the poet Skelton, poet laureate to Henry VIII., having fled thither to escape the vengeance of Cardinal Wolsey, whom he had lampooned in some verses full of caustic satire. At the instigation of the friars, the Bishop of Norwich called him to account for keeping a concubine. Skelton said he had always looked upon her as a wife, but did not declare it, because fornication in the clergy was thought a little sin, and marriage a great one.

To quote a further instance. When Margaret of Anjou received intelligence of the death of the Earl of Warwick in the Battle of Barnet, and of her husband's captivity, she at first took sanctuary in the Abbey of Beaulieu.

The subjoined list of some of the principal sanctuaries is from Dr. Pegge's "Sketch of Asylum or Sanctuary" in the "Archæologia" (viii. 41)—

Aberdavon, Wales.	London: St. Martin - le - Grand, Temple, and St. Mary-le-Bow.
Abingdon.	
Amethwaite, Cumberland.	
Beaulieu, Hants.	Manchester.
Beverley, Ebor.	Merton Priory.
Colchester.	Northampton.
Derby.	Norwich.
Durham.	Ripon.
Dover.	Wells.
Hexham, Northumberland.	Westminster.
Launceston.	Winchester.
Lechlade	York.

Sanctuary knockers are still said to exist at St. Gregory's, Norwich; St. Nicholas, Gloucester; All Saints, York; Adel Church, near Leeds; and at Hexham. At Durham, it has been suggested, the hollows for the eyes in the sanctuary knocker were probably filled with crystals or enamel. It has also been conjectured that the open eyes may have

been contrived to emit light from within the church, so as to guide the culprit by night to the very spot of his safety.*
But knockers on church doors, it has been pointed out, often of curious workmanship, are by no means uncommon. Three interesting examples, although of inferior design and execution to those already mentioned, and of coarser metal, remain on the church doors of the Suffolk churches of Mickfield, Stonham Aspall, and Grundisburgh, all within a few miles of each other.†

* Murray's " English Cathedrals," 243. Durham.
† See *East Anglian*, new series, i. 326.

CHAPTER XVI.

PEWS AND THEIR LORE.

THE gradual disappearance of pews from our parish churches is the lingering remains of a system which, apart from the gross abuses it occasioned, was the cause of much contention in times past, besides giving rise to many curious customs which nowadays would not be tolerated.

The arrangement and allotment of pews to the parishioners, according to their position and calling, was an invidious distinction which resulted in much bitter feeling, and oftentimes produced open warfare in the parish. At Eccles, Lancashire, it appears by documents (1595–1598) it was ordered that "the churchwardens, now for the time being, shall have power and authority to appoint places for the gentlemen of the same parish, and also for the vicar, according to their degrees and calling, and in like manner shall have authority to place the rest of the parishioners, as well Husbandmen and Cottagers, as others of mean estate and calling; having a special regard for their charges and payments which they have severally paid towards the repair of the said church and making anew of the said forms." * The allotment of pews varied in different places. At Assheton-under-Lyne, it was made by

* J. Harland, "Account of the Seats in Churches in the County Palatine of Lancaster," p. 9.

the lord of the manor; at Ludlow by the bailiffs of the town, and in some London parishes by the vestry. In the "History of Pews," the subjoined extract is quoted relative to the Church of St. Mary Woolchurch Haw, showing that the assignation of seats was under the authority of the Lord Mayor of London—

"Thys ys the copye of the ordynance in the boke of our Ladye of Woolchyrche hawe, . . . for the good rule of the same pysshe, made by all the bodye of the same pysse, w^t the consent of Syr John Benet, then pson, William Pyne, Brewer, at the Wyghte Cocke, made the 2 day of Jan. the yere of our Lord God 1457. . . . Also the sayd chyrche wardens shall be the autoryte of the Mayre of London, grauntyd in the Gyld Hall, that we shall set bothe ryche and pore yn the sayd chyrche in her pews yt longythe; and in case they will not be rulyed by the sayd wardens for the tyme being, they to ronne in payne that ys ordeyned in the Gylde Hall." But Mr. Heales * somewhat doubts the authenticity of this document; a search of the original records in Guildhall having failed to discover any such order as that referred to.

The following document is curious as showing the allotment, so far as was then arranged, of the seats in a country church, two hundred and fifty years ago, at a time when the sexes were divided in the sacred edifice—

"A Perfect order how men are to sitt in the chappell of Ashford by the Officiall Mr. Rowlandson and the neighbors of Ashford, April the 10th, 1632.

"The Minister and Churchwardens.

"1. Will. Nillus George Johnson Godfrey White during his life if he please and after his decease the neighbours are to dispose of the place.

"2. Ralph Atkinson Thomas Thorpe John Greauves,

* "History and Law of Church Seats and Pews" (1872), 77, 78.

Vnde the Pulpitt is for the ministers wife whomsoever she is.

"3. Nicholas Dale, John Harris, Widd: Goodwin Tho: Hayward.

"4. John Wright William Wright Feunell.

"6. Thomas Ragg William Low.

"North Side: 1. Place next the queer. Nicholas Dale wife John Harris Jon Greauves Wifes.

"2. Goodwife Thorpe, Fynney, Good: Wright.

"3. Good: Cheatam, Good: Cooper, Good: Platts.

"4. Widd: Nillus Edw: Heyward wife Ellen Toft, Good: White.

"5. John Brewell wife Widd: Bove Tho: Hayward Widd: Goodwin.

"6. Will: Milnes seat for his Tenants.

"7. George Johnson and Thomas Thorpe for Tenants.

"8. Will: Heaward George Brewell Tho: Wright, Will: Hayward Shoemaker.

"South side: 1. Place in the Queer—Will: Greauves, Will: Hayward, Micha: Hayward Henry Brownell.

"1. John Cheatam Will: Cooper Tho: Burrs, Robert Vickars.

"2. Will: Wright Edw: Hayward John Platts John Brewell Robs Brownell.

"3. Micha: Stone, Will: Rowland, Abrah: Goodwin, Tho. Greatback, Edw. Smith.

"Ralph White is to pay 8*s.* per annum to the minister or if he refuses to pay it Will: Milnes and George Johnson are to pay it and to take one with them that will pay it.

"John Thorpe is to pay 5*s.* per annum to the minister or else Ralph Attkinson Tho: Thorpe and John Greauves will pay it and take in one whom they please that will give it.

"All these that have any new seate in the church are to

leave their ould seats to the discresion of the Minister and Churchwardens.

"RALPHE HEATHCOTT, Minister.

Sign—

"Ralph ‡ Atkinson John Wright
Will 𝖯 Milnes John Greauves
Tho 𝟪 Thorpe Will: Cow
Geo ○ Johnson William Cooper
Nich ⊕ Dale Thomas Wright
Tho ✗ Thorpe Edward Heaward
Elizabeth F Goodwin Will: **Heaward ꝺe shop**
Thomas Heaward Will: Headwarde ꝺe Shoemaker." *

The following orders concerning sittings in church are extracted from **a seat-book for the** parish church **of Tewkesbury, in the diocese of** Gloucester, wherein **is numerically placed the several seats in** the said **church, and the several persons that** have right to sittings, **or** kneelings, **in the said seats, 1728**—

"Tewkesbury ⎱ Orders about sittings in church
In Com. Glour. 1595. ⎰ October 22, 1595.

"It was declared in the Chamber by common Consent, as the Ancient Custom of the Town, that no taker of any Seats or Rome [room] in the Church shall have property to challenge the **same** after one **yeare ended from** the **time of his** or her departure **out** of the Towne.

"**Item.** **That** uppon decease of any wife **in the Towne** it shall **be in the** Churchwardens **by consent of** the **Bailiffes (if need so** require) to place **any** other **woman in the same Rome fitt for that** place, there to **keep such rome upon a** Quarterly **Rent to** the **Church** until **the** husband **of the** deceased **woman shall marry again, and then** she to take **such place, and in mean tyme no husband to** challenge the **place.**

* "The Reliquary" (1861), ii. 98, 99.

"Item. That none be placed in any of the Mrs. sixe seates nor in the mydle rowe above the Clarckes pewe nor within iiij seates of the pulpitt below and so upward on both sides in the body of the Church without Consent of the Bailiffs, etc.

"WILLIAM GUILBECK, ⎱ Churchwardens."
"JOHN SCULLOWE,   ⎰

By 1711 the family system seems to have established itself, for we read—

"Mr. Thos Hale, Constant his wife, Thomas and Sacheverell his sons, the whole Seat with a room behind for a servant, gave £1 11s. 0d." *

In 5 Henry VIII., a curious award was made by the then Sir William Brereton, of Brereton, in a dispute between two neighbouring families, Moreton and Rode. The quarrel was about precedency, "which should sit highest in the church, and foremost goo in processions," which was referred to Sir William Brereton. After "examining xii of the most auncyent men of Astbury," Sir William Brereton's decision was "that whither of the said gyntylmen may dispend in lands, by title of inheritance, 10 marks or above more than the other, that *he* shall have the pre-eminence in sitting in the Church and in going in procession, with all the like causes in that behalf." †

In the parish vestry-book of Streatham Church, mention

* "Reliquary," 21, 64. It would appear, however, that parishioners did not always like to be confined to specified seats. At St. Michael's, Cornhill, we find an old vestry order on the subject—

"Order for keping their pewes on pain to forfeit ijd. the first time, and iiijd. the second.

"Item. Evy man that on the hollie day keepeth not his owne pewe, but setteth the service time in other pewes, for ye first tyme ijd. and the second time iiijd. to be emploied to the poore's box provided eny at the lessons & the smons the more better to heare may remove."

† Lysons's "Magna Britannia."

is made of an obstreperous pew-holder, who refused to pay back rent, and on the churchwardens writing to him to say that "if it was not paid by a certain date the pew would be locked against him," he replied that if that were done, he should attend the church and break it open. Steps were taken to prevent a disturbance in the church, but these appear to have been of a conciliatory character, for three years after, a resolution was passed at a vestry meeting, that as Mr. —— had not paid any rent for eleven years, the pew should be confiscated.*

Notices of locks to pews occur in old church documents, an abuse, however, which did not escape censure. On the 21st May, 1631, Dr. Neile, Bishop of Winchester, issued a monition upon this subject to the churchwardens of the parish of Elvetham, Hampshire : "Whereas I am given to understand that locks have lately been sett upon some pews in the parish church of Elvetham, and that, without any order from me or my chancellor, which I hould very unfitt to be indured. These are to will and require you and every of you, the churchwardens there, to remove all the lockes upon any the pews within the said church, between this and the feast day of Pentecost next insueing." Bishop Earle, three years before, had alluded to this unseemly practice in the character of " The She Precise Hyprocrite" : "She doubts of the Virgin Mary's salvation, and dares not saint her ; but knows her own place in heaven as perfectly as the pew she has a key to."† Later on Pepys speaks of the practice of locking pews as a common custom. "December 25, 1661. In the morning to church, where at the door of our pew I was fain to stay, because the sexton had not opened the door."

In the year 1604, four keys were made for the " Burges "

---

* Frederick Arnold's " History of Streatham " (1856), 51.

† Quoted in Mr. Heale's " History of Church Seats," 152.

pews in St. Margaret's Church, Westminster. And in 1600 the churchwarden's pew, at St. John Zachary, London, was supplied with two keys.

Further curious items of information connected with the old pew system of former days, illustrate the many abuses to which this custom gave rise. Accordingly, when pews were strewed with rushes and supplied with mats, " it was likely," says Mr. Heale, " that dust and vermin would accumulate." Hence, at St. Michael's, Cornhill, we find this entry: " 1469, payed for iij rat trappes for the chirche, vj*d.*" At St. Margaret's, Westminster, in the year 1610, sixpence was paid for salt to destroy the fleas in the churchwardens' pew.

Then there were the high pews "for the parishioners to sit or sleep in," an abuse which Bishop Corbet of Norwich thus exposed: " I am verily persuaded, were it not for the pulpit and the pews, many churches had been down that stand. Stately pews are now become tabernacles, with rings and curtains to them. These want nothing but beds to hear the word of God on. We have casements, locks and keys, and cushions—I had almost said bolster and pillows; and for those we love the church. I will not guess what is done within them, who sits, stands, or lies asleep, at prayers, communion, etc.; but this I dare say, they are either to hide some vice, or to proclaim one, to hide disorder, or proclaim pride." Indeed, the abuses which were the outcome of the old pews, are frequently alluded to in the literature of the past, and Swift, in his " Baucis and Philemon," speaks of—

> " A bedstead of the antique mode,
> Compact of timber many a load,
> Such as our ancestors did use,
> Was metamorphosed into pews ;
> Which still their ancient nature keep
> By lodging folks disposed to sleep."

At Branksea, Dorsetshire, was "a pew as large as a drawing-room, and magnificently furnished, and having a fireplace, and windows and blinds to secure privacy from the rest of the congregation. At Mertsham, Surrey, and at Mickleham, Surrey, were pews raised some feet above the level of the floor, comfortably fitted, and possessing a fireplace and table, by no means uncommon examples." *

In Little Berningham Church, Norfolk, a pew was erected by a shepherd in the nave, to afford accommodation for strangers and wedding parties, with this inscription—

> " For couples joined in **wedlock;** and my Friend,
> That stranger **is; This Seate I** did intend."

> " But (? built) at the coste and charge of Stephen **Crosbee.**"

> " **All you that do this** Place pass by
> As you are nowe, even soe was I ;
> Remember Death, for you must dye,
> And as I am, soe shall you be.
> Anno Domini 1640."†

At the south-west corner of the **pew a** skeleton **carved in wood** reminded those who used it—even **on the eventful** occasion of matrimony—that they would have to **die; a** warning which, perhaps, was not always appreciated at such a time.

The parish **books of** Chester-le-Street, Durham, contain the following entry: "**1612, 27** May. The churchwardens **meeting** together for seeking for workmen to mak **a fitt seete in a** convenient **place** for brydgrumes, **brydes, and sike** wyves to sit in, **two** shillings." **A document** relating to Warrington Church, dated 1628, **in mentioning** an allotment of sittings, refers to " the bryd's form."

At **Northorpe** Church, Lincolnshire, there was, in years past, a small pew, popularly **known as the** Hall Dog Pew,

* Heale's " History **of** Church Seats," 184.
† Blomefield's " History of Norfolk," **vi. 317.**

wherein the dogs, which followed the residents at the hall to church, were placed during divine service.

At St. Alphege, Cripplegate Within, a certain Mr. Loveday was presented in 1620 for sitting in the same pew with his wife, "which being held to be highly indecent," he was ordered to appear; but, failing to do so, "Mr. Chancellor was made acquainted with his obstinacy."

Many curious notices of separation of sexes, and the restriction of pews for women, occur in old parish documents of the fifteenth century. In the Cornhill accounts for 1473, there is an entry of two shillings and sixpence "for werkmanship and nayle for two women pewes;" and in the churchwardens' accounts for 1584, this item is recorded: "P'd for mendinge certeyn women's pews, ij*s.*; and in 1586, "Itm̄ for a hynge to one of y° women's pews, iiij*d.*" In a faculty for seats in Great Burstead Church, Essex, in 1611, the applicant was authorized to build one pew at the entrance of the chancel for the use of himself and sons, and companions and friends of the male sex; and another pew in the body of the church for the use of his wife and her daughters, and companions and friends of the female sex.*

A further distinction was made between married and unmarried women; the wives of the most eminent parishioners being placed in a more dignified position, while the young women were placed elsewhere.† In the accounts of St. Mary-at-Hill, for 1527, is a charge for workmanship of Mr. Rocke's maiden's pew,‡ and in those of St. Mary Woolchurch, London, under 1541 and 1542, occurs this item: "Paid for mending the mayden's pewe in the church, ij*s.*"

---

* "History and Laws of Church Seats," 70.
† Ibid., 132.
‡ Mr. Rocke afterwards became alderman, lord mayor, and knight.

Non-compliance with this custom occasionally gave rise to much unpleasantness, and a case is recorded in Archdeacon Hale's " Proceedings in the Diocese of London " (p. 242) of a young woman named Hayward, " that she beinge a young mayde sat in the pewe with her mother, to the great offence of many reverent women ; howbeit that after **I, Peter** Lewis, the vicar, had in the church privatlie admonished the said young mayde of her fault, and advised her to sitt at her mother's pewe dore, she obeyed ; but now she sitts againe with her mother." Proceedings were taken at Gateshead, Durham, against a Janet Foggard, " that she beinge a yonge woman, unmarried, **will not sit in** a stall wher she is appointed, but in a stall letten to another." *

Formerly, in many churches, there was **the " churching-pew ;" an institution** which, now and then, **gave rise to** some amusing contretemps. At the close of the last century, **it is related †** how " two dashing young unmarried women were journeying from London to Norfolk by coach, and from some accidental cause were compelled to spend Sunday at a village on their route. In the pride of beauty and finery, they made their way to church, and to the most conspicuous pew near the pulpit. But they soon wished themselves elsewhere when the clergyman commenced reading the ' churching service ' of the Church of England, and were still more dismayed when the clerk, at the close of the sermon, asked them for the customary fee for the additional service which their presence in the ' churching-pew ' had unluckily brought down upon them." Another amusing instance of a misadventure in a churching-pew is told in " A **Voice** from a Mask " (1861, 126-8), wherein the author says **that** the circumstance happened " to an un-

---

* " Injunctions and Ecclesiastical Proceedings of Bishop Burnes," Surtees Society, xxii. 124.

† *Notes and Queries*, **3rd series, viii. 500.**

married sister of one of my friends." This lady, after the churching ceremony, is beating a retreat from the pew, when the clerk asks her, " Have you a child to be christened, ma'am ?" Whereupon she rushes home to her friend in a very discomposed state. " My dear Charlotte ! what has happened to you?" asks Mrs. M——. " Have you been robbed or insulted?" " Worse, worse—much worse," hysterically sobbed the old maid, " I've been churched !"

At Boston Church, prior to its restoration, there was a churching-pew; and in the churchwardens' accounts of the parish of Cundal, this entry occurs : " 1636. A Childwife Pew. 26s. 8d."

There was also the "midwives pew," and in the year 1617, at St. Margaret's, Westminster, there was paid for making a new pew for the midwives, £2 5s. 0d., and also a further charge for making another new pew for the midwives adjoining the former.

Sir Thomas Widdrington, M.P. for York, in a speech in the House of Commons, told an extraordinary anecdote of a clergyman who was his friend and neighbour. A butcher in the parish was severely gored in the stomach by an ox, and only narrowly escaped death. Eventually, the wound being cured, the butcher desired to give public thanksgiving in the church for his safe deliverance. The puzzled clergyman, finding himself in a fix, anxious and willing to gratify his parishioner, and yet not knowing of any authorized form for such a public act, read the prayers for the churching of women.* The Rev. Frederic G. Lee relates a similar story in *Notes and Queries* (5th series, ii. 125). " In a church near Oxford, which I once served as curate, there was a special pew, capacious and high, at the entrance of the church, where only women worshipped who desired the office of benediction. One Sunday afternoon, three Oxford

* " Parliamentary History," ix. 455.

undergraduates, arriving during the evening service, hastily took their places in this particular pew, when, according to custom, towards the close of the service, the parson (who was shortsighted), looking up and seeing the pew occupied, immediately proceeded 'to church' these visitors, an act which he completed to the consternation of the congregation."

In 1515, a penny is charged in the accounts of the churchwardens of St. Margaret Pattens, London, for dressing of the "yrons" of the "shrevyng pew;" and at St. Michael's, Cornhill, such a structure was removed in the year 1548: "Item payd to the joyner for takynge down the shryvyng pew and making another pew in the same place. iij*s*."

What the form or nature of the shriving-pew was is doubtful; and from the rare mention of its existence in our parish churches, it was evidently, says Mr. Heales, "a most unusual thing," and was probably "an innovation not very long antecedent to the period of the Reformation, when their destruction might be safely anticipated." *

Occasionally a pew, it would seem, was the eminence upon which offenders did public penance, as the following story shows—

"'These witnes in dede will not lye,' as the pore man sayd by the priest, 'if I maybe homely to tell you a merry tale by the way.'

"'A merry tale,' quoth I, 'commith never amyse to me.'

"The pore man, quod he, had found y⁰ priest over famyliar with his wife, and bycause he spake of it abrode and could not prouve it, the priest sued him before y⁰ byshoppe's offyciale for dyffamatyon, when the pore man upon paine of cursynge (*i.e.* excommunication), was commanded that in hys parishe churche, he should upon y⁰ Sondaye, at high masse

<hr>

* " History and Law of Church Seats and Pews " (1872), 43. 44.

time, stande up and say, 'mouth, thou lyest.'   Whereupon for fulfilling of hys penance up was the pore soul set in a pew, that the people might wonder on hym and hyre what he sayd.   And there all a lowed (when he had rehersyd what he had reported by the priest), then he sett hys handys on his mouthe, and said, 'Mouth! mouth, thou lyest!' and by-and-by, thereupon he set his hand upon his eyes, and said, 'But eyen, eyen,' quod he, 'by y*e* Mass y*e* lye not a whitte.'"

In the Elizabethan period, the pew of the chief local family in country churches was florally ornamented.   "The dresser of a pew of this character," writes Dr. Doran,* "introduced with a sublime contempt for chronology, in the old play of 'Appius and Virginia,' says to one who had impeded her work :—

> "'Thou knave, but for thee, ere this time of day,
>   My lady's fair pew had been strew'd full gay,
>   With primroses, cowslips, and violets sweet,
>   With mints and with marigolds, marjoram sweet,
>   Which now lyeth uncleanly, and all along of thee.'"

Pews holding persons of less dignity were "strawed;" but in both cases this must have been at the expense of the occupants.

* "Saints and Sinners," i. 201, 202.

CHAPTER XVII.

A FAMILIAR object in the towers of many of our old churches was " Jack of the Clock-house ; " this automaton figure being variously represented, and known under different nicknames. Sometimes, he appeared " in knightly panoply with mace, maul, or axe in hand, ready to proclaim the flight of time upon the sonorous bell which hung near the venerable clock. Occasionally he stood forth in a state hovering on nudity, his only garment being a wreath of foliage about his loins, and having a goodly club for a weapon. Hence some people called him Hercules, while others denominated him 'the Savage' or 'Wild Man,' 'the Saracen,' 'the Giant,' but everybody knew him by the common appellation of 'Jack of the Clock-house.'" * Frequent allusions occur in the literature of bygone years to this well-known figure ; and Shakespeare, in " Richard II." (Act v. sc. 5) makes the king to say—

> " My time
> Runs posting on in Bolingbroke's proud joy,
> While I stand fooling here, his Jack o' the clock."

---

* See paper by Mr. H. Syer Cuming on this automaton figure in " Jour. of the British Arch. Assoc.," xxv. 281.

And in "Richard III." (Act iv. sc. 2) we find a further reference—

> "*K. Richard.*   Well, but what's o'clock?
> *Buck.*   Upon the stroke of ten.
> *K. Richard.*   Well, let it strike.
> *Buck.*   Why let it strike?
> *K. Richard.*   Because that, like a Jack, thou keep'st the stroke
> Betwixt the begging and my meditation."

The clock in old St. Paul's was furnished with Jacks to strike the hours, which are spoken of by Decker as "Paul's Jacks," who, writing in the year 1609, says: "The great dial is your last monument; where bestow some half of the three-score minutes to observe the sauciness of the Jacks that are above the Man in the Moon; the strangeness of their motion will quit your labour." But "Paul's Jacks" perished with the old cathedral in the year 1666.

From 1671, up to the early part of the present century, the Jacks at St. Dunstan's, Fleet Street, to which Cowper alludes in his "Table Talk," formed one of the regular sights of London:

> "When labour and when dullness, club in hand,
>   Like the two figures at St. Dunstan's, stand
>   Beating alternately, in measured time,
>   The clock work tintinnabulum of rhyme,
>   Exact and regular the sounds will be;
>   But such mere quarter-strokes are not for me."

It appears by the parish books, that, on May 18, 1671, Thomas Harrys made an offer to build a new clock with chimes, and to erect two figures of men with pole-axes to strike the quarters. His offer was accepted, with the exception of the chimes, and on October 28th, in the same year, at the completion of his task, he was voted the sum of £4 per annum to keep in repair. Strype (b. iii. 276), speaking of old St. Dunstan's Church, says: "It is a good, handsome, freestone building, with a fair dial hanging over into the street; and on the side of the church, in a handsome frame of architecture are placed, in a standing posture, two savages, or Hercules, with clubs erect, which quarterly strike on the bells hanging there." Ned Ward, in his "London Spy," mentions the moving heads and hands of these automata which he calls the wooden horologists at St. Dunstan's;" and the author of "London Scenes and London People," thus describes these famous Jacks: "The giants stood in front of the building, about thirty feet from the road, on a covered platform, each holding a club, the bell being hung between them, which at the quarters, as well as whole hours, they struck, but so indolently, that spectators often complained that they were not well up to their work. The mechanism, too, was rough and clumsy; you could not help noticing the metal cord inserted in the club, to which its motion was due." When the old church was pulled down, the clock and figures were purchased by the Marquis of Hertford, and removed to his villa in Regent's Park. The clock at Rye Church, Sussex, is noteworthy. The bells are struck by a pair of fat golden cherubs placed under a canopy on the north side of the tower. This clock is said, like the altar, to have been the gift of Elizabeth, but there are some doubts on this point. It is considered, however, the most ancient clock in England still actually doing its work.

St. Martin's, Carfax, Oxford, was once celebrated for its pair of Jacks, which were erected at the east end of the church, in the year 1624, an engraving of which may be seen in the *Gentleman's Magazine* for July, 1836 (p. 21). And at Horsham, Sussex, there was a " Jack Clock House," till about 1825.* Holy Trinity Church, Bristol,† which was demolished in 1787, had "a tapering spire, and in the

---

* "Reliquary," xxiii. 36.

† E. J. Wood, "Curiosities of Clocks and Watches," 107.

tower was a clock guarded by gigantic 'quarter-boys,' represented in two large figures, with ever-ready hammers to note the flight of time. They were placed under a semi-circular canopy on each side of the face of the clock. They wore brass helmets, and were partly habited in armour; each grasped a battle-axe, with which it struck the bell suspended over its head. It would appear that they were coloured and gilt with great care, according to the taste of the age." There is a Jack of the clock at Westgate, Exeter. It consists of three figures in the dress of the seventeenth century, and is popularly called "The Miller and his Sons."

In an arch in the tower of Blythburgh Church, Suffolk, is, or was, the figure of a man, four feet in height, which used to strike the hours on a bell. "He is habited," writes Mr. Syer Cuming,* "in plate armour, which is painted black, with the passe-gardes and borders of the coutes and genouillieres gilded; the crested helmet and gorget being white. A flowing beard gives this 'Jack' a venerable aspect, and loss of hands and occupation seem to make him look melancholy." At Southwold Church, in the same county, a "Jack of the Clock," in former years, proclaimed the hours. But "this curious figure is now removed from the tower to the vestry window open to the church, and though no longer toiling hour after hour, as of yore, is not altogether idle, for the parish clerk makes Jack toll the bell as the clergyman emerges from the vestry, as a signal that divine service has begun."

Another well-known instance of a "Jack of the Clock," is at Norwich. "Those persons," it is said, "who have inspected the curiosities at the cathedral of Norwich, will remember that the quarters for the use of persons within the building are struck by two similar, though much smaller

* "Journal of Brit. Arch. Assoc.," xxv. 281.

JACK O' THE CLOCK, SOUTHWOLD.   *Page* 200.

figures, placed **near two bells,** inside the church, in **one of** the recesses of **the south aisle, and that the arms communi-** cate with the abbey **clock by** two strings, which are visible **in** their whole course from the figures to the ceiling." *   Mechan- ical **clocks** of this kind, which were occasionally put up in churches, must be reckoned amongst the things of the past, **Jack** of the Church Clock House being a defunct personage.

Many entries are given in parish books of payments **to** the "clock-keeper," which would seem to have been a recognized appointment.   Allen, in **his** "History **of** Lambeth," quotes the following items **from** the church- wardens' accounts—

" 1585.   **Agreed that** Holloway shall **have iiij***s***. a year for** oyle, for the **clocke, and bells,** and for candle to the **clocke.**

" 1599.   **Payd to Lewis** Smalle, **for** keeping **the clocke, his wages, 1 2***s***.**

" 1605.   To Smalle, for keeping the clocke, **16***s***."

The churchwardens' accounts of **St.** Margaret's, West- **minster,** under the year 1548, record this item : "Also paid to the said John Ivery, for the keeping **of** the v a clock and viii a clock, for half a yere and half a quarter ended at the same feast, 16*s*. 8*d.*   In the parish accounts of Wigtoft, near Boston, Lincolnshire, for the year 1484, this entry occurs : "Item, paide to Ric. Anngell for kepyng of the clok, 3*s*. 4*d*."   **And in the** Proctor's accounts **for** 1469, **of St.** Mary's, Oxford, **is** this item : "Pro Custodia horilogij, vj*s*. viij*d*."; and in **1473, "Pro** Custodia hori- logij, iiij*s*."

Sometimes persons left special bequests **for the** clock- keeper.   The rents of **a** small piece **of land** called the "Clock Holt," at Haslingfield, Cambridgeshire, have been applied from time immemorial, says Edwards, in his "Remarkable Charities" (p. 208) "for the winding up and

---

* "Journal of Brit. Arch. **Assoc.,**" xxv. 280.

repairs of the church clock." From the same source we learn that "by indenture, 26th August, 1513, Roger Lupton, vicar of Cropredy, Oxfordshire, delivered to the church-wardens of Cropredy and Bourton, £6 13s. 4d., for which they covenanted for themselves and their successors, to find at their own costs some person to keep duly the clock of Cropredy." Sir Edward Lake, by his will, dated April 8th, 1665, gave as follows : "To the church or chappell of Normanton, near Pontefract, Yorkshire (if there be a church or chappell there, which I know not), where my paternall ancestors have lived for many years," a clock and a sum of money "for the maintaining and keeping of it for ever."

An indespensable adjunct of the pulpit in former years was the hour-glass, relics of which still remain in many of our old country churches. Its use in England, as a means of measuring time to the preacher, was coeval with the Reformation, as appears from the frontispiece prefixed to the Bishops Bible, imprinted by John Day, 1569. It was at this period in our church's history that long sermons came into fashion, when the preacher felt called upon to explain "tenets attacked, or eliminate doctrinal disputes." To regulate, therefore, the time accorded to the preacher for his discourse, an hour-glass was placed on the pulpit ; and in 1623 we read of a preacher "being attended by a man that brought after him his book and hour-glass."

Allen, in his " History of Lambeth," says, "when a new pulpit was placed in the parish church in 1522, in it was fixed an hour-glass, of which there are no remains ;" and in the churchwardens' accounts of this parish we find two entries respecting the hour-glass, the first being in 1579, when 1s. 4d. was "payd to York for the frame in which the hower standeth," and in the second, in 1615, when 6s. 8d. was "payd for an iron for the hour-glass." In the church book for St. Katherine's, Aldgate, under 1564, this entry occurs : " Paid for an hour-glass that hangeth by the pulpit, where the preacher doth make a sermon, that he may know how the hour passeth away, one shilling," and, in the same book, among the bequests of 1616 is an hower-glass with a frame of iron to stand in."   In 1592 the churchwardens of Leicester paid fourpence for "an oure-glass," and in 1597 in the Ludlow Church accounts, we find an item of twenty pence "for makinge of the frame of the hower-glasse."   In the churchwardens' accounts of St. Helen's, Abingdon, for 1599, fourpence is charged for an hour-glass for the pulpit ; and in the Chamberlain's accounts of Stratford-on-Avon, this is given : " **Paid to** Watton for setting up the hour-glasse, iiij*d*."   **In an** inventory, taken about 1632, of the goods and implements belonging to the church of All Saints, Newcastle-upon-Tyne, these items occur : " one whole-houre glasse," " one half-houre glasse," and many other similar entries elsewhere might be easily quoted.

Referring to some of the hour-glasses themselves, one of the finest in London is that of St. Alban's, Wood Street, which was first described in the *Gentleman's Magazine* for 1822 (xcii., pt. 2, p. 200).   According to the parish records, " Mr. Thomas Wadeson, parish clerk, gave a brass branch for the church, and two small ones for the pulpit and reading-desk, and a stand for the hour-glass."   The hour-glass at St. Dunstan's, Fleet Street, was taken down in 1723, and two heads for the parish staves made out of the silver.   And within memory there was an hour-glass stand affixed to the pulpit of St. Ethelburga's Church, Bishops-gate Street.   It is said that when Bishop Burnet was preaching at St. Margaret's, Westminster, before the House of Commons, he turned his hour-glass to show that he was about to continue his discourse, and that he was nearly interrupted by the applauding murmurs of his hearers—a strong testimony to his eloquence. Several versions of this well-known story are recorded; and Lord Macaulay tells us how the good bishop, after preaching out the hour-glass, would hold it in his hand, while the congregation "clamourously encouraged him to go on till the sand had run off once more." At the restoration of the Chapel Royal, in 1867, an eighteen-minute pulpit-glass was placed in the church, which was considered a protest on the part of her Majesty against long sermons.

In Shaw's work on "Dress and Decoration" is an engraving of the bracket and hour-glass belonging to Hurst Church, Berkshire. It is made of iron, painted and gilt, and of elaborate workmanship, and on the stem of the bracket are these words, "As this glass runneth so man's life passeth." The iron stand of the hour-glass remains in Chesham Bois Church, and at Keyingham Church, near Hull, there is an interesting example. At St. Michael's Church, St. Alban's, the hour-glass stand is affixed to the left of the reading-desk; and one with the date of 1636 is placed on a carved wooden bracket on the left side of the preacher in the pulpit of Cliffe Church, Kent. Fosbroke, in his "British Monachism," relates how "a rector of Bibury used to preach two hours, regularly turning the glass. After the text, the esquire of the parish withdrew, smoked his pipe, and returned to the blessing." It may be added the pulpit hour-glass was also common in Scotland, and Dr. Rogers, in his "Familiar Illustrations of Scottish Character," quotes the Rev. Peter Glas, minister of Crail, as saying, "It was a puir parish that didna hae a sand-glass."

Many of the hour-glasses throughout the country have gradually disappeared with the work of restoration. About thirty years ago an hour-glass was to be seen at Flixton, Suffolk, but it was destroyed during the work of restoration; and at Sacombe, a few miles from Hertford, before the church was restored, there was an old hour-glass frame fixed to the side of the pulpit which had come down from the period of the Commonwealth or thereabout. There was a preacher's hour-glass at Cuxham and North Moor, Oxfordshire, and one at East Worldham, Hampshire, where it remained till the body of the church was pulled down and rebuilt in 1865.

Among further instances may be mentioned those at Wolvercot and Beckley, Oxfordshire; Puxton, Somersetshire; Catfield, Sutton, Stalham, Lessingham, Hempsted, Salhouse, and Ledham, Norfolk; St. Edmund's Church, South Burlingham; and at Shelsley-Beauchamp.* In the "Oxford Glossary of Architecture" is a representation of an hour-glass stand at Leigh Church, Kent, and in Weale's "Quarterly Papers on Architecture" is an engraving of an hour-glass and frame in Compton Bassett Church, Wilts.†

We must not omit to notice some of the notable weathercocks which in years past created more or less interest. St. Mildred's Church in the Poultry, prior to its demolition, possessed a tower seventy-five feet high, surmounted by a vane representing a ship in full sail. The remarkable spire of St. Michael's, Queenhithe, destroyed in the great fire, was rebuilt by Wren in the year 1677. Its spire, one hundred and thirty-five feet, has long been famed for its gilt vane in the form of a ship in full sail, the hull of which has enjoyed the reputation of being able to hold a bushel of grain, the allusion being to the former traffic in corn at the Hithe. Then there is St. Sepulchre's Church, Skinner Street, with its tower, which, according to Malcolm, "is one of the most ancient in the outline in the circuit of London." This tower is noted for its four pinnacles with vanes, rebuilt

---

* See an interesting paper on Pulpit Hour-glasses in the "Journal of the Brit. Arch. Assoc." (1848), iii. 301–310.

† In the *Gentleman's Magazine* (1747, 264; 265), there are some remarks on the burial of an hour-glass with a corpse.

1630–33, and is one hundred and forty feet high. Hence it was that Howell wrote, " Unreasonable people are as hard to reconcile as the vanes of St. Sepulchre's Tower, which never looked all four upon one point of the heavens."

St. Peter's, Cornhill, has a tower and spire one hundred and forty feet high, surmounted by an enormous key, the emblem of St. Peter. Similarly, the steeple of St. Laurence Jewry, Cheapside, has for its vane a gilt gridiron, intended as the emblem of St. Laurence. The dragon of St. Mary-le-Bow, Cheapside, has long been famous. It is of copper, gilt, eleven feet long, and when it was regilded in the year 1820, a young Irishman descended from the spire point on the back of the dragon, pushing it from the cornices and scaffolds with his feet in the presence of thousands of spectators. It may be remembered that one of Mother Shipton's prophecies was that when the grasshopper of the Royal Exchange and the dragon of Bow Church should meet, London Streets would be deluged with blood. Although happily the last portion of this prophecy was not fulfilled, yet, curious to say, in the year 1820 both these vanes were lying together in the yard of a stonemason in Old Street Road. Washington Irving, who was an eye-witness of this event, thus writes : " The same architect has been engaged lately on the repairs of the cupola of the Exchange and the steeple of Bow Church, and, fearful to relate, the dragon and the grasshopper lie cheek by jowl in the yard of his workshop." The spire vane at Fotheringay Church, Northamptonshire, represents the falcon and the fetterlock, the badge of the Dukes of York.

In Wright's " History of Ludlow " (465) we are told " the north transept of the church is called the Fletcher's Chancel, and on its gable is an arrow, the ensign of the craft. It is a probable conjecture that this part was appropriated for the use of the archers who might possibly hold their meetings here." According to a local legend, this arrow was set in this position "in commemoration of a shot made by Robin Hood from the Old Field,—a long mile distant,—which hit the steeple."

There is the fine old copper-gilt weathercock of Portsmouth, which is in the fashion of an ancient full-rigged ship, with spread ensign aft ; the vessel is about six feet long, and the flag about four feet long. When the necessity arises of taking it down to clean and re-gild, it seems to be a local custom for any waterman from "the Hard," or thereabouts, whose wife has been lately confined, to take the child and lay it in the hull for a moment or two, just "for luck."

Another use to which church towers and steeples have been occasionally applied in times past, has been for the display of beacons. A beacon lamp was, in bygone years, placed in the centre of the steeple of All Saints' Church, York, for the benefit of travellers in the forest of Galtres. Edwards, in his "Remarkable Charities" (98), informs us that "John Wardall, by will, dated the 29th of August, 1656, gave to the Grocers' Company a tenement, called the White Bear, in Walbrook, to the intent that they should yearly, within thirty days after Michaelmas, pay to the churchwardens of St. Botolph, Billingsgate, £4, to provide a good and sufficient iron and glass lantern, with a candle, for the direction of passengers to go with more security to and from the water side, all night long, to be fixed at the north-east corner of the parish church of St. Botolph, from the feast day of St. Bartholomew to Lady Day. Out of which sum £1 was to be paid to the sexton for taking care of the lantern."

A similar bequest was bequeathed by John Cooke, September 12, 1662, "for the maintenance of a lantern and candle, to be of eight in the pound at the least, to be kept and hanged out at the corner of St. Michael's Lane, near

Thames Street, from Michaelmas to Lady Day, between the hours of nine and ten o'clock at night until the hours of four or five in the morning, for affording light to passengers going through Thames Street or St. Michael's Lane, £1." Formerly a lighted lantern at St. Mary's, Beverley, guided travellers over the wolds in the vicinity of the town. A curious story is told of the tower of Minster Church, Cornwall, which has long fallen into decay, and whose romantic ruins have thus been described by Mr. Hawker—

> "The Minster of the Trees ! a lonely dell,
>   Deep with old oaks, and 'mid their quiet shade,
> Gray with the moss of years, yon antique cell !
>   Sad are those walls : the cloister lowly laid,
> Where pacing monks at solemn evening made
>   Their chanted orisons : and as the breeze
> Came up the vale, by rock and tree delay'd,
>   They heard the awful voice of many seas
> Blend with thy pausing hymn, thou Minster of the Trees."

The story of the destruction of the tower runs thus : " It was seen through the gorge which now forms the harbour of Boscastle far out at sea. The monks were in the habit of placing a light in one of the windows of the tower to guide the worshippers at night to the minster. Frequently sailors mistook this, by day for some landmark, and at night for a beacon, and were thus led into a trap from which they could not easily extricate themselves, and within which they often perished. This accident occurred so frequently, that the sailors began at last to declare their belief that the monks purposely beguiled them to their fate, hinting, indeed, that plunder was their object. Eventually, a band of daring men, who had been thus lured into Boscastle, went to the abbey, and, in spite of the exertions made by the monks, they pulled down the tower, since which time it has never been rebuilt." *

* Hunt's " Popular Romances of the West of England," 439, 440.

CHAPTER XVIII.

LYCHNOSCOPES, OR **LOW SIDE** WINDOWS.

THE Low Side Windows, **found in the side** wall of the chancel—sometimes on the north, but more **often** on the south—in many **of** our parish churches, have long been **a puzzle to** most antiquarians. Numerous theories have been **advanced in** explanation of their use, but without any thoroughly satisfactory result. According to one popular **view,** they were openings for lepers to assist at Mass, hence called "leper windows." In support of the leper theory, it has been remarked that at the west end of the north side of St. Martin, Liskeard, is a curious opening consisting of three small square-headed openings, three inches and a half in width, one **foot** five inches in height, separated by monials five inches **in** thickness. There would be just sufficient space for **the** admission of a hand through **the** openings, and externally under the window is a small stoup **for** holy water projecting **from** the wall. About half a mile **from** Liskeard there formerly existed **a** hospital for lepers, which it seems had no chapel of its own.

It **has** been **urged,** however, that these openings could not have been used for this purpose, as "some are so close to the ground **that it** would be necessary for the leper to lie down to see through them," others are too high from

P

the ground for a person to reach, and the greater number do not command a view of the altar at all.

As the Rev. Henry G. de Bunsen says,[*] speaking of one of these so-called leper windows at Lilleshall Church: "In ancient times there were a number of lepers in England, and these were not allowed to enter the church, or to worship with the rest of the congregation, for fear of the leprosy spreading in the village. It seemed hard, however, to debar them from all the privileges of the rest; and accordingly those who built the north aisle had a little window made which should reach to the ground, as near as possible to the altar in that aisle (for there was an altar here as well as at the east end of the nave). Thus the outcast leper, one or more, would kneel out of doors by the side of the little window, and join his prayers to those of the congregation within. And whenever the Holy Communion was administered, by opening the little window he could receive it while kneeling outside. In this way did our forefathers think of the poor outcasts as well as those who were ' healthy and wealthy '; and while they provided lofty and roomy aisles for the many, the nook and corner for the miserable and wretched was not forgotten."

It has been suggested that the object of the Low Side Window was for the sacristan standing inside to ring the bell at Mass at the open window, so that it might be heard by the people outside. In support of this view, Mr. J. G. Cole writes in the "Journal of the Archæological Institute" for March, 1848: "That prior to the introduction of sanctus bell-cots, and commonly where these were not erected, then at the low side window—the only real opening in the church except the doors, and this unglazed, but provided with a shutter—the sacristan stood; and at the elevation of the Host, opened the shutter and rang the sanctus

* "Journal of the Brit. Arch. Assoc." (1861), xvii. 273.

bell, as directed, I think, in the most ancient liturgy : ' In elevatione vero ipsius Corporis Domini pulsetur campana in uno latere, ut populares, quibus celebrationi missarum non vacat quod idie interesse, ubicunque fuerint, seu in agris, seu in domibus, flectant genua ' (Constit. Joh. Peckham, A.D. 1281). This rule could be better observed by means of a Low Side Window, strictly regarding the words ' in uno latere' than by a bell cot, which was probably an innovation, though an elegant one."

But the Rev. J. F. Hodgson has pointed out in the " Antiquary " (xxi. 220) that the nature and position of many Low Side Windows militates against this theory. Some, for instance, are too narrow for the passage of a bell sufficiently large to be heard at any reasonable distance—that at Cockfield Church, Durham, being only six and a half inches wide ; at Downton, Wilts, the spaces between the bars measure only five inches by seven inches ; at Darsingham, Lincolnshire, the opening, about eighteen inches square, is closely filled with four pierced quatrefoiled circles in stone. Others, it is urged, are either too low or too high for this purpose, some being nearly on the ground, as at Hart and Elwick, Durham ; while in numerous cases a very long ladder would be required to reach the window, as at Winston, Durham ; Addlethorpe, Lincolnshire ; Lowestoft, Suffolk ; and Ingham, Norfolk. Then, again, it is further shown that occasionally the position of the Low Side Window precludes the idea of such a use, for at Staindrop and Barnard Castle Churches they occur in the western bay of the south aisle between the porch and the south-west angle. At Ludham, Norfolk, the opening is at the west end of the nave below the west window ; at Stanford-le-Hope, Essex, and St. Mary's, Guildford, at the west end of the north aisle.

A further objection put forth by the Rev. J. F. Hodgson is that Low Side Windows " are actually found in direct connection with eastern bell-cots—sanctus or other—or central towers, which for all practical purposes come to just the same thing." Thus, to quote two instances, at Rothersthorpe, Northants, he points out that the sanctus bell-cot and narrow grilled opening both remain; while at Boxwell, Gloucestershire, a small village church consisting of nave and chancel only, with an open bell-cot on the eastern gable of the nave, "there is a small and very narrow low side window, square-headed, and with a hood-mould, close to the eastern angle of the nave southwards. This, it is obvious, if the handbell theory were correct, would be quite superfluous, were it even wide enough to allow the passage of a bell, which it does not seem to be."

Another explanation of the Low Side Window is that it was intended for confession, and Mr. E. J. Carlos, writing to the *Gentleman's Magazine* (1846, ii. 380), quotes an extract from a letter of Bedyll to Cromwell : " We think it best that the place where these friars have been wont to hear outward confessions of all comers at certain times of the year be walled up, and that use to be foredone for ever." This recommendation applies only to the monasteries, but, as the same writer observes : "If an irregular practice of this kind existed in parochial churches, and there were places requiring to be walled up, it would be in the province of the ordinary to direct it to be done. It was not within the line of Bedyll's duty to notice such places, though the notoriety given to the practice by the visitation of the monasteries would necessarily produce a similar order from the ordinary to close them where found in parish churches." Mr. J. Lewis André in "The Antiquary" (xxi. 124), contributing to an interesting conference on "Low Side Windows" supports the confessional theory, and writes : " At Doddington, Kent, there is a stone book-rest placed in immediate proximity to the inside of the lychnoscope;

whilst at Sherringham, Norfolk, a Low Side Window has the splays inside corbelled off, and a seat placed inside the recess, the corbelling being exactly similar to that over several examples of sedilia in the same neighbourhood. These instances prove that the windows, where they occur, were intended to be used by some person either standing or seated by them, and this agrees perfectly with the confessional theory, for the priest waiting for penitents could sit and read during the intervals between the departure of one person and the arrival of the next."

Similar examples occur at Elsfield, Oxfordshire, and at Allington, Wilts, where there is a seat and a book-rest; and on the outside of SS. Mary and Margaret, Sprowston, there is a covered cell. Another similar Low Side Window exists at Melton Constable, near Holt, Norfolk, and is thus described by Mr. C. R. Manning :* "On the south side of the chancel, and on the east face of the tower, low down is a seat scooped out of the thick wall. In front of this seat, and projecting from the jamb and sill of a Low Side Window, is a stone desk for a book. The window is of one light, with a cinque-foiled head, and has a transom at the level of the top of the desk, below which the window is blocked, and no doubt had a shutter. The stone seat is now a somewhat uncomfortable perch, and may probably have been covered by a wooden stall and back, or canopy."

Mr. Paley (" Manual," p. 341) suggests another solution of the difficulty, and says : " I would call them offertory windows, since that was probably their real use. It appears that they originated from an order of recluses or *solitarii*, who had their oratories contiguous to, or adjoining churches, and who not being allowed to communicate with any assembly of men, had these little windows constructed, ' ut per fenestram possent ad missas per manus sacerdotum

* *The Antiquary*, xxi. 125.

oblationes offerre.' But the practice was doubtless extended from them to the general use of the laity, as very scanty notice can be found of such recluses, and a great number of ancient churches—from the twelfth to the fifteenth century—have such offertory windows." In many cases this would be impossible. The window at Dersingham Church, near Lynn, Norfolk, has the lower part transomed off. But " here the whole space does not open, so as to admit of the hand being passed through, but is pierced with quartre-foil openings in the square." * At All Saints, Hartley, Kent, there is an immovable grate over the aperture, and "in the south aisle of St. Peter, Ropsley, the loop is so small as to preclude the possibility of making an offering through it at all." † At St. Sennan, Sennen, Cornwall, it should be noted that the low side window was used for taking in the tithe milk of that parish.

Some have maintained that the Low Side Window was to give light to the reader of the lessons, most windows being filled in with painted glass. In the *Building News* for March 20, 1890, appeared the following letter on the low side window in the chapel or oratory of Prior Crauden, within the precincts of Ely Cathedral, wherein the writer says : " The chapel, a little gem of the Edwardian period is abundantly lighted by large eastern and western windows, as well as by two tall windows of two lights each on the north and south sides. In addition to this ample provision for the admission of light, the architect has introduced two lovely low windows, one on each side, west of the tall side windows just mentioned. The interior sills of these low windows are about two feet six inches from the floor of the chapel, and each ;of them has a stone ledge, not a seat, within its recess ; but the external sills are some ten or

---

* *The Antiquary*, xxi. 125.
† " The Reliquary," xxiv.

twelve feet from the ground, the chapel being built upon a large under-croft or crypt, and occupying the 'first floor' (to borrow a secular term) of an edifice with two stories. This fact disposes at once of the explanatory hypothesis 'of their being used by persons outside.' There could be no looking in from the outside by lepers, penitents, or ordinary witnesses of the sacred rites; and it is most unlikely that a sanctus bell would be rung at an open window of this private oratory, an appendage of the residence of the prior, attended, doubtless, only by himself and his household." Probably "the prior, elderly and dim sighted, wished for light thrown directly on his breviary, when he heard Mass said by his chaplains, and that his friend, Alan the sacrist, met his wishes by the insertion of these 'exquisite windows.'" This theory of the low side window having been intended to give light had the support of M. Viollet-Leduc, the eminent French architect, who was employed in the restoration of "La Sainte Chapelle," and who said that the low side window in that building was glazed with white glass covered by an internal shutter, which was closed when the window was not in use, in order not to interfere with the general effect of the "dim religious light" from the large windows.*

It has been suggested that the Low Side Window originated in the early custom of placing a light to scare away evil spirits from the churchyard. And a conjecture put forward by the Ecclesiological late Cambridge Camden Society, in their "Few Hints on Ecclesiological Antiquities," is that such windows were for the purpose of watching the Paschal Candle, hence called Lychnoscopes. It was an ancient tradition, to which reference is made elsewhere in the present work, that the second coming of Christ would be on Easter Eve, hence the sepulchre and light were watched

* "The Archæological Journal" (1847), iv. 326.

during the whole day and two nights between **Good** Friday and Easter **Day.** According to another theory, the Low Side Window was to enable the acolytes to pass the thurible through for **the purpose of having the charcoal blown up to** a red **heat in the open air before the** incense **was put on,** thereby avoiding **the** unpleasant fumes **which arose from** **charcoal when first lighted, but** it seems **"there are no** **records** or traditions **of such a** custom, **or directions for it in** **the rubrics of the Missal."** *

Then there is the symbolical **theory, that the** Low Side Window was intended to symbolize the wound in the side of our Saviour **on the cross, the church itself** being considered as representing **the body of Christ.** But there is no authority for this supposition, and the cases in which **there** **are two windows** opposite **to each other are fatal to this** **theory.** The suggestion that these **windows were for** purposes of ventilation is improbable, **for, as** it has been often urged, **"there seems no reason** for always choosing **the** **particular situation occupied** by these windows for **such a** **purpose."** †

Prior to the thirteenth century Low Side Windows are rare, **but after this period they** become comparatively **common,** **traces of them belonging to this and** the **two following** centuries **being numerous in** most parts **of the country.** The earliest example is probably that **at Caistor, Northamp-** tonshire, which **appears to** belong **to the Anglo-Saxon** period, while of the twelfth **century there are** instances at St. Margaret's at **Cliff,** Kent ; **North Hinksey,** Berkshire ; and at St. Giles's, **Northampton.**

Among thirteenth-century **examples may be** mentioned **those at Oakington,** Cambridgeshire ; Raydon, Suffolk ; **and** **at Elsfield and Bucknell, Oxfordshire.** Of those belonging to

---

* "The Archæological Journal," iv. 325.
† See "Archæological Journal" (1847), iv. 326.

the fourteenth century, instances occur at Garsington and at Ardley, **Oxfordshire; at** Offchurch, Lillington, Dunchurch, Long Compton, and at Cubington, Warwickshire; at Over, Cambridgeshire; **at** Whitwell, Rutlandshire; **and** the remarkable one **at Ely.**

Coming to the fifteenth century, Low Side **Windows are very numerous,** being occasionally insertions in earlier **walls.** Instances exist at Hellesdon, Norfolk; **at** Eccleshall, Staffordshire; at Swavesey, Cambridgeshire; at Blisworth, Northamptonshire; at Chaddesley Corbett, Worcestershire, and a late example at Wetherall, **Cumberland.**[*]

Two further specimens **of** Low Side Windows require notice, the **one being at** Othery, **near** Bridgewater, **which is thus described in the** "Archæological Journal" (iv. **323):** It **is not a separate** window, but merely **"a** square opening **in the lower part of** one light **of a late** two-light **Perpendicular window,** having the wooden **shutter** and **the ironwork** remaining. It is on the south side of the chancel, **but the** opening would be entirely concealed from almost **every** point of view by **a** buttress supporting the central tower, which projects immediately in front of **it,** and **so** close to it as to prevent any person from standing or kneeling **on** the outside of it. A hole is cut through **the** buttress in **a** direct line with this opening, either for **the** purpose **of** enabling **some** person **to see out, or to make a light in** the window visible to passers-by. **The distance from the** outside **of** buttress **to** the opening **appears too great** for the purpose of confession."

The other example occurs in Winchester College Chapel, on the south side. It is **about ten feet from** the ground, both inside **and** outside. **One of the** lights of a three-light **window is divided by a transom with** an arched head under

---

[*] " The Archæological Journal" (1847), iv. 314–321.

it. The hinges of the shutter remain. It is now blocked up by one of the buttresses of the tower, which was built about fifty years after the chapel, but as the foundations are known to have given way, this buttress is probably of later date.*

* "The Archæological Journal" (1847), iv. 323.

CHAPTER XIX.

THE EASTER SEPULCHRE.

IN some churches may be seen the remains of the Easter sepulchre, which was intended for the purpose of commemorating our Lord's entombment by means of a rubrical rite, which in some cases approached very nearly to a mystery, and partly originated from an ancient belief that His Second Advent would be on Easter Eve. There appears to have been no rigid rule of uniformity in the observance of this ceremony, which in general terms, writes Mr. A. Heales in his valuable paper on "Easter Sepulchres," * may be described as the deposit on Maundy Thursday of the consecrated Host and the crucifix from the high altar, in a place apart, where it remained concealed for a time, the spot being carefully watched and guarded. A light, too, was constantly kept burning, notices for the payment of which occur in old parish accounts. Thus, those of Great Yarmouth in 1465 contain charges for watching the sepulchre and tending the sepulchre lights; and in 1482, at St. Stephen's, Walbrook, London, this entry occurs: "Item, payd on Estren Evyn to William Breyt and to Ray's man pur wetchying of the Sepulcur, viij*d*.;" and in the following year, "Item, payd to the Clerkys when they wachyd the

* "Archæologia," xlii. (263–308): "Easter Sepulchres: their Object, Nature, and History."

sepulker for ther drynke and bred, iiij*d*." Under 1499, at St. Mary-at-Hill, London, we meet with these items—

" For the waching of sepulchre and the chirche to ii men, xij*d*.

" For brede and ale to them that wached, vj*d*.

" For a lampe and for tentyr hookes for the Sepulchre, j*d*. ob."

At St. Helen's, Abingdon, in the accounts for 1555 and 1558, these entries are made—

" To the Sextin for watching the Sepulter two nyghtes, viij*d*.

" To the Sexten for meat and drinck, and watching the sepulture according to custom, i*s*. x*d*.

" To the Bellman for meat, drinck, and cooles, watching the sepulture, i*s*. vij*d*."

At Lichfield three persons kept unbroken vigil, and a light burned in the sepulchre.

Occasionally, it would seem, guilds were formed for watching the sepulchre. In 1370 a guild in the parish of St. Botolph Without, Aldgate, was founded in honour of the body of Christ, and to maintain thirteen wax lights burning about the sepulchre in the time of Easter, and to find a chaplain. At Kirton-in-Lindsey, Lincolnshire, there was " the Guild of the Sepulchre of our Lord Jesus Christ," and in 1463 the will of John Baret mentions a Resurrection Guild at Bury, and bequeathes to it eightpence for eight tapers " stondyng at the Grawve of resurrec̃con gylde."

Naogeorgus says the people used to cast violets and all kinds of sweet flowers on the sepulchre, and make their offerings while the choir chanted a dirge. In some places the steps of the sepulchre were covered with black cloth, soldiers in armour kept guard, and in most churches there was a constant succession of watchers.

Very early on Easter morning, before sounding the matins bell, it appears that, in olden times, the cross was removed to its usual place upon the altar, and then there was performed, in some churches and cathedrals, a peculiar ceremony known as the "Office of the Sepulchre." At Durham, a framework with rich hangings of red velvet and gold embroidery was erected on Good Friday, and from it on Easter Day, between three and four o'clock a.m., two of the most aged monks took a figure of the risen Saviour holding a cross, and laying it on a crimson cushion, brought it to the high altar, singing *Christus resurgens.* Then it was carried to the south choir door, where "four ancient gentlemen held over it a rich canopy of purple velvet, faced with red silk and gold fringes, and so round the church, the choir attending with goodly torches, and great store of other lights, all singing and praising God till they came again to the high altar."* In some of the Edwardian inventories of Church goods, mention is made of certain articles for the sepulchre ceremonies; as, for instance, at Clapham, Surrey, where, under 1550,† we find these entries—

"Diverse Stayned Clothes and Stools for the Sepulchre.

"Diverse old stayned and painted Clothes for the doing of Ceremonyes lately used in the Church."

Lambarde ‡ has given an account of the resurrection by means of puppets as given at Witney, Oxfordshire: "In the days of Ceremonial Religion they used at Wytney to set forthe yearly in maner of a Shew or Enterlude the Resurrection of our Lord and Saviour Chryste, partly of Purpose to draw thyther some Concourse of People that might spend their Money in the Towne, but chieflie to allure by pleasant Spectacle the comon Sort to the Likinge of Popishe Maumetrie, for the which Purpose and the

* See Mackenzie Walcott's "Sacred Archæology," 243, 244.
† "Surrey Archæological Collections," iv. 44–109.
‡ "Alphabetical Description of the Chief Places in England and Wales" (1730), 459.

more lyvely thearby to exhibit to the Eye the hole Action of the Resurrection the Preistes garnished out certein small Puppets representinge the Parsons of Christe, the Watchmen, Marie, and others, amongest the which one bare the Parte of a wakinge Watcheman who (Espiinge Christ to Arise) made a continual noyce like to the sound that is caused by the Metinge of two Styckes, and was thereof comonly called *Jack Shacker* of Wytney."

Respecting the structure of the Easter Sepulchre, it appears to have been a temporary wooden structure, so designed as to be easily put up when required, and taken down and stowed away again when the ceremony was over. At Down, near Hayes, Kent, was "a sepulchre of wood;" at Sunninghill, Berks, a "sepulchre of timber;" at Barkstone, Lincolnshire, one is described as of "lattes," and those at Blyton, Lincolnshire, and Hanbury, Staffordshire, were of wainscot. At Durham the sepulchre is spoken of as being set upon Good Friday after the Passion, and in the treasury accounts of Norwich Cathedral for 1376, we find payments of two shillings for making the sepulchre, and the wages of workmen for four days. At Great Yarmouth payments occur in 1465 for setting up, taking down, and fetching it in, and for a new house in the vestry to put the sepulchre in ; and for the sepulchre of St. Mary-at-Hill, London, in 1493, several entries have been preserved—

"Paide to Christopher Bechen for a p̃ of tymber containing 11 feate, ... js. x*d.*

"Item to William Pavys for werkman ship and settyng of the sepulcre . . . . iijs. viij*d.*

"Item for a plank's ende for the one end . vj*d.*

"Item for a small quart next the wall behind the sepulchre . . . . . . ij*d.*

"Item to the smyth for 13 pynnes yryn . iij*d.*

Summa vj*s.* vj*d.*

In the churchwardens' accounts of the parish of Leverton, Lincolnshire, for 1553, these entries are given—

"For maykkyng of the Sepulkkure howysse, iij*d.*

"For payntyng of a clothe for the saym, ij*s.*

"For feycheyng of the sepulkcure cloth frome the paynt* att Boston, ij*d.*"

And at St. Helen's, Abingdon, similar payments for 1558 are recorded :—

"Payde for making the sepulture, x*s.*

"For peynting the same sepulture, iij*s.*

"For stones & other charges about it, iiij*s.* vj*d.*"

The sepulchre varied according to the size and wealth of the church. Its elaborate structure and new decorations appear by many records. Thus John of Gaunt by his will dated February 3, 1397, bequeaths his bed furniture, copes, tapestry, and "draps embroudés pur la sepulcre." An inventory of ornaments belonging to St. Margaret Pattens, London, 1470, mentions "a grete cloth of tapestrie werke to hang 'upon the Walls by hynde the Sepulcur ;" and at Chichester Cathedral, beginning of the sixteenth century, there was a very elaborate covering for the sepulchre : "A Clothe of fyne arays with a border of Clothe of golde of Crystys passyon contayning vj yards dim. pro sepulcro, xiii^{li} vj*s.* viij*d.*" The inventory of Lincoln Cathedral mentions the sepulchre there as having a white stained cloth of damask silk ; and at Ely Cathedral (1540) there was a red pall for the sepulchre. In the inventory of St. Paul's Cathedral (1552) are mentioned two rich cloths for the garnishing of the sepulchre, and two smaller ones of needlework, one of them of the Sepulchre and the other of the Resurrection. At Farley, Surrey, the sepulchre cloth was of red and green silk ; at Walton-on-Thames of white and red satin, and at Wimbledon were "ij clothes of cors clothe of gold for the sepulchre." *

* "Archæologia," xlii. 300–303.

But of these temporary structures, with their elaborate appendages, that at St. Mary Redcliffe, seems to have been most sumptuously arrayed. In Britton's "History of Redcliffe Church" (p. 47) these entries are given under 1470—

"Item, that Maister Canynge hath delivered this 4th day of July, in the year of our Lord 1470, to Maister Nicholas Petters, Vicar of St. Mary Redcliffe, Moses Conterin, Philip Bartholomew, Procurators of St. Mary Redcliffe aforesaid, a new sepulchre, well gilt with golde, and a cover thereto.

"Item, An image of Almighty God rising out of the same sepulchre, with all the ordinance that longeth thereto (that is to say), a lathe made of timber, and the iron work therto.

"Item, Therto longeth Heaven made of timber and stain'd clothes.

"Item, Hell, made of timber & iron work therto, with Divels to the number of 13.

"Item, 4 Knights, armed, keeping the sepulchre with their weapons in their hands; that is to say, 2 axes & 2 spears & 2 pavés.

"Item, 4 payr of Angels' wings for 4 angels, made of timber, & well painted.

"Item, The Fadre, the Crowne, and Visage, the ball with a cross upon it, well gilt with fine gould.

"Item, The Holy Ghosht coming out of Heaven into the sepulchre.

"Item, Longeth to the 4 Angels, 4 chevelers."

In many cases, as Mr. Heale * points out, "there are high or altar tombs set in a recess" on the north side of the choir or chancel, "which were probably inclosed within the framework, and served as the 'sepulchre' itself; some of these were expressly intended for the purpose, as appears by documentary evidence, and that others were so intended appears very evidently from their sculptured decoration."

* "Archæologia," xlii. 288.

Sir Thomas Tyrrell, for instance, by his will dated May 16, 1475, directs: "My body to be buried in the chauncell of the church of Essthorndon, in Essex, under the place where the sepulchre is wont to stonde their. And I woll that there be made a tombe of tymber or of stone for me and my wif, accordyng honestly for our degree."

At Stanwell, Middlesex, Thomas Windsor, by his will dated August 13, 1479, directed his body to be buried in the north side of the choir of that church, before the image of our Lady, "wher the sepultur of our Lord standeth, whereupon I will ther be made a playne tombe of competent hight to the entent that yt may ber the blissid body of our Lord and the sepultur at the time of Estre, to stond upon the same." This tomb, which was removed some years ago, stood on the north side of the chancel.* A similar instance was at Long Melford, Suffolk, where the tomb of John Clopton, 1497, was employed for the same purpose, as described in the manuscript of Roger Martin, who died in 1580. He speaks of a frame of timber to hold a number of fair tapers, and set up on Maundy Thursday, "the sepulchre being alwaies placed, and finely garnished, at the north end of the High Altar, between that and Mr. Clopton's little chappel there, in a vacant place in the wall, I think, upon a tomb of one of his ancestors. The said frame with the tapers was set near the steps going up to the said Altar." †

Thomas, Lord Dacre, by his will dated 1531, directs his body "to be buried in the parishe church of Hersemonceux, in the north side of the high awter there, where the sepulcre is used to be made, and one tombe to be made and ordeyned convenient for the making and setting of the said sepulcre, and apparell to be made and bought for the said sepulcre at my cost and charge in the honour of the most blessid sacra-

---

* See *Gentleman's Magazine* (1793), lxiii. **993.**
† Ibid. (1830), ii. 206.

ment." * Many other examples might be quoted, † but those already given are sufficient to show how common the practice was.

The purport of these holy sepulchres was occasionally rendered permanently apparent by a sculptured design on the front of the base, representing our Lord stepping forth from the tomb, while the Roman guard are sleeping. One of the most remarkable instances is that at Heckington, in Lincolnshire, which is of Decorated date.

At Lincoln Cathedral, the three seated soldiers are all that remain of the Easter Sepulchre, and at Gosberton are the remains of a stately sepulchre. The curious sepulchre in Patrington Church, Yorkshire, has three arches at its base, within each of which is seated a sleeping soldier, with pointed basinet and blazoned shield. The sepulchre in the chapel on Wakefield Bridge, in the same county, has a figure of Christ rising from the tomb, with an angel kneeling on each side, their hands clasped in fervent adoration, whilst the three soldiers beneath are gazing upwards in amazement. In 1846 Mr. Crofton Croker exhibited to the British Archæological Association, the bust of a knight from a holy sepulchre, stated to have been found in the Temple Church; a counterpart to the heads of the guard in the chapel on Wakefield Bridge. An Easter sepulchre in two stages remains at Bampton, in Oxfordshire.

Sometimes tombs or Easter sepulchres are found in a walled recess on north side of the chancel; instances of which exist at St. Peter's, Dorchester; Writtle, Essex; Tring, Herts; Cheriton and Hythe, Kent; Raveningham, Norfolk; Stanton, St. John, Oxfordshire; Gorleston, Suffolk; Walton-on-the-

* For further instances consult " Archæologia," xlii. 288–291.

† See " Sussex Archæological Collections," iv. 191. The tomb still remains. On the top are the full length recumbent effigies of Lord Dacre and his son Thomas in armour.

Hill, Surrey ; Bosham, Catsfield, Eastbourne, **Lancing,** and **Ore, Sussex ;** and **in All Hallows** Barking. * But **in** the majority **of cases, writes** Mr. Heales, "there is no such tomb-like recess," although very frequently we find a **small arched or** square-headed recess **to** the north-west **of** the **altar,** sometimes with a wooden door remaining, and always with the marks and hinges and bolt. This would **be** extremely suitable as the depository for the pyx, or pyx and crucifix, and it seems likely that it was intended to **receive** them in the holy week rather than entrust them to the temporary wooden structure." † Examples of such recesses on the north side of the chancel occur at St. Lawrence, Waltham, Berks ; **Wyke,** Hants ; Standground, Hunts ; St. Martin's, Canterbury ; Barfreston, Northfleet, **and** West **Wickham, Kent ;** Boston, and many others **in** Lincolnshire ; **Putney,** Surrey ; Amberley, Pevensey, Rustington, Salehurst, **and** Sompting, Sussex. Instances in the south wall exist **at Hayes,** Kent ; Hellesdon, Norfolk ; Chiddingfold, Surrey ; and **at** Pevensey ; while in the east wall are specimens at Hever, Kent ; at Alford, Lincolnshire ; and at Sompting, Sussex.

As in the case of Winchester Cathedral, the sepulchre was a chapel. The walls of this chapel—a building of the Early English period—are covered with paintings of **the** original **date,** representing **scenes** in the life of **our Lord** before, at, and after the Passion, but there is **none now** remaining of the resurrection.

Among further evidence bearing **on** the **Easter** sepulchre may be mentioned the representations of our Lord's resurrection which is engraven upon numerous monumental brasses, some **of** which, in all probability, "formed part of **a** sepulchral monument and Easter sepulchre combined." The scene generally "consists of a high tomb, out of which

* "Archæologia," xlii. 296.   † Ibid., xlii. 293.

our Lord is stepping, while in His left hand he bears a long cross-headed staff and *vexillum* or banner, similar to that with which St. John Baptist is usually figured; around the tomb are the guard of the Roman soldiers, varying from two to four, though four appears to have been the most correct number." Instances of such brasses exist at Swansea, to Sir Hugh Johnys, Knight, *circa* 1490; Great Coates, Lincolnshire, to Sir Thomas Barnardiston, 1503; All Hallows Barking, a tomb against the south wall, *circa* 1510; Narburgh, Norfolk, to Sir John Spelman, 1545; Slaugham, Sussex, to Richard Covert, Esq., 1547; and at Cranley, Surrey, to Robert Harding, alderman of London, 1503.

Another design which, it has been suggested, had reference to the Easter sepulchre, is a three-quarter figure of our Lord, seen above the edge of the tomb, quiescent and without the banner — rather resembling " The Man of Sorrows" of art—and the soldiers are wanting." * Examples exist at Stoke Charity, Hants, to Thomas Wayte, 1482; Burwell, Cambridgeshire, *circa* 1510 and at Stoke Lyne, Oxfordshire, to Edward Love, 1535.

Notice has been drawn to a brass at Macclesfield Church to Roger Legh, 1506, which is now fixed on a board. In the foreground is an ecclesiastic, known by his triple tiara to be a Pope, kneeling before an altar on which is a Chalice; and in the place of the *reredos* is a tomb with the three-quarter figure of our Lord, upright in it. From the Pope proceeds a scroll, and beneath is the following: " The pardon for saying of v. pater noster v. aves and a cred is xxvi. thousand yeres, and xxvi. dayes of pardon." On a certain occasion, runs the legend, when St. Gregory the Great was officiating at the Mass, one who stood near him doubted the Real Presence; thereupon, at the prayer of the

* " Archæologia," xlii. 293, 294.

saint, a vision was suddenly revealed of Christ Himself. According to another explanation, the same may originally have had reference to the fact of the Missal having been revised by him.

A similar device was discovered on the rebuilding of the church at Quatt, near Bridgnorth, Salop ; and against the north wall of a south quasi-transept in Childrey Church, Berkshire, is a tomb of a representation of the Holy Trinity, and of the deceased persons arising from the tombs at the last day.

The ceremony of the Easter sepulchre seem to have been in use for a considerable period, and notices of it may be traced down to the middle of the sixteenth century. But as the custom grew in ill-favour, the sepulchre itself was either destroyed or sold—entries to this effect occurring in many old parish records. In the accounts of St. Mary's, Reading, for 1551, these items are recorded—

"Receyvid of Henry More for the sepulker, xiij*s.* iiij*d.*

"Receyvid of John Webb for the toumbe of brycke, xij*d.*"

At Barnes, Surrey, an old sepulchre was sold for **2*s.* 6*d.*,** and at Wandsworth, broken timber and wainscot, together with the sepulchre, were sold for 13*s.* 4*d.* Church inventories taken in the reign of Edward VI. mostly record the same fate of the Easter sepulchres. A few were cared for, and the cloths converted to a covering for the communion table as at Wimbledon and Weybridge, Surrey. Out of those in Lincolnshire about one half were burnt, or broken, or sold, and defaced.* One was burnt in melting lead, whilst the rest were altered and converted to other purposes —some to make communion tables, and others became presses, biers, hen pens, steps, etc.

In the reign of Queen Mary "the making of the sepulchre" was revived, but on her death was soon put

* "Archæologia," xlii. 305, 306.

down again.   In the Visitation Articles of Bentham, Bishop
of Coventry and Lichfield, Article 21 directs : "That you
do abolish and put away, clean out of your church, all
monuments of idolatry and superstition, as holy water,
stocks, Sepulchres which were used on Good Friday," etc.
In the church inventories of Belton, Lincolnshire, under
1566, this entry occurs : "Item, a Sepulker with little Jack
broken in pieces this year by the said churchwardens."
The term "Little Jack" probably meaning the Pyx.   The
fact, says Mr. A. Heales,* "of there being no example of a
wooden sepulchre which has survived the general destruction shows the powerful prejudice against this Easter
ceremony which prevailed at the time of the Reformation."
Even the monumental brasses engraved with the Resurrection have almost all been displaced ; but a deep feeling of
respect for the spot on which the sepulchre was accustomed
to be placed, continued in many minds for some time after
the ceremonies had ceased to be observed, as notices like
the following indicate.   In 1559, Thomas Burrell, of
Stetchworth, Cambridgeshire, directs : "My boddie to be
buried in the holly sepulcre in the churche of Sainte Peeter,
of Stetchwourthe ;" and in 1569, Sir William Wareham, by
his will, directs : "My bodie to be buried in the chauncell
of the church of Ocle, Essex, by the highe Aultare, where
as the sepulchre was wonte to stand."

* "Archæologia," xlii. 307.

CHAPTER XX.

SOME parishes have long boasted of possessing two churches in one churchyard—a peculiarity which, in many cases, has a singular effect. St. Margaret's Church, close by Westminster Abbey, at once suggests itself as an interesting illustration, and at Ely, Holy Trinity Church was in the same yard with the cathedral. The church was pulled down about two hundred years ago, and the parish has used the lady chapel of the cathedral. At Bury St. Edmund's, the large and imposing churches of St. James and St. Mary stand but a short distance from each other in an extensive churchyard, to which the fine old Norman tower serves as a fitting portal. Another church, dedicated to St. Margaret, is said to have stood at the south-east corner, and at the northern boundary of the churchyard was the great Abbey Church ; there were in fact four churches in one churchyard. The originals of both St. James and St. Mary were removed in the twelfth century from their position near the conventional church to make way for the extension and increased grandeur of the great Abbey Church.

At Swaffham Prior, Cambridgeshire, the churches of St. Mary and St. Cyriac are in close proximity in one churchyard, the former being now in ruins.

Staunton, in the county of Nottingham, had two churches in the same churchyard, but a faculty was obtained for taking down the smaller one some years ago, much, it is said, to the regret of all those who were interested in the curiosity of the circumstance. Of Westbury-on-Severn, Sir Robert Atkyns, in the " Antient and Present State of Glostershire" (1711, 799), writes : "The old church, with an handsome wooden spire at the west end, is yet standing in the churchyard. It was dedicated to St. Peter. There has been an handsome new church built, 1530, in the same churchyard for the use of the parishioners. It has an aisle on each side supported by pillars, and is dedicated to the Virgin Mary."

At Trimley, in East Suffolk, within one mile of Felixstowe, there are the churches of St. Martin and St. Mary in one churchyard. At Overstrand, near Cromer, the new church is contiguous to the old, which is in ruins ; and at Antingham, in the same county, near North Walsham, a similar instance occurs. At Reepham, there were three churches in one churchyard, and at Thorpe, near Norwich, the new church and the ancient structure—now abandoned —were in the same churchyard ; also at Gillingham, Norfolk.

Among further instances may be noticed the churches of Alvingham and North Cockerington, near Louth, in Lincolnshire ; the churches of Holy Trinity and St. Michael, Coventry, in churchyards which, although separately walled, are divided only by a roadway. Furley, in his " Weald of Kent " (ii. 764), mentions an example of this peculiarity at Wantage, in Berks, and there are the churches of All Saints and St. Lawrence at Evesham. The churches of St. Andrew and All Saints in the parish of Willingale Spain, Essex, and of St. Christopher, at Willingale Doe, are built in the same enclosure. In speaking of the last, Morant, in his " History of Essex," writes : " The churches of these

THE WILLINGALES, ESSEX.

Page 232.

two Willingehalls **stand** in the same churchyard, **the reason** of which nothing now remaining shows."

And at Fulbourn, near Cambridge, there **are two churches in the same** churchyard, one of which was removed **by Act** of Parliament in the year 1776. The subjoined extract from the preamble **of** an old local Act (15 Geo. **III. c. 49)** is deserving of notice—

"Whereas there are within **the town of** Fulbourne, **in the** county of Cambridge, two parishes, the one called **the** parish of All Saints, the other the parish of Saint Vigors, both of which are united in **one** township, contributing **in** common to **the** relief of the poor, and having one set of officers for the relief thereof and the repair of their high- **ways,** and being **also** rated in common **for all** parochial charges and burthens, except for the repair **of** the churches belonging to **each** parish; That in the said town there are **two churches within** the same churchyard, the one belong- **ing to** and called the Rectory Church of Saint Vigors, in **the** patronage of the Master, Fellows, and Scholars of the College of St. John the Evangelist, in the University of Cambridge, the other belonging to and called the Vicarage Church of All Saints, in the patronage of the Bishop of Ely, each of which churches is repaired by the inhabitants of the respective parish to which it belongs; that a **great** part of the said Church of All Saints is fallen down, **and the same** cannot be made fit for divine **service** unless **it be entirely** rebuilt, **and** the said parish being small, **and** the inhabitants thereof **few in** number, and **of small** property, **they** are unable **to** rebuild the same; and whereas, when the said **Church of** All Saints was standing divine service was never performed in both the said churches, at **one** and the same time, but was performed on Sundays at each church alternately in the morning and evening, and at **each** alternately **on** holydays, and the inhabitants of both parishes were accommodated with seats in each of the said churches; but the marriages, christenings, and burials of the inhabitants of each parish were performed in their respective parish churches while they were both standing, and, since that time, within the said Church of Saint Vigors, by permission of the rector thereof."

Thus, instead of two churches in one churchyard, we have two incumbents in one church, and each of them appointed by different patrons.[*]

There are still existing in this country four round churches, consisting of a circular building, from which a rectangular chancel is built eastwards, a form of structure supposed to reproduce the distinctive outlines of the church built over the Holy Sepulchre in Jerusalem. The best known of these so-called " round churches " is the Temple Church, London, the other three being at Cambridge, Northampton, and Little Maplestead in Essex, while the ruins of a fifth round church may be seen at Temple Bruer, Lincolnshire. Much has been written on this style of architecture, and, according to Godwin and Britton in their " Churches of London," " round and polygonic buildings, respecting the origin of which there has been much disquisition, were erected in the earlier periods of civilization, when probably the form, a pleasing one, alone had influence."[†] It is further added that "after the introduction of Christianity and the institution of baptism, which was at first by immersion, a building for this purpose near or attached to the church, became necessary, and these were constructed either circular or polygonal, ' in order that the assistants might from all sides more easily view the cistern that served as a font,'[‡] and Helena, in whose reign many of

---

[*] *Notes and Queries*, 3rd series, xi. 372.
[†] See Britton's " Architectural Antiquities," i. 17.
[‡] Hope's " History of Architecture," 115.

these baptisteries were erected, when she built the church over the Holy Sepulchre at Jerusalem, gave to it the circular form, perhaps either from the remembrance of these or on the like principle, namely, that, the tomb being placed in the centre, it was the form best adapted to enable a number of persons distinctly to view at the same time the object of their pilgrimage."

The Church of St. Sepulchre, at Cambridge, was built in the reign preceding that which saw the gradual erection of the Temple Church, while the rotunda and chancel of the one at Northampton were originally of Norman workmanship; but in a succeeding century all the Norman chancel was pulled down, and rebuilt in the manner then in vogue; and at a later period the same thing happened to the upper part of the rotunda. The Essex example is small—"a porch has been added west of the rotunda, and there are but six pillars in the ring to sustain the tower and form the arcaded ambulatory round the building." *

In connection with these "round churches" may be noticed the round towers which occur so frequently in Suffolk and Norfolk. Altogether there are about one hundred and seventy-five examples existing, all of which, with the exception of about a dozen, are found in the two counties above named. Three of these exceptions may be seen in Cambridgeshire, two in Berkshire, two in Sussex, one in Northamptonshire, and one in Surrey. Most of these round towers bear every trace of antiquity, but opinions widely vary as to the reason of their having been built in this shape. According to a correspondent of *Notes and Queries* (4th series, ix. 249), "the round church towers in Norfolk generally appear, at any rate in the lower part, to be the oldest part of the church. The upper part of many of them seem to have been repaired or restored, and in

* *Chambers's Journal* (May 16th, 1891), 307.

some cases made octagonal, the base remaining round. The body of the church seem to have been built on to the tower; this is evidently the case with two very perfect ones near Norwich—viz. at Colney and Bawburgh. The door to most of them seems to have been placed six or eight feet from the ground, so that access could only be gained to them by a ladder. Moreover, the windows are splayed outwards and downwards; they are, in fact, arrow slits. It has been suggested that they were intended as places of defence; in fact, like some of the church towers on the English and Scottish border, they were peel-houses." In a paper "On the Round Towers of Churches in East Anglia," read in 1864 by Mr. E. Roberts before the British Archæological Association, the author remarked that they have in every case—though varying in diameter from two feet, seven inches to twelve feet—walls about twelve inches thick, with only one entrance, viz. from the east, and therefore into the body of the church. It was suggested that these towers were built round because they could be built more substantially of that form with the materials of the district, and it avoided the necessity of having large building stones for the angles.* Blomefield was of opinion that they were built by the Danes, and in the "History of Thetford" he says, "And from this time, the Danes becoming Christians, all over Norfolk and great part of Suffolk, began to divide the country among them, naming their shares, which became so many new villages, either after their own names, or that of their situations, but calling the Saxon towns and villages after their old names; and after some time, when Christianity was settled among them, they began to found churches in many of their villages, as the many round towers in this county which are now standing plainly demonstrate."

* See *Gentleman's Magazine*, 1864, 600, 601; *Notes and Queries*, 4th series, ix. 392, and "Archæologia," xxi.

But, wherever built, there can be no doubt of their antiquity.

Another interesting peculiarity of some of our old parish churches is their position within the boundaries of Roman camps. Bede informs us that "Paulinus built a church in Campodunum, which afterwards the Pagans, by whom King Edwin was slain, burnt, together with all the town." Although it is not certain where this Campodunum was situated, yet it is noteworthy that the people of Slack, now claimed as Campodunum, have a tradition that a church once was built there on the ruins of the old Roman camp. Dr. Stukeley supposes that the church of Kingsbury, "between Wilsdon and Edgware, stands within the area of a Roman camp, which was Cæsar's second station after he crossed the Thames." And at Moresby, near Whitehaven, Cumberland, there is a church standing within the enclosure of the Roman camp or station there, which Lysons, in his "History of Cumberland," thus describes: "The site is in a field on the side of the village towards Barton, called the Crofts, and the church stands (as is often the case) within its area." At Caistor, Horncastle, and at Ancaster, Lincolnshire; at Great Casterton, and at Market Overton, in Rutlandshire; at Porchester, Hants, and at Castor, Northamptonshire, the remains of Roman camps exist. "Within the boundaries of each," adds a correspondent of *Notes and Queries* (3rd series, v. 173), "and within a few yards of the western wall at each place, is a mediæval church." Ebchester church, Durham, is said to occupy the site of a Roman camp; and Mr. A. Lower, in his "Handbook for Lewes," under the head, "Church of St. John's, sub Castro," writes: "While in the churchyard, the visitor's attention may be called to the curious fact, that it occupies part of the site of a very small camp, supposed to be Roman, the vallum of which may still be traced." At Kenardington, Kent, writes Hasted:

" Below the hill, on which the church stands, and adjoining it south-east, are the remains of some ancient fortifications of earth, with a breastwork thrown up, and a small circular mount; and in the adjoining marsh below it is another, of a larger size, with a narrow ridge or causeway seemingly leading from one to another."

According to Mr. Matthew Bloxam, in his " Principles of Gothic Architecture," the tower of Rugby parish church, Warwickshire, was formerly used as a kind of stronghold for the inhabitants of the town to take refuge in cases of attack. The appearance, it is said, of this tower seems to justify a belief in this assertion. It stands at the west end of the church, " is of square form and lofty, and is perfectly without buttresses; the windows are singularly narrow, resembling the loopholes of a castle." * Cases of this kind do not appear to have been uncommon. The tower of the church of Burgh-by-Sands, Carlisle, is said to have been used for this purpose; and in Davies' " Handbook to Cheltenham," the tower of Swindon Church, about two miles distant, is thus described: " The tower is an unequal hexagon, with walls of massive thickness, and evidently built for the purpose of defence. There is one original window on each side of the top, each composed of two narrow loopholes, divided by a small column, but gradually shelving out, and having from the thickness of the wall, a deep recess both without and within. The doorway (square headed) is under a porch on the north-east side of this tower. When this porch was blocked up, the castellum would be only accessible by an exterior case on the west side, the marks of which are still visible on the west wall, where now a decorated window has been inserted." To quote a further instance, the tower of St. Botolph's Church, Northfleet, " is said to have offered so conspicuous a mark to pirates and other ' water thieves '

* *Notes and Queries*, 3rd series, x. 473.

sailing up the river that it was thought necessary to make it a fortress, like many of the church towers on the English borders. It has been partly rebuilt, but the steps which lead from the churchyard to the first floor are probably connected with its early defences."

A peculiarity of some churches is their sloping floors. The nave floor of St. David's Cathedral, being laid on a hillside, slopes downwards towards the doors. The church floor of Saxby All Saints, on the western edge of the Lincolnshire wolds, is sloped very considerably from west to east, to adapt it to the rise on the hill-side. And the church floors at Horkstow, on the same hill-side, are more or less sloped.

A correspondent of *Notes and Queries* (6th series, iii. 392), writing of the church at Gunnislake, says : "A beautiful little church, designed by Mr. James Piers St. Aubyn, was opened at Gunnislake in 1880. Gunnislake is on the western border of Cornwall, and the floor-line of the church is a continuous descent from the west door to the altar-table. The building stands upon mountainous ground, and, to humour the site, at every few yards the floor drops a step. The effect is by no means unhappy."

Mr. Dobson, in "Rambles by the Ribble" (part ii. 13), says : "There is one feature of Mitton Church which is very uncommon in our churches—the nave declines very much. Entering from the churchyard, we have to descend some steps to get into the nave; which declines till it gets to the screen, separating it from the chancel; and then some steps have to be descended to enter the chancel."

The old church of Standon, Herts, which is built on the slope of a hill, has a sloping chancel floor; and the church at Saundersfoot, near Tenby, has a similar peculiarity. The old church of Llanbadarn Fawr (once a cathedral), near Aberystwyth, had a sloping floor, but was altered in a subsequent restoration.

The church of St. Pierre-du-Bois, in Guernsey, has a similar peculiarity, the church being situated on the brow of a hill, falling rather rapidly to the westward. In a lesser degree the same peculiarity existed in the adjoining parish of St. Sauveur; but the building having been re-pewed, and a wooden floor substituted for the original irregular pavement, this feature has disappeared. But the ground on which this church is built is perfectly level.* Among further churches with sloping floors may be mentioned All Saints, Binfield, Berkshire; Worfield Church, Shropshire; Walpole St. Peter's Church, Norfolk, and Badingham Church, Suffolk.

St. Andrew's Church, Greenstead, has attracted much attention, and has been supposed to be of Saxon date. The nave, alone the original structure, is formed of trunks of oak or chestnut trees, "not, as usually described, 'half-trees,' since they have had a portion of the centre or heart cut out, probably to furnish beams for the construction of the roof and sills. The outside or slabs thus left, were placed on the sill, but by what kind of tenon they are there retained does not appear. While the upper ends, being roughly adzed off to a thin edge, are let into a groove, which, with the piece of timber in which it is cut, runs the whole length of the building itself, the door-posts are of squared timber, and are secured in the grooves by small wooden pins, still firm and strong—a truly wonderful example of the durability of British oak. . . . The outsides of all the trees are furrowed to the depth of about an inch into long stringy ridges, by the decay of the softer parts of the timber; but these ridges seem equally hard as the heart of the wood itself."†

Speaking of wooden churches—which although once numerous are now rare—there is in the "Journal of the

---

* See *Notes and Queries*, 6th series, iii. 392.
† A. Suckling.

Archæological Association" for 1850, a drawing of the original wooden church that preceded the cathedral at Manchester.   There was a wooden church at Newland, which was removed some years ago to make room for the Beauchamp almshouses.   Cuthbert Bede, writing of this church prior to its demolition, says : * "It is supposed to have been a grange belonging to the Priory of Great Malvern.   There is a wooden porch, a wooden bell-cot, and two-light windows with wooden frames.   It is supposed to have been erected in the fifteenth century."   There was a half-timbered church at Peover, in Cheshire, and an interesting little church built in the half-timbered style of the county exists at Trelystan, Montgomeryshire.   The oak-frame work at Ribbesford, Worcestershire, writes a correspondent of *Notes and Queries* (4th series, ii. 390), "is still perfect with an arcade of pointed arches on each side of the nave, now rendered more prominent by the scraping of the paint and removal of the flat plaster ceiling."

* *Notes and Queries*, 3rd series, i. 437.   See Noake's "Rambles in Worcestershire," iii. 7.

CHAPTER XXI.

CHURCHWARDENS.

In accordance with the long-established usage, the election of churchwardens takes place on Easter Monday, an event which reminds us of the many curious old customs connected with these parish officers in the course of their eventful, and memorable, history. It is related how George I., when landing at Greenwich, was elected churchwarden, but it became a matter of dispute whether a king could hold this office, a question which was the subject of debate in the Privy Council for two months. The Archbishop of Canterbury declared " he could not be both," and added that he could take his choice, and his crown again after he had served. But cases of this kind have been the exception, although occasionally it has been a matter of contention as to what invalidated the qualifications for the office of churchwarden. Thus, some years ago, a Quaker was required to serve, but he refused, his objection being upheld by Dr. Phillimore, who maintained that the tenets, doctrines, and habits of the Society of Friends " were recognized to be such as made it impossible to consider that they could discharge the duties of churchwardens." On another occasion it was argued that bodily infirmity incapacitated a parishioner from performing the duties of the office, and when the defendant prayed to be excused on account of deafness, his claim was disallowed, and he was ordered to discharge his office. It has even been contended that a woman is not exempt from this duty, although, writes Mr. Prideaux in his " Churchwardens' Guide " (1871, 5), "There can be little doubt that the Courts would relieve her from the burden of serving unless the necessity of the case required that she should do so."

There are numerous instances, however, of women serving as churchwardens, and in the old account books of the parish of St. Budeaux, Devon, many entries to this effect are recorded. Some years ago, it is said, the Hon. Maria Otway Cave, of Stanford Hall, Northants, presented herself at a visitation, and demanded to be sworn in, and her claim was allowed. For several years, the churchwarden of a rural parish near Bicester was a lady, and a correspondent of *Notes and Queries* tells us how he was present in the parish church of Bicester itself when Archdeacon Clerke admitted Mrs. Henry Hawkins to the office of churchwarden of Hardwick-cum-Pasmore, Oxfordshire. Among other parishes where women have served as churchwardens may be mentioned Goltho, near Wragby, Lincolnshire, and Maisemore and Randwick, Gloucestershire. It was stated also some years ago in a local newspaper, how Miss Trafford, sister of Sir Thomas de Trafford, had to serve the office of churchwarden of the old church in Manchester, but, " being both a female and a Roman Catholic, she appointed a deputy." Respecting the election of churchwardens, we find various customs observed in different places. In some cases it has been the immemorial custom for the parishioners to choose both, and in many parishes the election is, by custom, made by select vestries, a practice which, it is said, " seems to have grown from the custom of choosing a certain number of persons yearly to manage the affairs of the parish for that year, which by degrees came to be a fixed method."

Sometimes the election is by the lord of the manor, and at Doncaster it has been customary, time out of mind, for the vicar to appoint one of the churchwardens and the mayor the other, styled respectively the "vicar's churchwarden," and the "mayor's churchwarden." In the parish of Bodmin, a similar custom has prevailed; and Burn, in his "History of Henley," informs us that the churchwardens have been appointed by the Corporation of Henley for nearly six centuries. In the city of Wells, from the year 1378, when the records of the proceedings of the corporate body begin, to the year 1581, both churchwardens were appointed by the corporation. In the year 1582 a change took place, when the parishioners appointed one, and the corporation the other, a custom which has continued up to the present time. It appears, too, that the corporation exercised the right of allotting the church pews, besides having the control of the churchwardens' accounts.

Again, instances occur of the appointment being made by the old churchwardens, and a curious mode of election took place in the parish of Prestwich, in the county of Lancaster, which consisted of six townships. At the stated time, the outgoing churchwardens in one township presented two names to the rector to choose from, one of whom might be himself—in the remaining five respectively the inhabitants of the respective townships presented two names to the rector to choose one, and the six persons chosen by the rector became the churchwardens of the parish.

To quote a further case, it seems that in old city of London parishes the churchwardens are chosen by the parishioners, a mode of election which is based on a curious old custom connected with the transfer of land, and thus described by Prideaux: "In the city of London, by special custom, the churchwardens with the minister make a corporation for lands as well as for goods, and may, as such, hold, purchase, take, and devise lands for the use of the church, and sue and be sued on account thereof, as well as for goods and chattels; and this is alleged as a reason for that other custom, which hath also obtained in London, for the parishioners there to choose both churchwardens exclusive of the minister; for, say they, if the minister should there choose one of the churchwardens according to canon, he, with the said churchwarden as the major part of the corporation, may dispose of lands to the damage of the parish, and therefore it is not safe there to lodge so great a trust in him." Hence, in the city of London the leases of houses and lands, being parish property, often run in the names of the rector and churchwardens as lessors.

In a few cases the number of churchwardens has not been limited to the usual number—two—for in certain Norfolk parishes we read of three having been elected. At St. Michael Coslany, Norfolk, many years ago this was the case, but it would appear to have been unusual, for when the three presented themselves to be sworn the archdeacon jocosely exclaimed, "Any more churchwardens for St. Michael Coslany, gentlemen, any more?" At Attleborough, in the same county, a similar custom prevailed, and there is evidence, it is said, of the practice having existed as far back as the year 1617. It appears, also, says a correspondent of *Notes and Queries*, from the fourth bell at St. John, Maddermarket, Norwich, that in the year 1765 there were three churchwardens.

In connection with the duties of churchwardens in bygone years, we find many curious and interesting items of parochial lore. Thus, in "Reliquiæ Hearnianæ" (iii. 75), entered under date of July 23, 1731, there is the following extract from an old churchwardens' book of accounts at

Great Faringdon, Berks, bearing the date of 1518, and which no doubt is the form of admitting churchwardens at that period: "Cherchzewardenz thys shell be your charge to be true to God and to the Cherche for love nor favor off no man wythin this paroche to withold any ryght to the Churche but to reserve the dettye to hyt belongythe or ellys to goo to the Devell."

Among the ancient documents belonging to Walsall is a code of laws for "the goode rule and governaunce of the boroughe," drawn up in the year 1440 by the "maior and his bredren," one regulation of which relates to the churchwardens: "Also, it is ordeyned that the churchwardens, both of the body of the Churche of Our Ladye, Saynt Clement, Saynt Kateryn, and Saynt Nicholas, with alle other members, shall com to theyr accomptes uppon Saynt Kateryn's-day, before the mayer and five or six of his brethren, by the said mayer to be appoynted, and before such other of the brethren as will be there; and if they or any of them be not at the said day redy to make theyr accomptes, then they shall be so in defaute, to forfeit six shillings and eightpence, to be levyed as is before said, and to be put to the Burges Boxe."

One of their duties was to look after the spiritual and moral welfare of the parishioners, and to ascertain that there was some valid excuse for their absenting themselves from Divine service on a Sunday. In the church register of Aycliffe, Durham, we find this entry: "1599. A public admonition given the twenty-third day of December, for all Maysters and Dames to put away such servants and sojourners as wyll not usually come to churche."

Towards the close of the last century it was the custom at Manchester for the chief magistrate of the town, attended by the churchwarden and the police officers, to go out of the church while the first lesson was being read, and to compel all persons found in the streets to "come into the church, or pay a fee," which in the case of persons of the lower class was fixed at 1*s.*, and for those of higher rank at 2*s.* 6*d.* Indeed, neglecting to attend the parish church was no trivial matter in years gone by; and in the church books of St. James's Church, Bristol, it is recorded, under July 6, 1598, how Henry Austey, a resident in the parish, had, in answer to a summons, to appear before the vestry for not attending that church. At the same vestry, in the year 1679, four persons were found guilty of walking "on foot to Bath on Lord's Day," and were each fined 20*s.*

The following curious extract from the churchwardens' order and appointment book, St. Mary-le-Tower, Ipswich, is interesting as showing the active zeal displayed by these functionaries in bygone times—

"I heare by complaint of the Churchwardens of St. Marie Towers that the churchyarde of that pish church is noysomly kept and made a comon passage for horse and footemen and a sincke of all filthy excrem^te. And that pishioners of that pishe neither doe nor can receive the Blessed Sacram of the Lord's Supper in that church devoutly and orderlie as is lawfullie prescribed in that behalfe for the Administracon of that Sacram, and orderly receiveinge of it. Hereyne I admonishe and require you to haue speciall care that those passages in the churchyarde be stopped and barred up and that no such noysome use be longer contynued. And that you builde about the Comunion Table in that church where it is placed as by lawe is required, such convenient seates or stools where the Comunicants may receive that holy Sacram^t orderlie to be administered in the Chauncell or body of the Church without his cursitory passage to any of the saide Comunicants in their ordinary seates where they heare comon prayer red uppon daies appoynted for the same. And that you be respective that your minister doe not admitt any to that blessed Sacram[t] which doe not receive the same kneeleinge and not sittinge or standinge. And if any be refrectarie or willfull not to be rule in this behalfe certifie me there names and surnames the next Court in the Consistorie at Norwich after the Epiphany next ensuinge. Soe fare you well. Ipswich the xi[th] of October 1615.

<table>
<tr><td>"To the Churchwardens of the pishe church of St. Marie Towers at Ipswich."</td><td>"Yo[r] loving friend
(Unsigned).</td></tr>
</table>

Until a comparatively recent period it was also customary for the churchwardens on a Sunday to visit public-houses situated in their respective parishes during Divine service, and to make sure that no persons were in them during prohibited hours. The practice varied in different neighbourhoods. At Penzance, for example, it was usual for the mayor and corporation, with the macebearers and constables in attendance, to go once a month in state to St. Mary's Church. At the commencement of the first lesson the constables left the church to visit the licensed houses to see that there was no infraction of the law; returning to the church so as to be in readiness to accompany the mayor on his homeward journey.

But in the year 1872 the churchwardens and officials at Kirkheaton parish church were the transgressors. According to the *Sunderland Times* of May 18, 1872, it seems that on the day in question a police officer went to a certain inn, and there found the defendants. The account adds: "It appears to have been the custom, from time immemorial, of the churchwardens to go to service and remain in the church until the clergyman commenced reading the second lesson, and then leave the church and walk a short distance to the public-house in question and stay there until the church had loosed."

One of the most valuable duties of the churchwardens in olden days was to see that the vicar of the parish carefully filled in his registers, in accordance with the injunction issued by Thomas, Lord Cromwell, on September 29, 1538: "The curate of every parish shall keep one book of the register, which book he shall every Sunday take forth, and in the presence of the churchwardens, or one of them, write and record in the same all the weddings, christenings, and burials made the whole week before, and for every time that the same shall be omitted shall forfeit to the said church 3*s.* 4*d.*"

It should be added that the churchwardens' accounts themselves contain much curious information on parish matters in past days, and throw light on many a subject on which in other documents there is but scanty information. Thus, in the accounts of the parish of St. James's, Bristol, we find payments of money for sugar-loaves given to bishops, the price of such a gift being sometimes 15*s.* It was apparently the custom when the bishop of the diocese visited a church for the churchwardens to make an offering of this kind.

In the same accounts, too, occur these items—

"1627. Item. for warrant for her that laid the child at Mr. Sage's door, 1*s.*

"To the woman that kept the child, 1*s.*

"Spent at the Bell when he went about that child, 1*s.*

"More in charge about that church, 1*s.*"

An entry in the register of Prestmell, Lancashire, under 1655, states: "Received of the wife of George Hutton for swearing and other misdemeanours, 16*s.* 8*d.*"

The north aisle of St. Lawrence's Church, Reading, contains the monument of John Blagrave, who left a legacy for the encouragement of Reading maidservants. The churchwardens of each of the three parishes were to choose maidservants of five years standing, who were to meet and throw dice for a purse of £10 on Good Friday. "This is lucky money," says Ashmole, "for I never yet heard of a maid who got the £10, but soon after found a good husband."

It is said, according to the opinion of coroners, to be the duty of churchwardens to take into keeping the body of any one found dead. Upon this point, Mr. Edward Peacock contributed the following interesting communication to *Notes and Queries* (7th series, vi. 56) : " I think the opinion of coroners on this matter is correct. There is, I am pretty sure, no statute about it, but I believe by common law the churchwardens are bound to take care of the body of any one found dead from the time of the discovery of the body until the burial. In former days, there were in rural parishes no parish officers except the churchwardens (overseers of the poor and surveyors of the highways have been evolved out of him). The churchwarden's is a post of immemorial antiquity, probably as old as that of king or constable. His range of duties was a very wide one. Before the Reformation, christian burial was thought an important matter, and it naturally fell to that officer to provide that the stranger dead should be treated with reverence, and the rites of the Church provided for him. Had he neglected to do so, I make no doubt he would have incurred ecclesiastical censure. A pauper's funeral, such as we read of in books, and such as I have myself witnessed, would have shocked the feelings of the men and women of the Middle Ages. Now that we have a rural police, the duty of caring for dead bodies of this kind usually falls on them; but I cannot doubt that if the policeman were to neglect his duty, the churchwarden would be bound, in virtue of his office, to intervene."

CHAPTER XXII.

SEVERAL centuries ago the parish clerk was a very important person, and **up** to the period of the Reformation was frequently an ordained clergyman, instead of a layman. **His chief function, in olden times, was to assist the parish priest ; the** necessary qualifications for his office being **that he should be** proficient **in** reading, and have **a** knowledge **of music. About** the **year 1240, the** parish clerks **were** raised into a guild **or** fraternity **by Henry III.,** under the patronage of St. Nicholas, who was the chosen patron **of** the boy-bishop and choristers. **At** this period they so excelled in church music, that ladies and men of quality, on this account, became members ; and, on certain days in **the year,** public feasts or entertainments were held at which music and singing formed **a** prominent feature. **The performance** of sacred dramas and mysteries **was then highly popular. And it is** recorded how, in 1390, from **the 18th to the** 20th July, the London parish clerks gave **a three days'** performance before Richard **II., his** queen, **and court, at the** Skinner's Well, which was afterwards called, in compliment **to them,** the Clerk's Well, and is now known as Clerkenwell. In 1800, **a parish pump,** supplied by the stream from that well, was set up by the churchwardens of the parish, who, **in** the inscription which they **caused to be placed upon it,** stated that round the spring, " As history informs us, the parish clerks of London, in remote ages, commonly performed sacred plays. That custom caused it to be denominated Clerks' Well, and from which this parish derives its name. The water was greatly esteemed by the prior and brethren of the order of St. John of Jerusalem, and by the Benedictine nuns in the neighbourhood."

Henry VI. was the head of the parish clerks' patrons, as appears from a manuscript vellum roll in their possession dating from the year 1440 to 1525. In the " Diary of Henry Machin," published by the Camden Society, we find the following entry under 1555 : " The xxvij day of May was the Clarke's prossessyon from Yerdhall College, and ther was a goodly Mass be hard, evere clarke having a cope and a garlande with C stremers borne and the whettes playinge rounde Chepe, and so to Ledynhall unto St. Albro' (Ethelburga) Churche, and ther they put off ther gayre, and ther was the blessed sacrament, borne with torchlight abowt, and from thens unto the Barber Hall to dener."

Previous to 1560, the parish clerks met in the Chapel at Guildhall for evensong, and the next day to dinner at Carpenters' Hall; but two years after this, writes Mr. Timbs, in his " Curiosities of London," (417) they met in their own hall, receiving seven persons into their brotherhood, and attending " a goodly play of the Children of Westminster, with waits, regals, and singing." In 1592, the parish clerks commenced the Bills of Mortality, and in January, 1611, James I. re-incorporated them, in consequence of their brotherhood having been dissolved, and their hall and property seized. About 1625, they were licensed by the Star Chamber to keep a printing press in their hall, for the printing of the " Bills," which they were bound to make up every week, consisting of the births and burials, with some accounts of the diseases, age, etc., of the person dying. During the Great Plague, these "Bills" were very important; they are still to be seen in the Guild-hall Library, as well as others dating from 1657 to 1758. The "Weekly Bill" has long ceased to be issued from the Parish Clerks' Hall, and in its place, since July 1, 1837, the "Table of Mortality in the Metropolis" has been issued from the office of the Registrar-General, at Somerset House.* In former times, says Fosbroke, the London clerks, when country families thought it necessary, in case they came to town, to know the state of health there, used to communicate accounts of it. An instance of their doing so occurs in Gage's "History of Hengrave" (1822, 205), where this memorandum occurs: "Given in reward to the clerk of Coleman Street for oftentimes bringing bills of the sickness in town, twelve pence." But, in course of time, the parish clerks seem to have lost much of their intellectual and social status, and Sir John Hawkins, in his "History of Music" (iv. 362), alluding to their musical incompetence, writes: "In and about this great city, in above one hundred parishes, there are but few parish clerks to be found that have either ear or understanding to set one of these tunes musically as it ought to be; it having been a custom during the late war, and since, to choose men in such places more for their poverty than skill and ability, whereby this part of God's service hath been so ridiculously performed in most places, that it is now brought into scorn and derision by many people." Their want of culture was equally the subject of complaint; and, as the *Edinburgh Reviewer* remarked some thirty years ago, "the parish clerk is better known to most by the ear than by the eye. Who has not heard in our country churches, the cruel havoc wrought upon the responses of the service by his tasteless recitation, whether in lugubrious drawl, monotonous bawl, or drowsy rattle." Dr. Johnson

* Timbs's "Curiosities of London."

held parish clerks in high estimation ; and, when a friend expressed a wish that a better provision were made for them, he replied, "Yes, sir ; a parish clerk should be a man who is able to make a will, or write a letter for anybody in the parish."

As it was pointed out by a correspondent of the *Gentleman's Magazine*, at the commencement of the present century (lxxi. 1090), the reason of the ignorance and slovenly character of the parish clerk is attributed to the fact that the office is frequently bestowed on unsuitable persons, "the salary being so very small, that none but low mechanics will accept of it." He further tells us how, in the course of his travels, he was much surprised to hear the office of parish clerk performed by the waiter of the inn, notwithstanding it was the residence of the bishop.

At an earlier period, however, of their history, the same laxity was evidently not permitted. Towards the close of the sixteenth century, they were sometimes made the subject of inquiry in the articles of visitation. By Grindall's Injunction they were required to "read the First Lesson, the Epistle, and the Psalms"; and in the present century, it was customary in some parishes in Devonshire and Cornwall, for the parish clerk to read the First Lesson.

The Rev. R. Polwhele says, in his "Cornish Recollections": "A very short time since, the parish clerks used to read the First Lesson. I once heard the St. Agnes clerk cry out : 'At the mouth of the burning viery vurnis, Shadrac, Meshac, and Abednego, com voath and come hether.'" It is related of a Devonshire clerk who had to read this lesson, that, instead of repeating these three proper names, he said at their second and third recurrence, "the aforesaid gentlemen," and that in the same chapter, instead of repeating the words concerning the cornet, flute, harp, sackbut, psaltery, dulcimer, he said, "the band as before."

Many such anecdotes have long been current throughout the country, and Francis Grose, when writing about a century ago, "On Slip-slopping, or the Mis-application of Words," said: "Even the Church service itself is not exempt from this kind of slip-slopping. Almost every parish clerk is a lion, instead of an alien, among his mother's children ; and one I remember went to a length still more extravagant. In that verse in the chapter of Revelation describing the New Jerusalem, wherein it is said the doors were of agate and the windows carbuncles, the honest fellow read, 'the doors were of a gate, and the windows crabs ancles.'"

Towards the close of the seventeenth century, we find an inquiry made also in the visitation articles relative to their dress: "Have you a large and decent surplice (one or more) for the minister to wear, and another for the clerk, if he hath heretofore been accustomed to wear it when he assisteth the minister?" That the parish clerk was here intended, and not a clerk in orders, is clear from another question under the heading of "Parish Clerks": "Doth he wear a gown when he so attendeth, and a surplice over it, if heretofore the custom has been among you?" It would appear, says Lathbury, that the parish clerks in some churches wore a surplice, as in the case of singing men and choristers in cathedrals, and in many of our parish churches. "Until within the past quarter of a century, in many Oxfordshire and Buckinghamshire churches," writes a correspondent of *Notes and Queries* (6th series, i. 522), it was customary for the parish clerk to attend upon the parson at the communion table, and to kneel either at or within the rails. In some cases he wore a surplice. At Easington, near Chalgrove Field, in Oxon, I witnessed this myself, prior to the year 1840, when the parish clerk attended my father the rector. The same custom obtained at Towersey, Bucks, and at Tettesworth, in Oxfordshire, also at Thame, at Shabbingdon, and at Chearsley." Some years ago, at Lower Sapsey Church, Worcestershire, when the parson left the reading-desk at the end of Morning Prayer, and took up his position at the north side of the communion-table, the clerk would also go within the rails and kneel down at the south side of the table.*

The custom of allowing the parish clerk to give out notices in church, occasionally led to the most unforeseen results. Cuthbert Bede † has left two or three amusing instances. "Some thirty years ago," he writes, " I was told of a parish clerk who gave out in his rector's hearing this notice : ' There'll be no service next Sunday, as the rector's going out grouse-shooting '—the rector having inadvertently told him of the reason for his approaching absence. Another rector, who had lost his favourite setter, told his parish clerk to make inquiries about it ; but was rather astonished to hear him give it out as a notice in church, coupled with the reward of three pounds if the dog should be restored to his owner. But the following anecdote is perhaps one of the most amusing illustrations of the laxity of church discipline in bygone days. An old rector of a small country parish had sent his set of false teeth to be repaired, on the understanding that they should be returned ' by Saturday ' as there was no Sunday post, and the village was nine miles from the post town. The old rector tried to brave out the difficulty ; but, after he had incoherently mumbled through the prayers, he decided not to address his congregation on that day. While the hymn was being sung, he summoned the clerk to the vestry, and then said to him : ' It is quite useless for me to attempt to go on. The fact is, that my dentist has not sent me back

---

* *Notes and Queries,* 6th series, i. 356.
† *All the Year Round* (Nov. 6, 13, 1880).

my artificial teeth ; and as it is impossible for me to make myself understood, you must tell the congregation that the service is ended for this morning, and that there will be no service this afternoon.' The old clerk went back to his desk ; the singing of the hymn was brought to an end ; and the rector, from the vestry, heard the clerk address the congregation thus : 'This is to give notice ! as there won't be no sarmon nor no more sarvice this mornin', so you'd better all go whum (home) ; and there won't be no sarvice this aternoon, as the rector ain't got his artful teeth back from the dentist !'"

The Rev. Richard Polwhele, in his "History of Cornwall," relates that "at no great distance from St. Anthony, a wreck happening on a Sunday morning, the clerk announced to the parishioners just assembled that 'measter would gee them a holiday'"—a story of which there are several versions; one adding that when the parson saw his flock rushing from the church, he cried out, "Stop ! stop ! let us start fair !"

Although many of this class of stories are apocryphal, there can be no doubt that there was a familiarity between the parson and the clerk and the people, at which our feelings of decorum would revolt. An old story tells how at Kenwyn, Cornwall, two dogs, one of which was the parson's, were fighting at the west end of the church ; the parson, who was then reading the Second Lesson, rushed forth, and went down and parted them. On his return, doubtful where he had left off, he asked the clerk, " Roger, where was I ? " "Why, down parting the dogs, maister."

At Mevagissey, when non-resident clergymen officiated, it was, in past years, customary for the squire of the parish to invite them to dinner. On one occasion—a Sunday when the Athanasian Creed is directed to be read—the parish clerk asked the clergyman before he had begun the service whether he intended to read the Athanasian Creed that morning. "Why?" said the clergyman. "Because, if you do, no dinner for you at the squire's, at Penwarne."

Lord Teignmouth, in his "Reminiscences" (ii. 350, 351), writes: "My parochial portraiture would be incomplete without a passing notice of the old skilled blacksmith and respectable publican, who during thirty-seven years fulfilled the duties of clerk and sexton—'an odd-charactered man,' in the estimation of the neighbourhood. His nasal tone and notable mistakes in reading had been early brought into full play by his struggles for the mastery with the deaf rector, under whose auspices he commenced his performance. As there was no clock in the church, it was his custom, as he informed any stranger officiating, to ring the bell when he saw 'the lord,' *i.e.* the squire of Langton, cross the bridge; and meanwhile, as the time of Divine service approached, to beckon from the window to the congregation in the churchyard."

Of another parish it is related that when a clergyman had gone to take the duty for a friend, and was leaving the church, he looked at the sky, and made a remark to the clerk as to the probable weather on the morrow, when the clerk replied: "Ah, sir, they do say that the hypocrites can discern the face of the sky."

Again, in olden times, the parish clerk was occasionally a party man in politics, which was often the cause of acts of indiscretion on his part. Hence we find a parish priest, at the commencement of the last century, compiling "Thirty-six psalms of thanksgiving for the use of a parish church"; and amongst other reasons for omitting all the imprecatory psalms, he says: "Lest a parish clerk, or any other, should be whetting his spleen, or obliging his spite, when he should be entertaining his devotion." That such unseemly practices were indulged in, is illustrated by Bramston, the satirist, who thus denounces it—

> " Not long since parish clerks, with saucy airs,
>   Apply'd King David's Psalms to State affairs."

Among the many anecdotes told of singing psalms with a political bias, the following is related by Hume of King Charles I. : " Another preacher, after reproaching him to his face with his misgovernment, ordered the psalm to be sung—

> ' Why dost thou, tyrant, boast thyself,
>   Thy wicked deeds to praise ? '

The king stood up, and called for that psalm which begins with these words—

> ' Have mercy, Lord, on me I pray,
>   For men would me devour.'

The good-natured audience, in pity to fallen majesty, showed for once greater deference to the king than to the minister, and sung the psalm which the former had called for."

A correspondent of *Notes and Queries* informs us that in the excitement which prevailed at the trial of Queen Caroline, he remembers a choir, in a village not a hundred miles from Wallingford, Berks, singing with great gusto the first, fourth, eleventh, and twelfth verses of the thirty-fifth psalm in Tate and Brady's new version—

> " False witnesses with forg'd complaints against my truth combin'd,
>   And to my charge such things they laid as I had ne'er design'd."

When King William returned to London after one of his expeditions, Wesley's parish clerk gave out in Epworth Church " a hymn of my own composing "—

> " King William has come home, come home,
>   King William home is come ;
>   Therefore let us together sing
>   The hymn that's called Te Deum."

Some acts of indiscretion recorded of our old parish clerks prove that their conduct was not always what it should be. Instances have occurred wherein the parish clerk has been bribed to alter an entry in the parish register. Burn * tells of a search that was once made at Rochester by a person who used every means to rid himself of the clerk's presence; but finding that he could not be left alone, he offered the clerk a sum of money to assist him in the alteration of an entry which he pointed out. In a small work entitled "The Exaction and Imposition of Parish Fees Discovered," by Francis Sadler (1738), it is recorded how "one Phillips, clerk to Lambeth parish, ran away with the Register book, whereby the parish became great sufferers; and in such a case no person that is fifty years old, and born in the parish, can have a transcript of the Register to prove themselves heir to an estate. And in Battersea, the next adjacent parish, their late clerk had often been found tardy, and detected in registering boys for girls and girls for boys; and not one half of the Register book, in his time, was correct and authentic as it ought to be."

Accuracy and care on the part of the parish clerk were, in olden times, very necessary, when so much reliance was placed on them. Thus it was frequently customary for the parish clerk to keep notes, and for the clergyman to make up his register therefrom once a year. In the parish of St. Clement Danes, London, the entries were often made in the waste book in pencil. "An affidavit," writes Mr. Burn, "being required in the year 1829 of the entry of a burial in this register, it was found to be in pencil; and after waiting two months to see it properly entered in ink, the deponent was obliged to swear to the copy from the pencilled entry." In another parish, we read how the clerk

* "History of Parish Registers" (1862), 260.

was in the habit of demanding a fee for causing his memoranda to be entered in the parish book. A waste book was also in use in Chatham parish, called "a minute book," as appears by the letters of the minister in the year 1766, where he makes this statement : "The entries are chiefly brought from the minute-book carefully kept in the vestry-room, and it cannot be supposed that there should be any material variation in the case." But, if we are to be guided by the Rev. Christopher Hervey's description of the parish clerk's duties, it would seem that these, in his day, were not marked by those abuses which, in after times, gradually crept in—

> " The Church's Bible-Clerk attends
> Her utensils, and ends
> Her prayers with **Amen** ;
> Tunes psalms, and to the Sacraments
> Brings in the Elements,
> And takes them out again.
> Is humble-minded, and industrious-handed,
> Doth nothing of himself but as commanded."

In some instances the office of parish clerk has been held by a woman, although the Ninety-first Canon would seem to restrict the office to the male sex, which directs that he be twenty years at the least, and that he be known to the parson to be of honest conversation, and sufficient for his reading and writing, and competent skill in singing. But, as a woman can serve the office of an overseer, and as it was also decided in the case of Olive *v.* Ingram that a woman might be the parish sexton, it might be argued that she was legally entitled to serve the office of parish clerk.* That she has done so is proved by several cases which we quote below. According to a correspondent of *Notes and Queries*, at the close of the last century a Mrs. Sheldon

---

* Two papers on " The Parish Clerk," by Cuthbert Bede in *All the Year Round*, November 6th and 13th, 1880.

continued to discharge the duties which had been performed by her husband, the parish clerk of Wheatley, five miles from Oxford. From the same source we learn that in the parish of Avington, Hungerford, this post was held by a woman for twenty-six years; and an old sexton once remarked that he well remembered his astonishment, as a boy, whenever he happened to attend a neighbouring church service, to see a man acting in that capacity, and saying the responses for the people. At Ickburgh, Norfolk, a woman was acting as parish clerk in 1853, and up to 1832 Mary Mountford was parish clerk of Misterton, near Crewkerne, Somersetshire, for upwards of thirty years. About the year 1830, the female parish clerk of Sudbrook, near Lincoln, died; and Burn, in his "Parish Registers," quotes the subjoined extract from the parish register of Totteridge: "1802. March 2. Buried Elizabeth King, widow, for forty-six years clerk of this parish, in the ninety-first year of her age." A further example is given by Madame d'Arblay in her diary (1791, v. 206), who writes: "There was only a poor wretched ragged woman, a female clerk, to show us this church—Collumpton, county Devon. She pays a man for doing the duty while she receives the salary in right of her deceased husband."

Frequently the office of parish clerk has been hereditary, having been held by members of the same family for more than a century—an interesting example having occurred in a Derbyshire parish: "Mr. Peter Bramwell, parish clerk of Chapel-en-le-Frith, died January 23, 1854, aged eighty-six, after having held office for forty-three years. His father, Peter Bramwell, was parish clerk of the same place for fifty years; his grandfather, George Bramwell, for thirty-eight years; his great-great-grandfather, George Bramwell, for forty years; and his great-great-great-grandfather, Peter Bramwell, for fifty-two years. Total, two hundred and twenty-three years, by five members of the family, giving an average of forty-four years and nine months for each."

In modern times the parish clerk's salary has been mainly dependent on certain fees at baptisms, marriages, and burials, in addition to an allowance from the incumbent, by whom he has generally been appointed, although by custom the inhabitants have the right of election. By the common law, moreover, parish clerks have freeholds in their office; but by a statute passed in the early part of the present reign, they may be suspended by the archdeacon for misconduct, or neglect. They generally seem to have been scantily paid, reminding us of Sir Roger de Coverley, who " added five pounds a year to the clerk's place." In some places their income was supplemented, in olden times, by a contribution every Sunday from each householder in the parish for certain duties they performed; and, amongst other perquisites, they received a loaf at Christmastide from every house, some eggs at Easter, and corn in autumn.

CHAPTER XXIII.

PARISH BULLS AND COWS.

AN old charge levied in certain parishes upon the parson, was for keeping a bull for the use of his parishioners. Instances of this usage occurs in church records and other documents, from which it would seem that, as the rector was entitled to the tithe of calves, it was to his interest to promote increase of titheable produce. Such a custom formerly prevailed in the manor and parish of Marsh Gibbon, Bucks, and came to an end upon the laying in, dividing, and enclosing the common fields and commons. In the record of the Inclosure Commissioners' Proceedings, dated June 5, 1843, this minute occurs: "That the 'Bull Platts,' being held by the rector in consideration of his finding a bull for the use of the landowners depasturing in the common fields and commonable places within the parish, will now revert to the landowners, and be deemed by the Commissioners as part of the common lands within the parish, . . . the custom of maintaining a common Bull not being consistent with the altered circumstances of the parish when enclosed."

The inclosure award of the parish of Lower Heyford, Cheshire, dated 1802, acquits the rector of that parish and his successors from the pre-existing liability to keep a bull and a boar for the parishioners.

In the Hundred Court of the town and liberty of Kingston-on-Thames, in the fifteenth year of Elizabeth, a jury presented, by way of complaint, the vicar, a Mr. Pope, because " he hath not a bull at the Parsonage, according to the old custome ; " and it was ordered " that he have one from henceforth on payne of x shillings for every lackinge." * A correspondent of *Notes and Queries* (5th series, x. 354) informs us that " by custom of the parish of Quarley, Hants, the parson was bound to keep a public boar and bull for the use of the parish. This he had neglected to do, whereupon his parishioners refused to give him the tithe of milk." Mr. Bond, in his " Topographical and Historical Sketches of the Boroughs of East and West Looe, Cornwall " (1823), quotes in the appendix the following transactions relative to this custom, which is worthy of note—

" The 30th day of April in the year of our Lord 1666. Hereafter followeth a note of such anchant customs as hath bin used within the Parish of St. Martin's, as well in time past as this present and time out of minde observed and kept.

" Art. I. The Parishioners of the said Parish ought to have, by thare Custom, of thare Parson or his Proctor under him, a Bull alwaie remaining upon the Gleab of the Parsonage of St. Martin aforesaid, for the necessary use at all times when occasion shall searve."

After describing in Articles II. to XI. the tithes and other dues to which the parson was entitled, the note concludes thus : " Be it known to all men, by these presents, that I, Stephen Medhopp, Parson of the Parish of St. Martin's, and we, the Parishioners of the said Parish, whose names are under written, doe acknowledge that this award with us written was done with the consent and good liking, made by Richard Carew and John Wrey, Esquirse, and was

* *Notes and Queries*, 5th series, x. 248.

don with the consent and good liking of us all. In witness whereof we have subscribed our names."

Among further variations of this custom, it appears from the Appendix to the Report of the Commissioners on Municipal Corporations of England and Wales, the Mayor of Marlborough, in consideration of his finding a town bull, receives eightpence for every cow turned on a piece of land called "The Portfield," belonging to the Corporation. Among the items of expenditure by the Corporation of Nottingham, given in the same report (ii. 1972), one runs thus : "Paid for the bull for the Commons, £7 10s." Edwards, in his "Old English Customs and Curious Bequests and Charities" (1842, 65, 66), writes : "From a copy of Court roll of the Manor of Isleworth Syon, dated December 29, 1675, it appears that Thomas Cole surrendered 4a. 1r. of customary land lying in several places in the fields of Twickenham, called the Parish Land, anciently belonging to the inhabitants of Twickenham, for keeping a bull for the common use of the inhabitants, in trust for the use of the said inhabitants, for keeping and maintaining a sufficient bull for the use aforesaid."

"An entry in an old churchwarden's ledger of October 6, 1622, states an agreement between the vestry and Mr. Robert Bartlett, that he should hold the three acres and a half of the Parish Land with the Bull Mead, paying the same rent to the parish as he formerly did, with the condition that he, receiving a bull from the churchwardens for the common use of the parishioners, should keep the same at his own charge ; and if the bull should die, should provide another."

Similarly, among the entries of old church books, many curious bequests of cows for the maintenance of the parish, or for the use of the poor, are recorded. Sometimes the money derived from this source was devoted to the keeping of a light before the high altar of the parish church, or before the shrine of some saint. In 1531, Elizabeth Davye, of Pulham Magdalen, "bequethyd one kowe to ffynd one contynuall light before yᵉ sacrament in Pulham p d, and Wyllem Wyllyson to have yᵉ kowe to ferme for xvj*d.* by yer, and yᵉ seyd xvj*d.* to be ded to yᵉ chyrch wardeyns to see yᵉ lyght kept, and yᵉ kowe to be renewyd by yᵉ said chyrch wardeyns as they shall thynk best for yᵉ cotynuance of yᵉ seyd lyght." In the will of Thomas Byxley, alias Cowper, of Honyngham, Norfolk, 1533, occurs this bequest : "Itm. I bequeathe to the lyght of Oure lady in the same chirche, a mothys neete, and I wyll that with yᵉ yerly profite and ferme that come of yᵗ, wexe to be bought and to brenne before oure lady in maner and forme as the profite of other neet do in the sayd chirche en more to endure."

Another entry of the same kind is found in the will of Thomas Clerke of Rodney : "I bequeth to yᵉ p'ishe of Rodney viij*s.* or ellis a cow, price viij*s.*, to fynd a lamp afore I will (that) the p'ishe may light their candellis at yᵗ, and agayn to burn betwin Matence and Mass when the candellis be put owt, that they shall not nede to Rune hether and thether to mennis houses for fyer in great wynds and tempests, whereby gret vexacon, troble, and losse of goods other Inconvenience may chance and fortune." In the churchwardens' accounts of Bungay Trinity for the year 1539, it was noted that John Duke, resident of the town, gave six kine, and a legacy of five pounds to the parish ; the entries being as follows—

"1539. Itm. Rec. of xec' of Mr. Duke in ptye of payment of iiij*li.* x*s.* for the six kene, wᶜʰ were to the parish, xviij*s.* vj*d.*

"Itm. Rec. more in full payment for the said kene, iij*li.* xj*s.* vj*d.*

" Itm. Paid for an aquyttance for the exec' of Mr. Duke, for the vj kene, ij*d.*"

But no mention is made as to the manner in which they were appropriated to the benefit of the poor. In the inventory of Elmsett parish for 1542–3, there are numerous references to the parish cow, two entries of which we subjoin—

" I. First letyng a cowe to Thomas Prittey (Pattey ?), to find a lyght afore the sacrament, of the Gifte of Roger . . . and . . . is suretie for this cowe, that it shall be forthe comyng and the light honyestly kept during the yere.

"II. Itm. letyng another cowe by John Smyth and Thomas Pattey, churchwardens of the said p'yshe of Elmsett, to . . . Castard (?) to fynd the pascall and synging light of the gift of S. Nicolas Hanby, late p'sone of the said p'yshe, and . . . is suretie for this cowe, that it shalbe forthe comyng and the said light honyestly kept during the yere."

The sums at which the cows were let is not given, but from other lists it would appear that the " hyer " of each cow was " xx pence." *   In entries of this kind, it is curious to see how the object of the " sewerties " was practically defeated. One neighbour appears " to have been surety for another on condition that the kindness was returned to himself by the party whom he had befriended; and thus the parish had really no security against a ' conspiracy to defraud.' " †

The old account books of the parish of Pulham St. Mary Magdalen, Norfolk, extending from the year 1557 to 1620, show that an unusually large number of cows were at that time the property of the parish. In 1563, the total number of these cows was sixty-nine, which were farmed by the parishioners, the income arising from twenty-five of the

---

* *The East Anglian* (1864), i. 130, 131.   * Ibid., 67.

number being applied to the church, and the rest being given to the poor.*

The income arising from the cows given for the use of the poor was received by the "collectors for the poor," who kept a separate book of their receipts and payments until the year 1597. It does not appear to have been customary in this parish to require sureties from the farmers of the cows; and it is likely that the death of some of the cows, and the conversion of others into a money value, caused the gradual decrease of their number.†

Towards the close of the sixteenth century, the cows which then remained were rapidly converted into stock, and in 1601 the overseers of the poor received the income. The last reference to the cows in the account books of Pulham St. Mary Magdalen, relates to a lawsuit to recover from Robert Hannor (or Hanworth) the value of the cows or stock which he held of the parish. It seems that in the year 1573 Hanworth hired twenty cows (the gift of Thomas Palgrave) at twenty shillings a year, and two others (the gift of John Brown) at two shillings and eightpence a year, and he paid for the hire of these cows until the year 1582. But, after that date, he made no other payments, and probably repudiated the debt. The action, however, which appears to have been brought for one cow only, lasted five years. The total amount of the costs was £13 8s. 10d., and the churchwardens, in 1620, "rec⁴ of Robert Hanor at 3 severall tymes for the sewte, dependinge for the cowe which was due vnto the towen, xiij*li.* x*s.*" If, therefore, Hanworth paid no more than this, the parish gained only fourteen pence by the suit, and that after five years' litigation. The following are the entries referring to these legal proceedings—

* "Eastern Counties Collectanea," (1872-73), 5.
† Ibid., 5.

"1615.   It. payd to the register for the oaths of iiij witneses for the proof of hanors payment of xj*d.* by the yere for the cowe, iiij*s.* vj*d.*

"It. for v of o*ʳ* dyners ther, iiij*s.* ij*d.*

"It. for a sytation serven of the witnesses, xij*d.*

"It. for charges at Norwich at ij sessions, iiij*s.*

"1616.   It. for taken ovt the Depossions at Straton cort for hanor and my dynor, iiij*s.* ij*d.*

"It. to Mr. Talbot for his fee at Windam, when sentance pased against hanor for the town cowe, x*s.*

"It. for the sentance Drawen, vj*s.*

"It. for the Jvdges and registers fees for sentance for the Cowe, x*s.*

"It. for other charges then, xvj*d.*

"1617.   It. to John Baker, pt of charges for distraynen of hanor, iiij*s.*

"1618.   It. for charges at Norwich, being sited by Robt. hanor, xx*d.*

"1619.   It. Layd ovt at Norwich for search of the books that were transmitted for hanors swet, xj*s.*

"It. for my charges at Norwich Cort, xij*d.*

"It. payd unto Mr. Agas for y*ᵉ* books for hanors carse, xij*s.*

"It. for Mr. Tabut, who was Covnsell for the town at the sentance in hanors carse, vj*s.*

"It. more, Mr. Agas had then that he layd ovt of his purse for that case, v*s.*

"It. for charges then, ij*s.*

"It. for the judges fees and registers fees when sentans was past at Norwich fo hanors Carse, xx*s.*

"It. for my diner and horsmet then, xij*d.*

"It. for senden to Mr. Agas, when hanor did site me to loud! vij*d.*

"1620.   It. to the p'ctor at London, for charges when

sentance pased against hannor for the cow money, iij*l.* ix*s.*

"It. to Mr. Agas for fees and other charges when the sentance mony was payd at Norwich Cort, which wase x*s.*

"It. to Mr. Agas for his fees for pcedinge at Straton and Norwich, against hanor, iij*li.* x*s.*

"It. for charges at that Cort then, x*s.*

"It. for maken ij aqvittances for Robt. hanor vj*d.*"

These items are also interesting as affording some idea of legal expenses at this period.

Among further old cow charities, it is recorded by the Charity Commissioners that James Goodaker, of Barnston, in the parish of Woodchurch, Cheshire, in 1525, left twenty marks to buy twenty yoke of bullocks, which were subsequently replaced by cows, and given to the poor of Woodchurch, every parishioner that had a cow or cows paying yearly for each to the overseers the sum of 2*s.* 8*d.* every Friday before Whit-Sunday, which hire was to be a stock for the benefit of the poor for ever. A table of benefactions in the parish church of Bebington, Cheshire, records how William Hulme, of Poulton, A.D. 1620, gave three cows to be disposed of by the minister and churchwardens, to the poorest and godliest parishioners at eight groats a year, and this hire to be employed for the increase of parish cows. It is further added that in 1625, Christopher Smallshall gave three cows for the same purpose, and that in 1661, John Briscow, of Poulton, gave £2 10*s.* for the buying of a parish cow. In years past, each individual contributed 5*s.* a year for the use of his cow, and on the 25th April, in every year, the cows were exhibited for the inspection of the rector and churchwardens, when every person was required to find security for the proper care of the cow with which he was entrusted. Each cow was branded on one horn with the initial letter of the parish, and on the other with those of the rector.

A curious cow charity, at Minehead, Somerset, originated in the operation of an Act passed in the eighteenth year of Charles II., " against importing cattle from Ireland and other parts beyond the seas," wherein it was enacted that the importation of cattle from the 2nd of February, 1660, should be a common and a public nuisance, and that if any great cattle should, from and after the day above mentioned, be imported, or brought from beyond seas into England, it should be lawful for any constable, etc., to seize the same, and that the same should be forfeited, one half to the use of the poor of the parish where they should be seized, and the other half to the persons seizing. By another Act, 20 Charles II., every vessel importing cattle was to be liable to the like seizure, and the monies arising from the sale thereof, were to be applied as aforesaid.

In 1669, it appeared that a number of cattle were unlawfully imported from Ireland into the port of Minehead, and that the same, together with the vessel importing them, were seized and sold pursuant to the powers contained in the two Acts, and that a moiety of the sum produced from the sale thereof, was, by the direction of the churchwardens and overseers of the said parish of Minehead, invested in the purchase of a freehold estate in the parish of Ottery St. Mary, Devonshire, which was conveyed to certain persons as the trustees for the parish of Minehead, and that a book was kept in the said parish called the " Cow-money book," in which entries were made of the rents and profits received from the said charity estate, and of the distribution thereof.

CHAPTER XXIV.

WELLS AND WELL-CHAPELS.

CONNECTED with the "holy wells" throughout the country, we find a host of curious legends and superstitions which have invested them with an importance, and an interest, apart from their religious associations. Indeed, so extensive is the legendary lore which, in the lapse of years, has clustered round our "holy wells" that a volume might be devoted to this subject alone, illustrative of the strange fancies and romantic stories which our forefathers have handed down. In many cases some sacred influence has been supposed to subsist between the church and the neighbouring well, a fact which would partly explain the mysterious powers so frequently attributed to the latter.*

The holy wells of Cornwall, which have long been a source of interest to the antiquarian student, may be divided, says Mr. J. T. Blight,† "into two classes, viz. those which were used as baptisteries in connection with the churches near which they were situated, and those which are to be found by the side of some little chapel or hermitage, in remote and retired places, and may or may not have

---

* An interesting series of papers have lately appeared in "The Antiquary," by Mr. R. C. Hope, on "Holy Wells, their Legends and Superstitions."

† "Reliquary," ii. 126–133.

T

been used for baptismal purposes. As so much veneration was paid to certain springs, previous to the introduction of Christianity, the early missionaries of the Christian faith are supposed to have appropriated them to the services of their own creed, and dedicated them to saintly patrons. These wells being thus adopted by the Christians, many of them were merely used as baptisteries; near or over them small chapels were erected, in which the baptismal ceremonies were probably performed—such structures having been sometimes called "Well Chapels." Many of these wells were much resorted to as places of divination, and are still visited by young persons as "Wishing Wells."

Judging from its appearance, St. Madron's well-chapel, now in ruins, is one of the oldest in Cornwall, and about a mile from the church. Many remarkable cures are said to have been effected at this well; an allusion to which is made by Bishop Hall, in his "Mystery of Godliness," where he speaks of the good office which angels do to God's servants, adding, "of whiche kinde was that noe less than miraculous cure whiche, at Madern's Well, in Cornwall, was wrought on a poor cripple, whereof, besides the attestation of many hundreds of the neighbours, I saw him able to walk and get his own maintenance. I took strict and impartial examination in my last triennial visitation. I found neither art nor collusion, the cure done, the author an invisible God." Borlase relates how "to this miraculous fountain, the uneasy, the impatient, the fearful, the jealous, and the superstitious, resort to learn their future destiny from the unconscious water. By dropping pins or pebbles into the fountain, by shaking the ground around the spring, or by continuing to raise bubbles from the bottom, on certain lucky days, and when the moon is in a particular stage of increase or decrease, the secrets of the well are presumed to be extorted." He further adds that the fame of this celebrated well was known far and wide throughout the county in years past, on account of " the supposed virtue of healing, which St. Maderne had thereinto infused, and many votaries made annual pilrimages unto it, as they do even at this day unto the well of St. Winnifrede, beyond Chester, in Flintshire, whereunto thousands do yearly make resort, but of late St. Maderne hath denied his pristine aid, and he is coy of his cures." One of the seats beside St. Madron's Well was known as St. Madron's Bed, on which the sick folk who came to be cured, reclined ; it having been also customary, for those who derived benefit from the spring, to leave a donation for the poor in Madron Church, a practice which prevailed till the middle of the seventeenth century.

One of the Cornish well-chapels in the best state of preservation is that of Dupath, near Collington, which is of the sixteenth century.   It is built of granite, the roof being "constructed of enormous slates hung with fern, and supported in the interior by an arch, dividing the nave and the chancel.   The building is crowned by an ornamental bell-cote." *   A legend connected with this spot has been poetically described by the Rev. R. S. Hawker.   It appears that two " gentle knights " here fought for a lady's hand : the " noble Siward " was mortally wounded, and when told by the leech that his " passing hour was nigh "—

> " ' Bring me,' he said, ' the steel I wore,
>   When Dupath spring was dark with gore ;
>   The spear I rais'd for Githa's glove,
>   Those trophies of my Wars and Love. '
>   *   *   *   *   *
> " A roof must shade that stoned stream
>   Her dying lord's remember'd theme,
>   A daily vow that lady said
>   Where glory wreathed the hero dead.

---

* R. C. Hope, " Holy Wells," *Antiquary* (1890), 30.

> "Gaze maiden ! gaze on Dupath Well !
> Time yet hath spar'd that solemn cell ;
> In memory of old love and pride,
> Hear how the noble Siward died."

The well-chapel of St. Cleer, which is in ruins, was probably erected about the same time as that at Dupath. The well is supposed to have been used, in olden times, as a bowsening or boussening pool, for the cure of mad people, a mode of cure which, as formerly performed at a holy well at Altarnum, Carew has thus described : "The water running from St. Nun's Well fell into a square and enclosed wall plot, which might be filled at what depth they listed. Upon this was the frantic person set to stand, his back towards the pool; and from thence, with a sudden blow in the breast, tumbled headlong into the pool, where a strong fellow, provided for the nonce, took him, and tossed him up and down, alongst and athwart the water, till the patient, by foregoing his strength, had somewhat forgot his fury. Then he was conveyed to the church, and certain masses sung over him, upon which handling, if his right wits were returned, St. Nun had the thanks; but if there appeared small amendment, he was bowsened again and again, while there remained in him any hope of life or recovery."

The well-chapel of St. Euny, about two miles from Sancreed Church, now in ruins, was in past years the scene of many supposed magical cures, in connection with which Dr. Borlase writes : "I happened luckily to be at this well upon the last day of the year, on which, according to vulgar opinion, it exerts its principal and most salutary powers. Two women were here, who came from a neighbouring parish, and were busily employed in bathing a child. They both assured me that people who had a mind to receive any benefit from St. Euny's Well must come and wash upon the three first Wednesdays in May."

In the parish of St. Cleather may be seen the ruined well-chapel of St. Basil, and at Menacuddle, near St. Austell, remains an ancient Gothic structure, the well here situated having been reputed to possess medicinal virtues. A holy well-chapel also existed at Helston, and one of the smallest and most ancient in this county was that of St. Julian at Mount Edgecumbe, its internal dimensions being only six feet three inches by four feet nine inches. The "proportions are as simple as they are beautiful, and the details and character of the masonry fix the period approximately as that of the early part of the fourteenth century. This little structure was a few years ago restored by the Earl of Edgecumbe." *

St. Neot's Well was arched over in granite by the late General Carlyon ; and of St. Ruan's, or St. Rumour's Well, Whitaker, in his "Ancient Cathedrals of Cornwall," thus writes : " Here, near to the site of St. Grade's Church, at the village still denominated St. Ruan from the fact, did St. Runon live, having a cell for his habitation and a chapel for his devotions, regardless of the wild beasts around him, seeing them, perhaps, in his walks, hearing them, perhaps, in his prayers, yet beholding them to flee the face of this strange intruder on their privacies. About a quarter of a mile to the north-east of Grade Church is a noted well, from which is fetched all the water used in baptisms at the church."

Among further Cornish wells may be mentioned that of St. Roche, and the one at Ludgvan, which was commonly reported to preserve those who had been baptized with its waters from ever being hanged. At Cardynham there are the remains of a holy well, eighty feet long and forty-two feet broad. Polwhele says, " It may be classed among the first Christian places of worship," and adds, " it was sacred

* "Journ. of the Arch. Assoc." (1883), xxxix. 355, 356.

before all saints." The site of the well-chapel of St. Ninnie, popularly designated the "Piskies' Well," is still pointed out, while the properties of the famous Well of St. Keyne have been immortalized in Southey's popular ballad—

> " If the husband of this gifted well
> Shall drink before his wife,
> A happy man henceforth is he,
> For he shall be master for life.
> But if the wife should drink of it first,
> God help the husband then."

Alluding to the wells found by the side of little chapels, or hermitages, in remote situations, Mr. Blight writes : "Some of these in Cornwall are on the sea coast, and were probably constructed near a spring, for the convenience of the hermit. Spenser describes the situation of "a lowly hermitage" near "a christall streame" ("Faerie Queene")—

> " Far from resort of people that did pass
> In traveill to and froe ; a little wyde
> There was an holy chappell edifyde
> Wherein the hermit dewly wont to say
> His holy things each morne and eventyde ;
> Thereby a christall streame did gently play,
> Which from a sacred fountaine welled forth alway."

In this case, however, the ,"hidden cell" was "by a forest side," but in Cornwall such structures were sometimes placed on the very edge of the most fearful cliffs, or even occasionally on isolated rocks, where they were exposed to every gale. The foundations of a seaside chapel may still be seen at the Gurnard's Head, on the north coast of West Cornwall.* Near the edge of the cliff is the ruin of the ancient baptistery or well of St. Levan, who, according to tradition, supported himself by fishing.

Derbyshire and parts of Staffordshire have long been

---

* "Reliquary," ii. 126–133.

noted for the custom of "well-flowering," or "well-dressing," on Ascension Day; Tissington, near Ashborne, and Buxton having been specially enthusiastic in this respect;[*] a practice also observed at Endon, Shropshire, on May 29th or 30th, and at St. Boniface's Well, Bonchurch, on the saint's festival. A well, a short distance to the north of the church of St. Alkmund's, Derby, is known as St. Alkmund's Well. The custom of dressing this well with flowers was revived in 1870, and annually the clergy and choir of St. Alkmund's meet in the church and walk there in procession. A noted well in Derby is that of St. Thomas à Becket. According to the "Derbyshire Archæological Society's Proceedings" (xii.), there was a chapel over it, or close by its side. In 1652 a small building was again erected over it, which was restored in 1889.[†] Trinity Well, to the southwest of the ruined chapel of the Holy Trinity at North Lees, in the parish of Hathersage, is sheltered "by four slabs of gritstone, one as the bed, two as upright stones, and the fourth as a covering. Close by the well is a flat stone, on which are rudely sculptured a small cross, and the letters "I. S." This chapel was built by the Romanists in the time of James II., and destroyed by a Protestant mob when William III. came to the throne."[‡]

A Devonshire well, which has long been famous, is that of St. John-in-the-Wilderness, Morwenstowe, a spot on which Mr. Hawker has written these lines—

> " Here dwelt in times long past, so legends tell,
> Holy Morwenna, guardian of this well;
> Here on the foreheads of our fathers pour'd
> From this lone spring the laver of the Lord !

---

[*] See "Book of Days," i.
[†] *Antiquary* (1890), 93-95.
[‡] Ibid., 98, 99.

> If, traveller, thy happy spirit know
> That awful font whence living waters flow,
> Then hither come to draw—thy feet have found
> Amid these rocks a place of holy ground !
> Then sigh one blessing—breathe a voice of praise
> O'er the fond labour of departed days !
> Tell the glad waters of their former fame,
> And teach the joyful waters Morwenna's name ! "

The following is recorded in the endowment deed, dated 1296, relative to this well, and is preserved in Bishop Brantinham's register : " The church land is said to extend eastward *ad quendam fontem Johannis.* Water wherewithal to fill the font for baptism is always drawn from this well by the sacristan, in pitchers set apart for this purpose. It stands midway down the cliff on the present glebe ; around it on either hand are rugged and sea-worn rocks, before it the wide sea." *

Many wells have been popularly designated " pin-wells," from the superstitious custom of passers-by dropping in pins for luck. At St. Helen's Well, Sefton, Lancashire, this practice is still observed, and a few years ago the bottom was covered with them.† Near Keyingham, Yorkshire, is St. Philip's Well, into which young girls used to drop pins when wishing.

Allusion has already been made to the healing properties of certain holy wells, which have been much resorted to on this account. The water of St. Austin's Well, Leicester, was once in high repute as a remedy for sore eyes, and a spring at Holly Well Dale, near Winterton, Lincolnshire, was equally famous for its medicinal properties ; the bushes around it being covered with rags as votive offerings. ‡ About a mile to the west of Jarrow, near Newcastle-on-Tyne

---

* Quoted in *The Antiquary*, (1890), 145.
† *Notes and Queries*, 5th series, i. 158.
‡ See Taylor's " Prim. Culture."

there is Bede's Well, to which, up to the middle of last century, it was customary "to bring children troubled with any disease or infirmity. A crooked pin was put in, and the well laved dry (?) between each dipping." * At Oxford, St. Edmund's Well was frequented by those suffering from various distempers, and "Our Lady's Well," at Wombourne, Shropshire—supposed to have been sacred to the virgin in mediæval times—is said to have possessed curative virtues. St. John's Well, at Harpham, Yorkshire, is believed to possess the power of subduing the wildest and fiercest animals, and William of Malmesbury says that in his day the most rabid bull, when brought to its waters, became quiet as the gentlest lamb. †

In Yorkshire there is St. Diana's Well, whose pure water has long been proverbial—

> " Whoever eats Hammer nuts, and drinks Diana's water,
> Will never leave Witton while he's a rag or tatter."

St. John's Well is about a mile from Moxley Nunnery, over which was formerly, writes Mr. Hope, "an ancient building, consisting of a small dome of stone and brick. There is still discernible the remains of a causeway leading from the nunnery in the direction of this well. The water is said to possess medicinal properties, and there is a large and convenient cistern built on the east side, into which the water is admitted for the purpose of bathing. It was much resorted to in the days of superstition, and there are still the remains of stone steps for the more easy descent thereto. Near the mouth, which admits the water into the bath, is a large stone, called the ' wishing stone,' and many a faithful kiss has this stone received from those who were supposed never to fail in experiencing the completion of

---

* Brand's " Newcastle," ii. 54.
† See *The Antiquary* (1891), 112.

their desires, provided the wish was delivered with full devotion and confidence."

Wells have occasionally been found in churches. Somewhere on the north side of the choir of Canterbury Cathedral was the famous well of St. Thomas, of which no trace is now visible. The dust and blood from the pavement, after the murder, are said to have been thrown into it. The spring changed four times into blood and once into milk, and constant miracles were wrought by the water. This marvel did not appear, however, until the fourteenth century, and is unknown by the earlier chronicles. From its recorded effects it seems to have been slightly chalybeate, like the well of Zem-Zem at Mecca.

In April, 1879, while the restoration of the choir of Beverley Minster was being carried out, two very old and much worn steps were discovered, which had been hidden, the upper one by the footpace of the altar, the lower by the foundation on which the rail at the south end of the altar rested. These, on subsequent examination, were found to have been used as an approach to a well.

In Carlisle Cathedral there is a well which was closed during the late restoration. The water was raised by a windlass; and a similar well, regularly formed, and with sides of squared stone, exists in the north transept, but has been covered. Besides supplying water for the use of the church, such wells may have been of special service in border churches, which, like the cathedral of Carlisle, served as places of refuge for the inhabitants, in case of sudden alarm or foray.* It is said that the late dean had it covered over for fear of it or the water in some way affecting the music. There is a well in the eastern part of the crypt of York Minster, where King Edwin is said to

* R. J. King, "Handbook to the Northern Cathedrals" (1869), pt. i. 192, 193. *Notes and Queries,* 3rd series, xii. 235.

have been baptized in the year 627. A wooden oratory was erected over it before the stone building was thought of. The crypt is about forty feet by thirty-five feet.[*] In the crypt of Glasgow Cathedral, on the south-east corner, there is a well, and one exists within the cathedral of St. Patrick, Dublin.

In the nave of Marden Church, Herefordshire, is a spring protected by stonework, and called St. Ethelbert's Well. It is said to arise from the spot in which the body of St. Ethelbert was first interred.

Close to the west end of East Dereham Church, Norfolk, is St. Withburga's Well, the spring which is said to have burst forth from her grave. It is in a small enclosed spot, full of flowers, having at one end an arch (not of early character) with an inscription, recording that Withburga, youngest daughter of Annas (Anna), King of the East Anglians was once buried there. The spring was famous for its miraculous cures, and was resorted to by numerous pilgrims. During her life at East Dereham, St. Withburga and her maidens are said to have been miraculously fed by two milch deer, which came every morning to a certain bridge, and waited there to be milked. But a man in the place, "instigated by the devil," took bow and arrows, and killed both the deer, after which he was "smitten with jaundice, consumed away, and miserably died."[†] And within the Church of St. Michael, near Tenbury, a well was sunk to supply the font with pure water.

[*] *The Antiquary* (1891), 113.   [†] Murray's "Norfolk," 268.

CHAPTER XXV.

CHURCH LIBRARIES.

AN important institution, in years gone by, was the church library. When books were scarce and dear, and the incomes of the clergy far from large, the libraries founded in the numerous parishes throughout the country proved an incalculable boon to the parson and his parishioners ; oftentimes affording them opportunities for study and research which otherwise would not have been within their reach. Placed in the church, occasionally in a room over the church porch, or in the parson's house, or in the parish grammar-school, such libraries gained a more than local interest, as from time to time, they were enriched by private munificence ; and, at the present day, some idea of their value may be gathered from those which still exist, here and there, in different parishes.

But, unfortunately, these old church libraries have suffered sadly in the past, books having only too often been borrowed and never returned ; and instances have occurred where they have been sold "with the goods and chattels of deceased incumbents, or deceased schoolmasters, and where the tenure of such offices has extended to thirty or forty years, it is not difficult to see how this may have occurred. Such books sometimes turn up long afterwards in second-hand stores." *   In the year 1708, through, it is said, the exertions of Dr. Bray and Lord Chancellor King, an Act was passed " for the better preservation of Parochial Libraries, in that part of Great Britain called England," from which we gain an interesting glimpse of the value attached to them at this period : " In many places," it states,† "the provision of the clergy is so mean that the necessary expense of books for the better prosecution of their studies cannot be defrayed by them, and whereas of late years several charitable and well disposed persons have by charitable contributions erected libraries within several parishes, but some provision is wanting to preserve the same. Be it enacted—that in every parish or place where such a library is or shall be erected, the same shall be preserved for such use or uses as the same is or shall be given, and the orders and rules of the founders of such libraries shall be observed and kept. And for the encouragement of such founders and benefactors, and to the intent that they may be satisfied that their charitable intent may not be frustrated, Be it enacted— That every incumbent, rector, vicar, minister, or curate of a parish, before he is permitted to use or enjoy such library, shall enter into security—for preservation and due obser- vation of the rules and orders belonging to the same," etc. For a time the passing of this Act gave a decided impetus to the church library movement, many having been founded in various parishes, partly through the munificence of Dr. Bray.

In the course, however, of the present century, our church libraries have been sadly neglected. "In some instances," writes Mr. **T. W. Shore**, "the books have disappeared by the old method of having been taken out and not returned,

---

* Transaction of the Library Association, 1879 : " Old Parochial Libraries," by T. W. Shore.

† Ibid., 51, 52.

as at Wimborne and Barnstaple, or by being sold as at Reepham, or sold by the cart load as at Boston, or by having been given away.

Referring to Boston library, it may be noted that in 1635, upon the request of the Rev. Anthony Tucker, Vicar of Boston, it was ordained by the Archbishop of Canterbury, (Laud), then on his visitation at Boston, "that the roome over the porch of the saide Churche shall be repaired and decently fitted up to make a librarye, to the end that, in case any well and charitably disposed person shall hereafter bestow any books to the use of the parish, they may be there safely preserved and kept."

In one instance, the books were not improbably burnt, for as long ago as 1807, a writer in the *Gentleman's Magazine* complained of seeing one of the books at Westerham acting as a fender to the clerk's fireplace, and in 1856 the books had all disappeared, and the catalogue only was left."

A correspondent of *Notes and Queries* (6th series, vi. 294) says that when visiting St. Mary's, Beverley, in 1852, he was shown " in one of the vestries in the north transept, a small library, consisting mainly of good folios, chiefly theological, covered with dust, in a most dilapidated condition ; the fires in the church had been usually lighted from this literary source for some time."   On visiting the same in 1865, the same correspondent informs us that the small collection in the library was apparently reduced to one book, a copy of the Hexapla.*

The late Mr. William Blades, in his " Biographical Mis-cellanies," † relates an amusing anecdote as told him by Mr.

---

* In George's *Westerham's Journal* (April 1st, 1844), we are told how one, Charles West, gave to the parish by will in 1765, a library of books, consisting of several hundred volumes, many of them curious and rare.   The catalogue of these books is carefully preserved in the parish chest, but the books themselves are nowhere to be found.

† " Books in Chains," p. 27.

Stibbs, bookseller, of Oxford Street, showing how church libraries have, in one way or another, got dispersed: "About twenty years ago, I was in the vestry of the church of All Saints', Hereford, in which there were about two hundred chained volumes of old divinity. One of the churchwardens accompanied me, and I remarked to him, 'How useless these old books must be without any one to look at them.'

" 'That's true,' he said; 'they are quite useless.'

" 'Well,' I replied, 'why not let me have them? I will give you £100 for them, which will obtain for the use of the parish a really useful lot of books.'

" 'Well, that's a good offer, and I'll lay it before the vestry,' was his reply. A short time after, I was informed that the vestry meeting had been held, and my offer accepted. I went down to Hereford, paid the £100, took possession of the books, chains and all, and brought them up to London. I immediately made a catalogue of them, but had hardly finished, when I received an urgent request from one of the churchwardens not to part with one of them on any account, for that the Dean of Windsor, whose consent ought first to have been obtained, had positively refused to sanction the sale. Having been at considerable expense in travelling to Hereford three times, besides time wasted in cataloguing, I declined to deliver up the books, but as considerable ill-blood, and probably legal proceedings would have ensued, I at last sent them back, upon payment of all expenses, and they are now restored to their original position. I will only add, that arrangements had been partially made for the sale of the whole to an American dealer."

To give another example of the same kind—

The following is from the fly-leaf of "A Treatise of Ecclesiastical Benefices and Revenues," by the learned Father Paul, translated by Tobias Jenkins, 1736: "Bibliotheca de Bassingbourn in Com. Cant. Dono dedit Edvardus

Nightingale de Kneesworth Armiger Filius et Hæres Fundatoris. Feb. 1ᵐᵒ. 1735."

This book was purchased some years ago at a sale in Oxford.

In some cases it would seem that, with the work of Church restoration, the library has been subjected to somewhat rough treatment. During the restoration of Cirencester Church, Gloucestershire, in 1867, it is said the chained books disappeared from the church, and in 1852, when the church at North Denchworth, Berks, was undergoing repairs, the room over the church porch, which had long served as a library, was removed, and "was replaced by an ugly lean-to," which has since been converted into a gable-porch. At the time of these alterations in 1852, the library was taken bodily into the vicarage, and the chains removed, except a few which remain as specimens. Of the original library but a few books remain. It contained the "Golden Legend," printed by Caxton, in 1483, which was sold in 1843 to Messrs. Parker, of Oxford, and by them to the Bodleian Library. The proceeds were applied to the re-binding of books, and enlargement of book-cases. There are still remaining a Cranmer's Bible, four black-letter volumes of Aquinas, one of Ancient Homilies, a copy of Bishop Burnet on the Articles, given by the author himself, and a life of Christ by Ludolphus Saxo, which once belonged to Bishop Juxon, with chain attached.*

But these are not the only ways in which our Church libraries have been injured, for it appears that in the parish church of Impington, Cambridgeshire, some years ago, in consequence of the books being subject to constant mutilations, they were removed from the church by the clerk, who for many years had charge of them in his own house. After his death, the books found their way into an

* See *Notes and Queries*, 6th series, iv. 304, 305.

old granary on a farmstead, in close proximity to the church. "I rescued their remains," writes the vicar, "and after removing the cobwebs and filth to which they had been exposed, they presented a very dilapidated appearance. Happily there still remained a few links of the chains, and other metal ornaments used in the binding, which stimulated the idea to rebind the tattered fragments." *

There was a library at Doncaster, of which there is a catalogue in Miller's History of Doncaster. It was founded in 1714 by a society known as the Society of the Clergy, which existed at Doncaster from 1714 to about 1760. The library perished in the fire which destroyed the late church in 1853.

The beautiful church of Hanmer, Flintshire, unfortunately burnt down about three years ago, contained, among other treasures, four books chained to two desks.

A correspondent of *Notes and Queries* (1st series, vii. 438) tells how he found the library at Swaffham Church, Norfolk, "in a most disgraceful state, covered with dust and the dung of mice and bats, and many of the books torn from their bindings." It contains, among other valuable books, some of the Elzevir classics. A fine copy of Cranmer's Bible was given away by the churchwardens.

Among some of the most curious and interesting church libraries may be mentioned that at St. Mary's, Bridgnorth, Shropshire, which was established by Dean Stackhouse in 1750. It contains eight hundred volumes, chiefly divinity, besides many valuable fragments of illuminated manuscripts, dated 1460.†

---

* "Biographical Miscellanies," 1890; W. Blades, "Books in Chains," 29.

† Additional Manuscripts, 28732, at the British Museum, contains foundation deed of the library, with will of founder, list of books, etc., 1743.

In a room over the south porch of the parish church, Chelmsford, are the remains of a good theological library, which, it is said, was bequeathed by John Kingsbridge, D.D., for the use of the clergy of the town of Chelmsford and its environs. Castleton Church, Derbyshire, has a large library of over a thousand volumes. Mr. James Croston, speaking of Castleton Church in "On Foot Through the Peak," writes : "In the vestry there is an excellent library, the gift of a former vicar, the Rev. James Farrer, to which considerable additions have been made by his daughter and Captain Hamilton. It contains upwards of a thousand volumes, chiefly in divinity, history, and biography, many of them being rare and valuable works. They are lent to the parishioners at the discretion of the vicar for the time being—a wise provision, which tends to ensure their pre-servation."

The vestry room of the Abbey Church, Bath, contains a library of about three hundred volumes, the larger number of which are folios, and to which great interest attaches. Mr. C. P. Russell, referring to this library at the first annual meeting of the Library Association, said : "The present church was commenced by Bishop Oliver King, about 1490. It remained unfinished until about 1614; and it would appear that shortly after that date, or between 1616 and 1626, efforts were made to establish a library in connection with the church."

In an interesting old record, written on vellum, entitled, " A Catologue of the Benefactors towards the Labrarie in the Church of Saint Peter and Paule in the City of Bath," the first entry runs thus : "The Right Reverend Father in God, Arthur Lake, Bishop of Bathe and Welles, beganne this worthie Work, giving to the said Church Two Volumes of the renowned works of our late Sovereign Lord King James, the one in Latine the other in English." Then follow a list of other benefactors and the works presented by them ; among the names recorded being some of great interest.   Thus, Sir William Waller, the Parliamentary General, presented five works, among them a copy of Jacob de Voragine's " Legenda Aurea ; " the celebrated writer William Prynne, Recorder of Bath, and his publisher, Michael Sparkes, of London, presented a long list of books, among them many of Prynne's own works ; Elias Ashmole, founder of the Ashmolean Museum, gave " The Institution, Laws, and Ceremonies of the Most Noble Order of the Garter ; " and Thomas Radcliff, " Fellow of Universitie Colledge in Oxford," gave several works.   In the vestry-book of the parish occurs this entry, under the date of March 27, 1722-23 : " Order'd that Mr. John Anstey, Churchwarden, doe repair the Book, etc., in the vestry, and that the Books left by the pious Dr. Kenn, late Bishop of the Diocese of Bath and Wells, be brought from Longleyeat and set up in this vestry." *

The library at Skipton parish church was removed in 1880 to the new Skipton Grammar School. " This library," writes a correspondent of *Notes and Queries* (6th series, vi. 258), " is known as the Petyt Library, after the name of its founder, Mr. Sylvester Petyt (1640–1719), a native of the parish, and sometimes Principal of Barnard's Inn." The library, which at its best numbered more than eighteen hundred volumes, was contributed during the years 1708 to 1715, principally by Petyt, but also by Mr. Christopher Bateman, " of Pater Noster Row, Citizen, Stationer, and of the Common Councill of London, and one of the most Eminent Booksellers in England," † and Mr. William Busfeild, of the Inner Temple, London. The library has been

* See " The History and Antiquities of the Cathedral Church of Salisbury and the Abbey Church of Bath," 1723.

† From the inventory which accompanied his gift.

very badly used, many of the books having been either stolen or lost.

The library belonging to St. James's Church, Bury St. Edmunds, was formed in 1595, and from a catalogue entitled, "A copy of an Inventory indented of all the books which do remain in the library of the Parish Church of St. James, in Bury St. Edmunds, the 13th day of October, in the 41st year (1599) of the reign of our Sovereign Lady, Queen Elizabeth, to be delivered in charge to John Mann, and William Briggs, now Churchwardens, and by them to be accounted for to the said Parish," it appears that upwards of two hundred of the most valuable books were at that time in the library. But in 1847 the books, consisting of four very ancient manuscripts and four hundred and seventy-five printed books, were removed to the Guildhall, where they at present remain.*

At Gorton, Lancashire, there is a valuable church library ; † and that at St. Margaret's, King's Lynn, Norfolk, contains, in addition to some valuable books, "a curious little manuscript of the New Testament, very neatly written, a (mutilated) black-letter copy of the Sarum Missal, and many fine copies of the works of the Fathers, and also of the Reformers." ‡

In the rectory house at Whitchurch, in Shropshire, there is a valuable library, left as an heirloom by the request of Jane, Countess Dowager of Bridgewater ; who in 1707, having purchased from his executors the library of the Rev. Clement Sankey, Rector of Whitchurch for £305, left it for ever for the use of the rector for the time being. The number of the volumes was two thousand two hundred and fifty, among which are a fine copy of Walton's Polyglott Bible, some of

* *Notes and Queries*, 6th series, vii. 117.
† See Cheetham Society, 1855.
‡ See *Notes and Queries*, 1st series, viii. 93.

the Ancient Fathers, and other theological works. This collection was afterwards increased by a bequest from the Rev. Francis Henry, Earl of Bridgewater, founder of the Bridgewater Treatises, who by his will, dated in 1825, gave the whole of his own books in the rectory house at Whitchurch to be added to the others; and left also the sum of £150 to the rector to be invested in his name, and the dividends thereof expended by him, together with the money arising from the sale of the wines and liquors in the cellars at Whitchurch, in the purchase of printed books for the use of the rector, and that parish, for the time being.*

It should be added that the same noble earl presented to the rector of Middle, Shropshire, a small collection of books as the nucleus of a library there; and bequeathed by his will the sum of £800, to be applied, under the direction of the rector of Middle for the time being, for augmenting this library. He further left a sum of £150, to be invested in the name of the rector, and the dividends thereof expended by him in the purchase of books, in the same manner as he had done at Whitchurch.

The library at Bromham Church, near Bedford, was founded by Thomas, second Baron Trevor, of Bromham, and on a slab let into the outside wall on the eastern side of it, is the following inscription :—

> This small library was founded and freely given
> For the use of the Minister and the Parish of Bromham,
> By Thomas, Lord Trevor, in the year 1740.
>
> No book to be taken out without leave of the minister
> or lord of the manor.

The library at Totnes, which was established before the year 1656, contains folio editions of the works of SS. Chrysostom, Augustine, and Ambrose; but the books which

---

* *Notes and Queries,* 1st series, viii. 570.

are in the vestry-room are said to be perishing from damp. An amusing though incorrect notice of this library occurs in "A Graphic and Historical Sketch of the Antiquities of Totnes" by William Cotton (1850), 38: "I know not what the library contains. I believe nothing more than theological lumber. It is always locked up, and made no use of by those who keep it, and it is inaccessible to those who would wish to examine it. I was once there by accident and looked into some of the books, which were all on divinity."

In the preface to the "Life of Lord Keeper Guilford," by Roger North, it appears that Dudley, a younger daughter of Charles, and grand-daughter of Dudley Lord North, dying, "her library, consisting of a choice collection of oriental books, by the present Lord North and Grey, her only surviving brother, was given to the parochial library of Rougham, in Norfolk, where it now remains."

In Ballard's "Memoirs of British Ladies" (1775, 286), we are further told that this library was founded "for the use of the minister of Rougham, and, under certain regulations and restrictions, of the neighbouring clergy also, for ever." Among the choice collection of books there is, in particular, one very neat pocket Hebrew Bible, in 12mo, without points, with silver clasps to it, and bound in blue turkey leather, in a case of the same materials, which she constantly carried to church with her. In the first leaf of all the works that had been hers when they were deposited in that library, was a Latin inscription, setting forth the names of the late owner, or the donor of these books.

For many years a parochial library was deposited in the room over the south entrance of Beccles Church, Suffolk, but in the year 1840 it was handed over to the public library, after many of the books had apparently been lost; the room where they had been kept having been used as a repository "for discarded ecclesiastical appliances, and latterly, for charity blankets during summer." In the vicarage of St. Mary's, Marlborough, there is a library in excellent condition. The following extract from a terrier of the lands and profits of this vicarage, taken in the year 1698, records the origin of the library : " Item. The library of Mr. White, late rector of Pusey, in the county of Berks, given to Cornelius Yeate, and his successors, vicars of St. Marie's, in Marlborough, which Books are now in possession of the said Mr. Yeate till a more convenient place can be assigned for them, and the catalogue of the books is in the Chest of the Mayor and Magistrates."

At Basingstoke, in the room over the south porch, is a library chiefly of Puritan theology ; and a copy of the Latin Chronicle of Nuremberg may be seen in a small library adjoining to the church at Langley, Buckinghamshire, which library is, by the appointment of the donor, under the care of the inhabitants of an almshouse at the same place." *
About fifty folio volumes, chiefly Benedictine editions of the Fathers, are in the rectory house at Wendlebury, Oxford- shire, and at Halifax, Yorkshire, the books are kept in a room under the chancel.

Among further libraries of this kind may be noticed those at Brent Eleigh, Suffolk ; Tong, Shropshire ; Sutton Courtenay, Berkshire; St. Peter's-in-East, Oxford; St. Peter's, Maldon, Essex ; and at Gillingham, Dorset.

---

* *Gentleman's Magazine*, 1792, pt. ii. 1181. Mr. Edwards, in his "Memoirs of Libraries," says this library was given by Sir John Kederminster, in 1632, and is placed at the west end of the Keder- minster Chapel."

CHAPTER XXVI.

BOOKS IN CHAINS.

THE custom of fastening books to their shelves was formerly an important feature of many of our church libraries, interesting illustrations of which may still be seen in some country parishes. The practice of chaining single books in churches would seem to have originated in the injunctions given by Edward VI. to "the Clergie and the Laitie" in 1547, in which they are ordered "to provide within three moneths after the visitacion one boke of the whole Bible of largest volume in English, and within one twelvemonth after the saied visitacion, the Paraphrasis of Erasmus, the same to be sette uppe in some convenient place within the churche." This injunction was repeated by Queen Elizabeth in 1559, and "although nothing was mentioned about chains, it seems very probable that the churchwardens would, for their own sake, adopt that plan of protecting their property." *

In the churchwardens' accounts of the sixteenth century, mention is frequently made of the purchase of certain books in compliance with such injunctions. In those of Wigtoff, Lancashire, under 1549, we find these items :—

* W. Blades, "Books in Chains" (1890, 10), which contain a carefully arranged list of chained books.

"It. payd for the paraphrases of Erasmus, 7*s*.

"It. payd for a chayne for y* paraphrases, 4*d*." *

The churchwardens' accounts of Leverton, Lincolnshire, contain similar entries :—

1549. "It'm p'd for ij newe Salters, x*s*.

"It'm p'd for the second booke and tome of homelies, iiij*s*. viij*d*."

1570. "It'm p'd for half Mr. Juylles boke called the Appologie of Ingland, iiij*s*.

"It'm p'd for the cariage of the same boke iiij*d*."

Many entries of a similar character occur in the churchwardens' accounts of St. Margaret's, Westminster :—

1548. "Paid for the half-part of the Paraphrases of Erasmus, 5*s*."

1551. "Paid for a book of articles 2*s*."

1559. "Paid for a Bybyl and a Parafrawse 16*s*."

. 1566. "Paid for two books of Praises, set out by the Bishop of Canterbury, to be read Sundays, Wednesdays, and Fridays, 6*d*."

1581. "Paid for a book of the Abridgement of the Statutes to remain in the Church, 9*s*."

Archbishop Parker required Jewel's "Defence of the Apology" to be placed in parish churches, and Archbishop Bancroft prescribed that a copy of his collected works (edit. 1609, 1611) should be similarly placed, together with Erasmus's Paraphrase.†

An ancient desk and chain, preserved in the library at Lincoln, may, it has been suggested,‡ have been used for the Bible which Henry VIII., in 1537, ordered to be placed in all churches for the perusal of the common people, who

---

* Nichols' "Illustrations of Manners and Expenses," 1797.

† Ayres' "Life of Jewel," Parker Soc. edit. of his Works, vi. p. xxviii.

‡ "Traditions and Customs of Cathedrals," 122.

came, some to read and some to listen. Bale records in his narrative of Anne Askew's examination, how she said, " As I was in the minster reading upon the Bible, the priests resorted unto me by two and two." Erasmus saw in the nave of Canterbury " some books fixed to the pillars, among them the gospel of Nicodemus."

Out of two thousand volumes in the library of Hereford Cathedral, about fifteen hundred are chained, this, probably, being the largest chained collection in existence. But, notwithstanding this precaution, many books are missing, whilst others have suffered from the rough handling which chains necessitate. The method of chaining has thus been described : To attach the chain, a narrow strip of flat brass is passed round the left-hand board and rivetted to it in such a manner as to leave a loop in front of the edge of the board, wide enough to admit an iron ring, one inch and a quarter in diameter, to which one end of the chain is fastened. The book is placed on the shelf with the fore-edge turned outwards, and the other end of the chain is fastened to a second ring rather larger than the former, which plays along an iron bar. Here it was, in 1798, Southey read the legend of the " Old Woman of Berkeley," in Matthew of Westminster, which, as it was fastened to the top shelf by a very short chain, he was compelled to read standing on a number of books piled upon a lectern once used by the librarian.*

The library at Wells Cathedral was a chained one, many of the chains still hanging on the shelf, although there are no chained books. At Salisbury Cathedral the books were chained before printing was invented. One of the canons, Thomas Cyrcetur, who died in 1452, gave some books to the cathedral library, in two of which occurs the following memorandum, written in a fifteenth-century hand upon the

* " Traditions and Customs of Cathedrals," 123.

inside of the cover: "Cathenād⁹ in libraria noua eccłiæ ad dei honorē." *

Wimborne Minster has long been famous for its chained library, which consists of about two hundred and forty volumes. They are in a room over the vestry, and mostly belong to the seventeenth century. A catalogue of the books, made in 1725, exists in manuscript, under lock and key, and another made in 1863 by William George Wilkinson, was printed, a copy being kept in the library. The chains are made of rod-iron bent into a figure of eight, each chain is about three feet long, and has at one end a ring which runs along an iron rod, and permits the book being moved some little distance. The present shelving "is modern, and the old desks, which afforded a resting-place for the volumes when consulted, have unhappily disappeared. A glass case has quite recently been put over the table, so as to cover up a few selected books, with the result that the old-world look of this library has altogether taken flight, and a show-room appearance substituted. All the books having the chain fixed to the fore-edge are placed back just on the shelves, and have to be released by pulling the chains.†

In 1598 a chained library was presented to the church of Grantham, Lincolnshire, and placed in a room over the south porch. There are two hundred and sixty-eight books in the library, of which seventy-four have chains still attached to them. In Turton parish church, Lancashire, there is to be seen an oak case, with shelves and folding doors, fitted with two iron bars, to which are chained the books presented by Humphrey Chetham in 1651. In the year 1855, writes the late Mr. W. Blades, "the books were restored by re-binding as nearly as possible to their original

* "Books in Chains," 39.
† *The Antiquary* (November, 1890), 210.

state, the chains being fixed, cleaned, and the oak case
polished. It now stands in a conspicuous place near the
chancel." In 1651, also, Humphrey Chetham left by will
certain books to be chained in the parish of Bolton-in-the-
Moors, Lancashire, which are now deposited in the Grammar
School Library.

There are two hundred and ninety books in the vestry of
Cartmel Church, Lancashire, and amongst them a fine copy
(4to) of Spenser's "Faerie Queene," 1560. This library was
in existence in 1629, for in that year the churchwardens
ordered "That the books given unto the Church may bee
more convenientlie laid and chained, according to the directions of the donors." In the "Journal of the British
Archæological Association" (1883, ix. 394), is a list of the
books kept in the parish schoolroom of Chirbury, Shropshire, which number two hundred and seventeen, dating
from 1530 to 1684. At the present time the chains remain
on only a hundred and ten, although there are indications
that originally all the books were chained.

In many cases books were left by bequest to the church
library, on the distinct understanding that they were to be
chained. The following extract from the will of Sir Thomas
Lyttleton, dated 1481, quoted in "Testamenta Vetusta," is
an illustration of this practice : " I will and bequeth to the
Abbott and Convent of Hales-Oweyn a book of myn called
' Catholicon ' to theyr own use for ever, and another boke
of myn wherein is contaigned the ' Constitutions Provincial '
and ' De Gestis Romanorum ' and other treatis therein, which
I will be laid and bounded wyth an yron chayn in some
convenyent parte within the said Churche at my costes, so
that all priests and others may se and rede when it plesith
theym."

Humphrey Oldfield, by will, dated April 30, 1684, left
his theological books to be deposited in the chancel of

Salford Church, Lancashire, "with three pounds for the woodwork and chains that they might not be stolen. They became much dilapidated, and early in the present century many were rejected and cast out as waste paper. The remnant, seventy-two volumes, are now safely housed in the Salford Free Library." * From the same source we learn that " According to the will of Humphrey Chetham, dated 1651, two hundred and two books were placed and chained in the Jesus Chapel, Collegiate Church, Manchester. Their disappearance, says Mr. Chancellor Christie, is one of the most discreditable chapters in the history of the Wardens and Fellows. In 1830 the books were sent to the Chetham Hospital; but nothing appears to have remained, save the desks, a few old tattered books, and remnants of loose chains. Soon after they—about one hundred volumes— were sold to a bookseller of the town." †

In Rutter's "Somerset" (258), we are told that " Against the north wall of the old nave was a curious old tablet, dated 1669. At the top, was the portrait of Captain Samuel Sturmy, of this parish, who published a mathematical treatise, in folio, entitled ' The Mariner's or Artisan's Magazine,' a copy of which he gave to the parish, to be chained and locked in the desk, until any ingenious person should borrow it, leaving £3 as a security in the hands of trustees," etc.

Among further existing specimens of chained books to be seen, here and there, in different parishes, may be mentioned those at the fine old church of St. Andrew Undershaft, Leadenhall Street. This small library includes Fox's " Book of Martyrs," and Erasmus's " Paraphrase on the Gospels." Several of the books were re-bound some years ago, but one still has attached to it a chain about three feet long, with a swivel in the centre.

* " Books in Chains," 39.
† Ibid. 36..

At All Hallows' Church, Lombard Street, is a glass case containing "The first tome or volume of the Paraphrase of Erasmus upon the Newe Testament. Enpriented (*sic*) at London in Flete Strete at the signe of the Sunne by Edwarde Whitchurch the last daie of Januarie Anno Domini 1548." The second volume is dated "the ii daye of June, 1552." On the first volume is a rude chain of sixteen links attached to the top of the left-hand cover, and to the bottom of the right-hand cover of the second volume a similar chain is attached. The third volume is "The Holy Bible," 1613, the pages of which are wanting after Rev. xviii. 12. These three volumes were originally chained to a desk in St. Leonard's Church, Eastcheap. They were rescued in 1666 when the church was burnt, and the parish, after the Great Fire, having been united to St. Benet's, Gracechurch, they were deposited there until this church was destroyed in 1864, and united to All Hallows, when they were located in their present position.

At St. Clement's, Eastcheap, two books are preserved which were once in chains, these being "Pearson on the Creed" (presented by the author himself), and the other Comber's "Companion to the Temple."

An entry in the churchwardens' books of All Saints', Derby, of about the year 1525, gives a curious list of chained books—

"These be the bokes in our lady chapell tyed with chanes yᵗ were gyffen to Alhaloes Church in Derby—

"Imprimis, one boke called Summa Summarum.

"Item. A boke called Summa Raumundi.

"Item. Anoyer called pupilla oculi.

"Item. Anoyer called the Sexte.

"Item. A boke called Hugueyon.

"Item. A boke called Vitus patsum.

"Item. Anoyer boke called Pauls pistols.

"Item. A boke called Januensis Super Evangeliis dominicalibus.

"Item. A Grette Fortuose.

"Item. Anoyer boke called Legenda Aurea." *

In Breadsall Church stands an old double reading-desk, with folding lids that can be fastened by a simple padlock at the top. There are four volumes on each side, all secured with chains attached to the binding, viz. : Jewell's Works, 1609 ; Burnet's "Reformation," 2 vols., 1679 and 1681 ; Cave's "History of the Fathers of the Church," 1683 ; Cave's "Antiquitates Apostolicæ," 1684 ; Cave's "History of the Primitive Fathers," 1687 ; "A Collection of Cases to recover Dissenters," 1694 ; and Josephus's Works, translated by Roger L'Estrange, 1702.

At Egginton Church, in the same county, there is kept in the vestry a black-letter copy of Erasmus's "Paraphrase," the binding of which shows traces of having been chained ; and at Wolverley, Kidderminster, there is in the vestry "A Defence of Jewell's Apology," with a chain attached to it.

At Wootton Wawen Church, Warwickshire, there are on a desk several chained works ; and at Newport Pagnell, Buckinghamshire, there is "The Defence of the Apology of the Church of England," with chains attached to it ; and at Barcheston, Warwickshire, there is "Musculus, Wolfgangus. Common Places of Christian Religion" (4to, London, 1578), with chain attached, as also a copy, with chain, of Erasmus's "Paraphrase on the New Testament."

At Chelsea Church, Middlesex, there are five chained books, and amongst them "The Vinegar Bible" (1716–17) ; and at Leyland, Lancashire, there are four chained volumes, one being "A Preservative against Popery in Several Select Discourses upon the Principal heads of Controversy between

---

* "The Collegiate Church of All Saints', Derby," by Rev. Dr. Cox and Mr. W. H. St. John Hope.

Protestants and Papists," which was written by Edmund Gibson, successively Bishop of Lincoln and London.

At Christchurch, Hants, there is a library of about one hundred volumes, all chained; and a correspondent of *Notes and Queries*, writing some years ago of the Church of St. Mary the Virgin, Wiggenhall, says: "In this church may be seen fastened by chains to a wooden desk in the chancel: Fox's 'Book of Martyrs,' in 3 vols., all chained to the same staple; 'Book of Homilies'; The Holy Bible; 'The Works of Bishop Jewel,' in 1 vol. The title-pages are lost from all; in other respects they are in a fair state of preservation."

There are three chained books at St. Michael's Church, Southampton; and a black-letter Bible, with chain attached, may be seen at the parish church of Stratford-on-Avon. Some years ago a desk with Fox's "Martyrs" lying upon it was affixed to one of the pillars in the nave of Holy Trinity Church, Hull. At Cunmor, Oxfordshire, there is a chained Bible; and at Bromsgrove, Worcestershire, there is a copy of Bishop Jewel's "Defence of the Apology for the Church of England," 1609, chained to a desk in the church.

Connected with Great Yarmouth Church library is an ancient reading-desk—an ingenious contrivance to enable the reader to arrange the works of reference he may require, and then to bring each one before him by simply giving the desk a turn. It has six shelves with an aggregate length of 24¾ feet, and is so cleverly arranged that the shelves severally maintain one angle, while all else is revolving. There are about three hundred and twenty volumes in the library, and amongst them a copy of Cranmer's Bible; a Roman Missal; a manuscript roll, containing the Book of Esther, written in Hebrew, unpointed and illuminated; and Matthew Paris's "History of London" (1571).

But, as it has oftentimes been remarked at the meetings of our Archæological Associations, it is sad to think how many of these chained books have disappeared. A correspondent of *The Antiquary* (Nov., 1890, 211), says : " An American gentleman whom the writer met last summer at a house of European fame, confessed to having in his possession five old chained books that had come from English churches."

Occasionally we find books chained to tombs.   In the will of Sir Thomas Ormond, Earl of Ormond, dated July, 1515, in this direction: " I will my sawter boke, covered with whyte lether, and my name written with myne owne hande in th' ende of same shall be fixed with a cheyne of iron at my tombe, ther to remain for the service of God."   He directs his body to be buried in the church of St. Thomas Acon, upon the north side of the " high aulter, where the sepulture of Almighty God is used yerely to be sett on Good Friday," *i.e.* the Easter sepulchre.*

Wm. Lyndewood, Bishop of St. David's, author of the " Provinciale," by his will dated November 22, 1443, directed that a copy of his book should be kept chained in the upper part of St. Stephen's Chapel, at Westminster, where he was buried, to serve as a standard test to which all future editions should be referred—

" Item, volo quod liber meus quem compilavi super Constitutiones Provinciales reponatur in cathenis et inferratus sit ut salvo et secure custodiatur in superiori parte capelle Sci. Stephani predicte vel alias in vestiario ejusdem capelle ut quotiens opus fuerit pro veritate scripture primarie ejusdem pro correctione aliorum librorum ab eodem tractatu copiandorum recurri poterit dum sit opus." †

* *Notes and Queries*, 7th series, xi. 367.
† " Archæologia," xxiv. 419.

x

CHAPTER XXVII.

SOME CHURCH SUPERSTITIONS.

IT was not to be expected that the Church should have escaped the influence of the great witchcraft movement, which it has been justly said fills " one of the blackest pages in the annals of British superstition."   Hence, in many of our old parish documents, we find all kinds of references to this wretched delusion, for, it must be remembered, " witchcraft was formerly an offence against the Church, which was not directly punishable by the civil power before the change of religion in England." *   The first penal statute against witches was enacted in the year 1541, when the clergy were strictly enjoined by Cramner " to seek for any that use charms, sorcery, enchantments, witchcraft, soothsaying, or any like craft invented by the devil."

In 1563, some commotion was caused by Bishop Jewell's preaching before Elizabeth on the wickedness of disobeying the scripture precept to put witches to death ; † and later on Richard Baxter " positively exulted in the legal murder of a poor old crazed vicar, nearly eighty years of age, who, after being a minister for fifty years without reproach, was accused of dealings with the devil."   Before the poor old

---

* R. E. Chester Waters, " Parish Registers in England " (1887), 58.
† " Jewell's Sermons," Parker Society, p. 1028.

man was hanged, they extorted from him a confession which Baxter gravely reproduces "for the conversion of the sadducee and the infidel" :—

"Among the rest an old reading parson named Lewis, not far from Framlingham, was one that was hanged, who confessed that he had two imps, and that one was always putting him on doing mischief, and (being near the sea) as he saw a ship under sail, it moved him to send him to sink the ship, and he consented, and saw the ship sink before him."

But down to the close of the seventeenth century, persons were supposed to die from the effects of being bewitched. In the register of Holy Island, Northumberland, this entry occurs : "1691. William Clough, bewitched to death, buried 16 July." A similar entry occurs in the register of Coggeshall, Essex, " 1699, December 27. The widow Comon, that was counted a witch, was buried."

Even in the following century the belief in this superstition occasionally asserted itself with so much vigour that "many accused persons felt themselves compelled by public opinion to clear their characters by a voluntary submission to the accepted tests of guilt." * A curious case of this kind of ordeal occurred in 1759, when Susanna Hammokes, an elderly married woman, residing at Wingrove, near Ailesbury, was accused by a neighbour of bewitching her spinning-wheel so that she could not make it go round. Accordingly her husband insisted on vindicating his wife's character by a trial by the church Bible. On February 25th, 1759, Mrs. Hammokes was solemnly conducted to the parish church, where she was stripped of all her clothes to her shift, and weighed against the great parish Bible, in the presence of all her neighbours. The result was that, to the no small mortification of her accuser, she out-

* R. E. Chester Waters, "Parish Registers," 61.

weighed the Bible, and was triumphantly acquitted of the charge.*

Beneath the choir of St. German's Cathedral, in the Isle of Man, is a fine crypt. In this desolate dungeon, "reached by thirty steps—the dead above, the booming of the sullen sea below piercing through the crevices of the floor of rock —Eleanor, Duchess of Gloucester, was imprisoned on a charge of witchcraft." According to another piece of superstition, her spirit, after death, was supposed to take the form of a spectre hound, the Mauthe Dhoog of "Peveril of the Peak" which, Waldron tells us, was a "terror to profane soldiers." †

Occasionally horse-shoes are nailed on the doors of some Devonshire churches, as at Haccombe, Stampford Peverell, and elsewhere; these, no doubt, having been intended, in days gone by, to serve as charms against evil influences. Near the south doorway of Stanningfield Church, Suffolk, is the figure of a horse-shoe, said to have been placed there in order to prevent witches from entering the church.‡

In Tymm's "Family Topographer" a curious account is given of "The Witches' Cauldron," preserved in the vestry of Frensham Church, Surrey, hammered out of a single piece of copper, and "supposed to be a remain of the ancient parochial hospitality at a wedding of poor maids. Aubrey supposes it to have been used for the church ales. Tradition reports it to have been brought from Borough Hill, about a mile distant; where if any one went to borrow anything, he might have it a year or longer, provided he kept his word as to the return. On this hill lies a great stone, about six feet long; the party went to this stone, knocked at it, declared what was wanted, and when they

---

* "Annual Register" (1759), ii. 73.

† Mackenzie Walcott, "Traditions and Customs of Cathedrals," 224, 225.

‡ "Proceedings of the Suffolk Institute of Archæology," iii. 309.

WITCH'S CALDRON, FRENSHAM CHURCH.

Page 308.

would return it; and a voice answered appointing a time when they would find the article desired. This kettle, with the trivet, it is said, was so borrowed, but not returned at the time fixed; and though afterwards carried back, it would not be received, and all subsequent applications have been fruitless. Another tradition ascribes the place whence it was borrowed to have been the neighbouring cave, called Mother Ludlam's Hole."

According to Grose,* Mother Ludlam, when properly invoked, assisted the poor neighbours by lending culinary utensils, etc., the business being thus transacted: "The petitioners went to the cave at midnight, turned three times round, and thrice repeated aloud, 'Pray, Mother Ludlam, lend me such a thing (naming the utensil), and I will return it within two days.' On the next evening the requested moveable was found at the entrance of the cave. This intercourse being continued until once, a person not returning a large cauldron according to the stipulated time, Mother Ludlam was so irritated that she refused to take it back, when afterwards left at the cavern, and has never since accommodated any one with the most trifling loan."

The story adds that the cauldron was afterwards carried to Waverley Abbey, and after the dissolution of the monastery, deposited in Frensham Church. But Salmon, in his "Surrey" (139), says, "The great cauldron which lay in the vestry, beyond the memory of man, was no more brought thither from Waverley than, as report goes, by the fairies," and adds, "It need not raise any man's wonder for what use it was, there having been many very lately to be seen, as well as very large spits, which were given for entertainment of the parish at the wedding of poor maids."

In the parish register of Wells, A.D. 1583, is recorded the perishing on the coast of fourteen persons (seamen?) coming

* "Antiquities of England," v. 112.

from Spain, "whose deaths were brought to pass by the detestable working of an execrable witche of King's Lynn, whose name was Mother Gabley; by the boyling, or rather labouring of certayn eggs in a payle full of colde water; afterwards approved sufficientlie at the arraignement of the saide witche."

A curious instance of tracking a church robbery by magic has been handed down in the parish history of Holbeach. The story goes that in the reign of Henry VIII., the parish church of Holbeach was robbed of a considerable amount of its money and jewels, an event which led to the superstitious practice of trying to ascertain the culprits by means of magic. In an interesting paper by Mr. W. J. Hardy on the subject, which appeared in the *Antiquary* (Jan. 1890, 4–6), we are told how, in the general consternation which was occasioned by this serious loss, the leading men of the parish adopted what was then evidently the customary course at such times by resorting to "one Edmund Nasche, dwellyng at Cicestre towene," in order that they might learn from him "the namys of the theffez, and to know where the seyd money and goods was bycom." Although by trade Edmund Nasche was a "wheeler," it would seem he added largely to his income by practising "the craft of inchantement and wichecraft.".

· But, in order to make the discovery of the thief more certain, the good people of Holbeach secured the services of "a certain John Lamkyn of Holbeach," who in addition to practising witchcraft, was supposed to possess the additional accomplishment of sorcery.

Accordingly, a conference took place at Cirencester, and, "for a certeyn rewarde," Nasche and Lamkyn undertook to give the parishioners of Holbeach the names of the thieves, and the whereabouts of the money and church goods.

Their terms, it seems, were promptly accepted; for, it is recorded how then and there these soothsayers named one John Patriche as having been concerned in the robbery at Holbeach parish church. The party immediately returned home to Lincolnshire; and, despite the fact that John Patriche had hitherto borne a good character, they reported that " he was one of the thevez, and of those that shuld be the robberez of the seyd churche." The story was at once credited by the people of Holbeach, and poor John Patriche was "brought into infamy, slander, and owte of credenz, so that ' such as afore thys tyme haue been conversant with hym, withdraw his company, and such as afore this have been his frendes, have hym now in mistrust withowt cause, and withdraw their friendshippe and favour from hym to hys utter undoying in this worlde for ever.'" As a proof of his innocence, John Patriche sought for personal redress in the Star Chamber, at the same time urging that it was against the laws of God for any person to use and exercise "any inchauntement, sorcery, or wichecraft."

Only Lamkyn made answer to the charge preferred against him by Patriche, in reply to which he urged that at the time of the robbery, he had long been resident at Holbeach, gaining his livelihood by teaching and instructing children "in the sciens of gramer." He went on to say that soon after the robbery at the parish church, information was given to the churchwardens, and to the leading inhabitants of Holbeach, that Edmund Nasche was " an expert man in the knowleg of thynges stolen," by reason of which he, Lamkyn, at the request of the churchwardens, went to Cirencester and saw Nasche, and demanded "of hym what knowlege he cowde tell of the sayd robbery, shewyng to him a payer of gloves of lether which were founde in the revestry of the saide churche immedeately after the said robbery was knowen to be done." He denied the possession of any supernatural power, but admitted that he had taken every possible trouble to gain such information as might lead to the discovery of the robbery.

But Lamkyn, adds Mr. Hardy, "makes no direct statement of opinion one way or the other as to Patriche's guilt; his object was simply to clear himself of the charge of being a practitioner of magic, or one who would avail himself of the aid of the black arts as a means of ascertaining the truth on an obscure point, and thus, in detecting crime, commit it."

At Ripon Cathedral, one of the most interesting sights is St. Wilfrid's needle, which is said by Camden to have been used as an ordeal for women accused of unchastity. If they could not pass through it they were considered guilty. Many years ago, a correspondent of the *Gentleman's Magazine* tells us he was once witness to an amusing ordeal of this kind. "While I was making my sketches," he writes, "one of the gentlemen of the party led a young lady to the ominous 'needle,' and entreated her to try the touchstone of female honour. After some preparatory excuses the blushing fair put her head into the opening, her friend being in the choir avenue on the other side of the opening, in order to assist her efforts; then her body; at last she literally forced her whole body through the 'needle,' to the inexpressible joy of him who proposed the trial, and to the great mirth of the bystanders." *

According to the late Prebendary Mackenzie Walcott,† "like similar preparations in tombs at St. Didier and St. Menoux," the so-called St. Wilfrid's needle, "was an imitation of the Basilican transenna." He considers it probably served as a place for poor palsied folk to creep through in

* See Murray's "Handbook to the Northern Cathedrals" (1869), pt. i. 170, 171.
. † "Traditions and Customs of Cathedrals," 224.

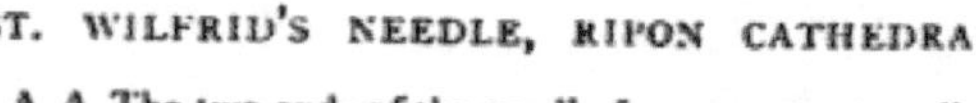

ST. WILFRID'S NEEDLE, RIPON CATHEDRAL.   *Page* 312.

A A The two ends of the needle from passage to cell.

the expectation of being healed. A touchstone resembling the ordeal of the needle at Ripon existed in Boxley Church, Kent, in the shape of a small figure of St. Rumbald, which only those could lift who had never sinned in thought or in deed.

Speaking of the cures of disease, we may note that a special virtue has long been supposed to reside in "Sacrament money"—a form of superstition which, with some variation, prevails more or less throughout the country. In the west of England it is customary to collect a certain number of pennies, and then to change them into one silver piece from the offertory, which is made into a ring and worn. Mrs. Latham, in her "West Sussex Superstitions" ("Folklore Record," i. 39), says that sometimes one may observe a silver ring on the wedding-ring finger of a single woman. Such rings are worn for the cure of fits, and are made out of sixpences which have been begged from six young bachelors. The same superstition largely prevails in the northern counties, and on one occasion the vicar of Danby, near Whitby, was asked for half a crown, after Holy Communion, by a farmer, the thirty pence being proffered in exchange.[*]

A similar belief attaches to Sacramental wine in Sussex ; and Mrs. Latham relates how a farmer's daughter one day called with a message from her mother to ask whether she could procure some Sacramental wine. "For," said the girl, "mother thinks, as she has tried everything else that she can hear of, and it has done the baby no good, that a little of the Sacramental wine might save it."

[*] Henderson's "Folklore of Northern Counties," (1879), 146.

CHAPTER XXVIII.

HATS WORN IN CHURCH, ETC.

It is notorious that much irreverence in divine service prevailed during the latter part of the sixteenth and the beginning of the seventeenth centuries. One custom which prevailed, more or less, at this period, was that of men wearing hats in church during sermon time; frequent allusions to which practice are to be met with in the literature of that day.

In Strype's "Life of Bishop Parker," is a copy of a representation made to Queen Elizabeth concerning the irregular manner in which the service was conducted, and proceeds to state that "some minister in a surplice, others without, some with a square cap, some with a round cap, some with a hat," etc.

Cardinal Pole, in 1556, ordered veiling of bonnets and bending knees in Hereford Cathedral, when the words were sung, "Et incarnatus ex spiritu," and "Et Homo factus est." A picture of Bishop Coe's funeral, in 1581, showed the large congregation sitting in the choir of Ely, to hear the sermon, "having their bonnets on."

In Foxe's "Acts and Monuments," is an illustration representing Dr. Cole preaching at St. Mary's, Oxford. He wears an ordinary out-door cap, and so do many of his clerical hearers.

When Queen Elizabeth visited Cambridge in 1564, the preacher, on Sunday morning, put off his cap out of respect to the Queen ; but when he had advanced some way in his sermon, " she sent the Lord Hunsdon to will him to put on his cap, which he did to the end."

As showing that King James I. and his Court sat during sermon time with their hats on, Mr. B. Nicholson quotes from Ar. Wilson's " Life of King James " (1653), pp. 151, 152 ; and says it is certain that "the Lord Treasurer would not have acted so differently from his master, in a point of religious etiquette in his master's presence : "—" An. Christ, 1620. For about this time one of his own chaplains, preaching before him at Greenwich, took the text 4 Matt. 8 —so that he concluded the devil to be a great monarch, and no doubt he had his Vice-Royes, Councill of State, Treasurers, Secretaries [etc.], . . . he gives a character of every particular officer, who were fit to be the devil's servants, running through the body of the Court, . . . and when he came to describe the devil's treasurers, exactions, and gripings, he fixed his eye upon Cranfield, then Lord Treasurer, and pointing at him with his hand, said with an emphasis, that man (reiterating it), that man makes himself rich, and his master poor, he is a fit treasurer for the devil. This the author heard, and saw, whilst Cranfield sat with his hat pulled down over his eyes, ashamed to look up; the King who sat just over him, smiling at the quaint satyre so handsomely coloured over."

The custom was persisted in by the Puritans as late as the middle of the seventeenth century, as appears by a letter written from the Episcopal Palace, at Gloucester, in 1639, by Jno. Allibond, to Dr. Heylin, the friend of Laud, and one of the King's chaplains, in which, speaking of Alderman Pury, of Gloucester, who was a candidate for the representation of that city, he says, " Old Pury, sometime a weaver, now an attorney, whom I think nothing has so much indeered as his irreverence in God's House, sitting covered when all the rest sit bare." This letter was published in the *Gloucester Journal,* January, 1874, and has since appeared in the calendar of State Papers (domestic).

"If one passing through a church shall put off his hat, there is a giddy and malignant race of people (for indeed they are the true malignants), who will give out that he is running post to Rome " ("Howell's Familiar Letters," *temp.* Charles I.).

In a sermon preached by James Rowlanson, B.D., chaplain to the king, at the consecration of Pear-tree Church, Southampton, in the year 1620, the following passage occurs :—

" How unmannerly are a many that carry themselves with more lowlinesse in a Gentleman's Hall (for there they will uncouer) then in the House of God ? A French fashion, indeed, but very ill-fauored, though it be naturalized amongst the most, and growne English euen in our greatest congregations, where the apprentice that stands bare-headed all the weeke long in his master's shop, must need have his hat on in the church. Grant it an indulgence to the aged and the weake, who yet to testifie reuerence might put off hats, and to confesse a weaknesse, might keep heads warme enough with some other fit and graue covering. But what priuiledge, but pride and wantonnesse can be alledged for the strong and healthfull in times and places of no extremity of cold ? I may say of it, as Tacitus speaks of astrologie, *semper vetabitur, semper retinebitur :* there is little hope of redresse, yet still it desueres (mee thinkes) to bee rebuked."

On one occasion when Dr. Donne was preaching in the ordinary course at St. Dunstan's Church, he thus referred to this custom—

" And is not this the King of kings' house ? or have

they seen the king in his own house use that liberty to cover himself in his ordinary manner of covering at any part of divine service?   Every preacher will look, **and justly,** to have the congregation uncovered at the reading **of his text;** and **is not** the reading of the lesson, at **time** of prayer, the same word of the same God, to be received with the same reverence?   The service of God is one entire thing; and though we celebrate some parts with more or less reverence, some kneeling, some standing, yet if we afford it no reverence, we make that no part of God's service.   And therefore **I** must humbly entreat them, who make **this** choir the place of their devotion, to testify their devotion by more outward **reverence** there," etc.*

Edmund Rossingham, writing to Edward, Viscount **Conway, in** a letter dated June **8,** 1640, referring to the Canons, **and** Articles of Visitation, says—

" There is another Article to inquire who keep on their **hats** during divine service and in sermon-time, for the keeping off of hats has been much urged in many churches **in** and about the city.   On Sunday, last week, the parson of St. Giles-in-the-Fields took so great scandal at two earls that were in the Church, for putting on their hats in sermon-time, that he went out of the Church [in great] discontent. One of these earls taking notice afterwards to his Grace (the archbishop) **by way** of offence at the parson, his **Grace** replied in the **Doctor's** behalf that he had been very diligent **for a long** time **to** bring his parishioners **to a decency of** behaviour in the Church."

One of the Articles of inquiry **at** Bishop Hackett's **second** triennial visitation in 1668, is " Do your parishioners behave reverently **in** Church, men and youths with their hats off?" Similarly, Bishop Cosin, in his " Primary Visitation of Durham Cathedral, 1662," speaks of " some who come into the

* **Donne, sermon** preached at S. Dunstan's, **ed.** Alford, v. **354.**

quire in their furre and nightgowns, and sit with their hats on their heads at the reading of the lessons." In 1689 King William gave great offence because he would wear his hat in church, and if he ever uncovered it during the liturgy, always resumed when the sermon began.*

But, as Mr. T. H. Overton remarks in his "Life in the English Church, 1660–1714," "In dealing with the subject (that of irreverent behaviour in church generally) we must be upon our guard against applying the standard of the nineteenth century to the habits of the seventeenth. For instance, it seems very sad to think that the restorers of Church order had to wage incessant war against the habit of wearing the hat during divine service, or at any rate during parts of it. But it must be borne in mind that the hat was not infrequently worn indoors during the seventeenth century." Pepys evidently considered it an unnecessary piece of strictness to insist on the bare head in church, for he tells us contemptuously how he heard a "simple fellow [in a sermon] exclaiming against men's wearing their hats in Church."

The popular usage of "smelling the hat" would appear to be somewhat old. The term is derived from a little boy in *Punch* asking his father why gentlemen "smelled their hats on going into church." The following extracts are interesting as illustrating this practice:—

"And after a good while I grew so infirm, through this continual pain, that it was all I could do, when Assumption Day came, to venture to go and sit down and hear a sermon. And as I put my hat before my eyes, I fell into a swoon from very weakness," etc.†

---

* *Notes and Queries*, 7th series, i. 458.

† From MS. of Rulman Merswin, one of the "Friends of God," or Mystics of the Fourteenth Century, extracted from introductory notice to "John Tauler's Life and Sermons," edited by Susanna Winkworth (1857). 148.

And again : " When the master [John Tauler] came and saw that there was such a multitude, he went up into a pulpit in a high place, that they might hear him all the better. Then he held his hood before his eyes, and said, ' O merciful Eternal God.' " *

The late Prebendary Mackenzie Walcott says this fashion came in from the hall when kneeling went out in church. Gratiano, in the " Merchant of Venice " (ii. 2)—

> " [I will]
> Wear prayer-books in my pocket, look demurely ;
> Nay more, while grace is saying, hood mine eyes
> Thus with my hat, and sigh, and say amen."

According to a correspondent of *Notes and Queries* (7th series, i. 113), the following passage from the regulations issued by the Vice-Chancellor of Cambridge previous to the visit of James I., in the year 1615, seems to show that smoking in church was at that time not unknown in England :—

" That noe Graduate, Scholler, or Student of this Universitie, presume to resort to any inn, taverne, ale-howse, or tobacco-shop, at any time during the aboade of his majestie here ; nor do presume to take tobacco in St. Marie's Church, or in Trinity Colledge Hall, uppon payne of finall expellinge the Universitie." † But it has been suggested by another correspondent that the term " take tobacco," more probably referred to snuffing rather than to smoking. " Not only," it is added, " was the latter operation usually at that period designated ' drinking tobacco,' but snuffing was especially in favour with ' the faculty,' and recommended by them as the best preventive and cure for cold in the head." On the other hand, it has been urged that King James,

---

* Ibid:, p. 49. See *Notes and Queries*, 6th series, i. 374.
† Nichol's " Progresses of King James the First " (1828), iii. 44.

in his " Counterblaste to Tobacco," constantly speaks of " taking tobacco " in the sense of smoking, and not of snuffing. The subjoined passage has been adduced as an example of the term " taking tobacco " being applied to smoking—

" Surely Smoke becomes a kitchin far better than a dining-chamber, and yet it makes a kitchin also oftentimes in the inward parts of men, soiling and infecting them, with an unctious and oily kind of soote, as hath been found in some great tobacco takers, that after their deaths were opened " (Arber's reprint, 111).

Among the strange stories told of Blackburn, Archbishop of York, may be quoted the following relating to his smoking in church. It is contained in a letter written by John Disney, Rector of Swindon, Lincolnshire, to James Granger, dated Dec. 13th, 1773 :—

" The anecdote which you mention is, I believe, unquestionably true. The affair happened in St. Mary's Church, in Nottingham, when Archbishop Blackburn (of York) was there on a visitation. The archbishop had ordered some of the apparitors, or other attendants, to bring him pipes and tobacco, and some liquor into the vestry for his refreshment after the fatigue of confirmation. And this coming to Mr. Disney's ears, he forbad their being brought thither, and with a becoming spirit remonstrated with the archbishop upon the impropriety of his conduct, at the same time telling his Grace, that his vestry should not be converted into a smoking-room." *

A similar story is told of Dr. Parr, who smoked in the vestry at Hatton, before his sermon, while the congregation

---

* " Letters between the Rev. James Granger, M.A., and many of the most Eminent Literary Men of his Time," edited by J. P. Malcolm, p. 198. The Mr. Disney mentioned was grandfather of the writer of the letter.

were singing. For, as the doctor justly remarked, "My people like long hymns, but I prefer a long clay."

Sir Walter Scott, in his " Heart of Midlothian " (chap. xlii.), has given an amusing instance of smoking in church, the smoker being one Duncan, of Knockdunder, a person of some local importance :—

" So soon as the congregation were seated after prayers, and the clergyman had read his text, the gracious Duncan, after rummaging the leathern purse which hung in front of his petticoat, produced a short tobacco pipe made of iron, and observed almost aloud, ' I hae forgotten my spleuchan. Lachlan, gang down to the Clachan, and bring me up a pennyworth of twist.'

" Six arms, the nearest within reach, presented, with an obedient start, as many tobacco-pouches to the man of office. He made choice of one with a nod of acknow-ledgment, filled his pipe, lighted it with the assistance of his pistol-flint, and smoked with infinite composure during the whole time of the sermon. At the end of the discourse he knocked the ashes out of his pipe, replaced it in its sporran, returned the tobacco-pouch or spleuchan to its owner, and joined in the prayer with decency and attention."

CHAPTER XXIX.

CHURCH-ALES AND RUSH-BEARINGS.

An important festival in many of our old country parishes,
was the Church-ale, which, originally instituted in honour
of the church saint was, in after years, frequently kept up
for the purpose of contributing towards the repairs of the
church. Existing at a period prior to the establishment of
church-rates, the contributions levied at this season were a
real necessity if the fabric of the church was to be kept in
proper order. On such an occasion, it was the business of
the churchwardens to have brewed a considerable quantity
of strong ale, a custom which, it is said, led "to a great
pecuniary advantage, for the rich thought it a meritorious
duty, besides paying for their ale, to offer largely to the
church fund." In Francis Beaumont's "Exaltation of Ale,"
we find this allusion to the church-ale—

> "The churches much owe, as we all do know,
>   For when they be drooping and ready to fall,
>   By a Whitsun or Church-ale up again they shall go
>   And owe their repairing to a pot of good ale."

But, like other festival gatherings, the church-ale, in
course of time, was abused; and it is recorded how actually
in the body of the church, when the people were assembled
together for devotion, they not only turned their attention

to diversions, but even introduced drinking. Another cause of complaint arose from the church-ale being occasionally celebrated on Sunday; and in a sermon preached by one William Kethe, at Blandford Forum, in 1570, this passage occurs: "Which holy day, the multitude call their revelyng day, which day is spent in bull-beatings, beau-beatings, dicyng, cardyng, daunsynges, drunkenness, etc." Stubbs, in his "Anatomie of Abuses" (1585), is somewhat severe in his strictures on the church-ale as observed in his day, and says, "In this kind of practice they continue six weeks—a quarter of a year—yea, half a year together. That money, they say, is to repair their churches and chapels with, to buy books for service, cups for the celebration of the Sacrament, and other such necessaries. And they maintain their extraordinary charges in their parish besides."

There seem to have been some ground for these remarks of Stubbs, for, in some parishes, several of these ales were held in the course of the year, sometimes one or more parishes agreeing to keep a certain number of them. It is related, for instance, how "the parishioners of Elvaston and Okebrook, in Derbyshire, agree jointly to brew four ales betwixt this (the time of the contract) and the feast of St. John Baptist next coming; and that every inhabitant of the said town of Okebrook shall be at the several ales; and every husband and his wife shall pay twopence, and every cottager one penny; and all the inhabitants of Elvaston shall have and receive all the profits and advantages coming of the said ales, to the use and behoof of the said Church of Elvaston."

By the Canons of 1683 it was enacted that "the Churchwardens or questmen and their assistants shall suffer no plays, feasts, banquets, supper, Church-ale drinkings . . . in the Church, Chapel, or Churchyard."

How closely the festivities of the church-ale were associated with the sacred fabric itself may be gathered from the fact that several pieces of sculpture in Cirencester Church commemorate these old merry-makings. In the church porch of Chalk Church, Kent, have been preserved some grotesque figures, illustrating the festive scenes as witnessed at a church-ale. On the beam of a screen in the church of Thorpe-le-Soken, near Walton-on-the-Naze, is the following inscription, in raised Gothic letters, on a scroll held by two angels: " This cost is the bachelors, made by ales theen he ther med." The date of the screen is, as far as can be ascertained, about the year 1480.*

But the memorials of this kind that have come down to us of the church-ale are scanty. " I have," writes Mr. Edward Peacock, in " The Archæological Journal" (1883, xl. 14), " met with two—one a piece of stained glass, and the other sculpture, which I think are representations of church-ales. Where the glass now is I know not. There is an engraving of it in *The Gentleman's Magazine* (1793, i. 397). It is a small roundel, seemingly of late fifteenth or early sixteenth century work. In the centre stands a gigantic work—the demon of the feast—and around him are human figures—two women, a priest, a soldier, and a blind crippled beggar with his dog, all of whom seem to be in various stages of intoxication ; in the upper part of the picture are two large tubs and sundry ale pots. The engraving is rude and probably by no means accurate.

" The sculpture is on two of the bench ends in the church of Stevington, Bedfordshire. The one represents a man lying down hopelessly drunk, and the other two men crouched down drinking out of a large bowl which they hold between them. From the Certificate of Chantries it seems that there was in this parish, before the Reformation, certain lands

* *Notes and Queries*, 6th series, x. 244. See "Journal of Archæological Association," x. 183.

given for the purpose of drinking there. Their rent in the second year of Edward VI. was four shillings and eightpence."

"Drinking Bush Hill," adds Mr. Peacock, "was the name of a place on the western side of the parish. When the people were in the habit of beating the bounds, a hole was dug on this spot, and certain men used to jump into it, and drink as much as they could. Whether this practice was a genuine relic of old heathendom, or whether it was a kind of symbolic representation of the church-ale kept up after the feast itself had fallen into disuse, it is impossible to say."

In addition to the feasting and merrymaking at the church-ale, it appears that certain amusements were provided for the recreation of the visitors. Hutchins, in his " History of Northumberland," tells us that in the northern counties these festivals were held under tents and booths erected in the churchyard. Interludes were performed, " being a species of theatrical performance, consisting of a rehearsal of some passage in Holy Scripture personated by actors." Miss Baker, in her " Glossary of Northamptonshire Words " (1854), describing a Whitsun or church-ale early in the present century in a barn at King's Sutton, says that it was specially fitted up for the occasion. The lord, as the principal, carried a mace made of silk, finely plaited with ribbons, and filled with spices and perfumes for such of the company as desired it. Six morris-dancers were among the performers. From the same source we learn that at an ale kept at Greatworth, in the year 1785, all those who misconducted themselves were obliged to ride a wooden horse; " and if still more unruly were put in the stocks which was termed being my lord's organist." In Coates' " History of Reading," under the churchwardens' accounts of St. Mary's Church, we find this entry : " Payed to the Morrys dansers and the mynstrelles mete and drink at Whysontide, iij*s*. iiij*d*."

To defray the expenses of the church-ale, persons often-

times left in their wills special bequests for this purpose.
Sir Richard Worsley, in his " History of the Isle of Wight,"
speaking of the parish of Whitwell, tells us that there is a
lease in the parish chest, dated 1574, "of a house called
the Church-house, held by the inhabitants of Whitwell,
parishioners of Gatcombe, of the lord of the manor, and
demised by them to John Brode," in which is contained the
following proviso : " Provided always, that if the quarter
shall need at any time to make a quarter-ale, or church-ale,
for the maintenance of the Chapel, that it shall be lawful
for them to have the use of the said house, with all the
rooms both above and beneath, during their ale."

Edwards, in his " Old English Customs and Charities,"
mentions "an ancient customary donation of a quantity of
malt made annually at Whitsuntide by the proprietors of
Kempton mill, near the parish.   The malt was always
delivered to the overseers of the parish for the time being,
and brewed by them into ale, which was distributed among
all the poor inhabitants on Whit Tuesday."

"Something of the nature of a church-ale," says Mr.
Peacock,* "seems to have survived at Bicester till the year
1816, and at Kirton, in Lindsey, existed until within my
own memory.   The church-house had long been swept
away, and no money for the fabric was raised by the ale,
but the salary of the sexton was in part paid by a feast given
at his house, to which all persons could go who were willing
to pay for what they consumed."

Speaking of the church-house, this, Mr. Peacock adds,
" seems to have almost entirely passed away.   As far as I
have been able to ascertain, not a single undoubted specimen
has been spared to us.   Though it is not improbable that
the half-timbered building attached to the west end of the
church at Langdon, in Essex, and now called the Priest

* " The Archæological Journal," xl. 14.

House is really one of these. There is hardly an old Churchwardens' account-book that does not contain some reference to a building of this kind. They continued to be used for church purposes long after the Reformation. The example at All Saints', Derby, stood in the churchyard, and was in existence in 1747. The church-house at Tetbury, Gloucestershire, was sold a few years ago for the purpose of raising money for the repair of the church. At Ampthill there is still remaining—adjoining the churchyard on the south—a half-timbered cottage which may have been one of these structures, but its identification is very uncertain."

Aubrey, in his introduction to the " Natural History of Wiltshire," tells us that there were no rates for the poor in his grandfather's days, the church-ale of Whitsuntide doing the business. According to his account, "in every parish was a church-house to which belonged spits, crooks, and other utensils for dressing provisions. Here the house-keepers met. The young people were there too, and had dancing, bowling, etc."

Carew, in his "Survey of Cornwall," thus describes the church-ale and its festivities: "For the church-ale the young men of the parish are yearly chosen by their last foregoers to be wardens, who make collections among the parishioners by whatsoever provision it pleaseth them voluntarily to bestow. This they employ in brewing and baking against Whitsuntide, upon which holidays the neighbours meet at the Church-House, and there merrily feed on their own victuals. When the feast is ended the wardens yield in their accounts to the parishioners, and such money as exceedeth the disbursement is laid to defray any extraordinary charges arising in the parish."

It is worthy of note that at Horton, near Slough, Buckinghamshire, a public-house, known by the sign of the Five Bells, with a small garden attached to it, is let by the churchwardens, and the income derived therefrom is devoted to the repair of the church and churchyard. The title by which the property is held is unknown; but it is probable, writes Mr. Peacock, that the Five Bells "stands on the site of the old church-house, and that there are no deeds belonging to it because it has come down from churchwarden to churchwarden from a very early time." *

Closely allied with the church-ale was the rush-bearing, a festival which was attended with no small amount of merry-making and rejoicing. In the "Sussex Archæological Collections" (1857, lx.), the Rev. G. Mills Cooper thus writes : "Though few are ignorant of this ancient custom, it may not perhaps be so generally known that the strewing of churches grew into a religious festival, dressed up in all that picturesque circumstance whereof the old Church knew well how to array its ritual. Remains of it linger to this day in remote parts of England. In Westmoreland, Lancashire, and districts of Yorkshire, there is still celebrated between haymaking and harvest, a village fête called the rush-bearing. Young women, dressed in white, and carrying garlands of flowers and rushes, walk in procession to the parish church, accompanied by a crowd of rustics, with flags flying and music playing. There they suspend their floral chaplets on the chancel rails, and the day is concluded with a simple feast. The neighbourhood of Ambleside was one of the chief strongholds of this popular practice. Up to the passing of the Municipal Reform Act, the town clerk of Norwich was accustomed to pay to the subsacrist of the cathedral an annual guinea for strewing the floor of the cathedral with rushes on the Mayor's Day, from the western door to the entrance into the choir."

A correspondent of *Notes and Queries* (5th series, iv. 163), in an account of the rush-bearing at Grasmere, says

* "The Archæological Journal," lx. 9.

the following notice was posted up at one of the entrances of the churchyard :—

"The rush-bearing notices for 1875. Mr. Dawson will give his gratuities of 6*d.* only to such bearers who are attending the parochial day, infant, and Sunday schools during the present school quarter. Rush-bearing standards for dressing by ladies will be received at the school, only between the hours of 4 and 6 on Thursday next, after which no standard will be taken. The number of standards so received for dressing at the school will be limited to fifty—that is, to the fifty first brought to the school; all beyond this number will be refused, as the ladies cannot undertake a larger number.

"All rush-bearings must be on the churchyard wall not later than six o'clock on Saturday, the 17th inst.—July 10, 1875."

The following hymn has been in use for many years in Grasmere Church, at the rush-bearing festival :—

HYMN FOR THE RUSH-BEARERS.

"Our fathers to the house of God,
    As yet a building rude,
Bore offerings from the flowery sod
    And fragrant rushes strew'd—

"May we, their children, ne'er forget
    The pious lesson given,
But honour still, together meet,
    The Lord of earth and heaven.

"Sing we the good Creator's praise,
    Who gives us sun and showers
To cheer our hearts with fruitful days
    And deck our world with flowers.

"These, of the great Redeemer's grace,
    Bright emblems here are seen ;
He makes to smile the desert place
    With flowers and rushes green.

> "All glory to the Father be,
>   All glory to the Son,
>   All glory, Holy Ghost, to Thee,
>   While endless ages run.   Amen."

Rushes were strewn in the choir of Canterbury in 1655. And the ancient custom of strewing the choir of Bristol with sweet-smelling herbs is still observed when the mayor visits the cathedral in state.[*]

At Runcorn and Warburton, Cheshire, the rush-bearing was carried out in an imposing manner. Another correspondent of *Notes and Queries*, describing one of these scenes some years ago, thus wrote : "A large quantity of rushes—sometimes a cart-load—is collected, and being bound on the cart, are cut evenly at each end, and on Saturday evening a number of men sit on the top of the rushes, holding garlands of artificial flowers, etc. The cart is drawn round the parish by three or four spirited horses, decked with ribbons, the collars being surrounded with small bells. It is attended by morris-dancers fantastically dressed; there are men in women's clothes, one of whom, with his face blackened, has a belt with a large bell attached round his waist, and carries a ladle to collect money from the spectators. The party stop and dance at the public-house on their way to the parish church, where the rushes are deposited, and the garlands are hung up to remain till the next year."

Many curious bequests in years past were made for the strewing of the church with rushes. According to Edwards,[†] the parish of Clee, Lincolnshire, possesses "a right of cutting rushes from a piece of land called ' Bescars ' for the purpose of strewing the floor every Trinity Sunday. A small quantity of grass is annually cut to preserve this right."

---

[*] "Traditions and Customs of Cathedrals," 132.
[†] "Old English Custom and Charities," 216–219.

At Wingrave, Buckinghamshire, a piece of land was left to furnish rushes for the church on the feast Sunday; and, in accordance with an old bequest, it has been customary for the mayor to go to St. Mary Redcliffe Church, Bristol, on Whitsunday, when the church is strewn with rushes.

Occasionally, instead of rushes, hay was used for strewing the church floor. Bridges, in his "Northamptonshire," speaks of a custom observed at Middleton-Cheney, of strewing the church "in summer with hay gathered from six or seven swaths in Ash Meadow." At Old Weston, Huntingdonshire, "a piece of land belongs by custom to the parish clerk for the time being, subject to the condition of the land being mown immediately before Weston feast in July, and the cutting thereof being strewed on the church floor, previously to divine service on the feast Sunday, and continuing there during divine service." A close, called the "Church Acre," was set out on the inclosure of Glenfield, Leicestershire, "in lieu of lands in the open fields, the rent of which has always been paid to the clerk of the parish, as a part of his salary. In respect of this land the clerk is obliged to strew the church with new hay on the first Sunday after the 5th July, and for this purpose he is allowed to take a cut of hay from off the land."

In the parish account books of Hailsham, Sussex, charges occur for strewing the church floor with straw or rushes, according to the season of the year; and in the books of the City of Norwich we find similar entries for pea-straw used for such strewing.

Fennel was strewn round the shrine of St. Etheldreda at Ely, and at the coronation of George III. the King's herb-woman and six maids strewed the abbey with sweet herbs.[*]

In the churchwardens' accounts of St. Mary-at-Hill, London, these items are given:—

* "Traditions and Customs of Cathedrals," 132.

"1493.   For 3 Burdens of rushes for yᵉ new pews 3*d.*

"1504.   Paid for 2 Berden Rysshes for the strewing the newe pewes, 3*d.*"

In the parish register of Kirkham, Lancashire, are entries to this effect: "1604.   Rushes to strew the church cost this year 9*s.* 6*d.*"   Under 1631: "Paid for carrying the rushes out of the church in the sickness time 5*s.*"   But, after 1634, disbursements for rushes never appear in the Kirkham register when the church was flagged for the first time.

CHAPTER XXX.

CAREFULLY preserved in many of our parish churches are sundry antiquarian curiosities, some of which have a legendary and historical interest. Among the treasures preserved at York Cathedral is the celebrated so-called horn of Ulphus, which is really a portion of the tusk of an elephant, about three feet long. It dates from a period shortly before the Conquest, when Ulph, the son of Thorald, the lord of great part of eastern Yorkshire, laid this horn on the altar in token that he bestowed certain lands on the Church of St. Peter. This famous horn is encircled about the mouth by a belt of carving, representing griffins, a unicorn, a lion devouring a doe, and dogs wearing collars. The griffins stand on either side of a tree, which at once recalls the conventional sacred tree of Assyrian sculpture.

At the time of the Commonwealth this horn disappeared, but it afterwards came into the hands of Lord Henry Fairfax, who restored it in 1675 to the Minster authorities. Its gold ornaments had been removed, but a brass silver-gilt chain and bands were attached to it by the chapter. The legend connected with this horn tells how "a certain Ulphus, son of Thoraldi, was king, or sub-king, of the western portion of Deira, in the days when the Danes ruled their Saxon brethren in these parts. Of Ulphus's four sons, Adelbert, the eldest, was slain in battle, and the others, even in their father's lifetime, quarrelled and strove about the succession to his estates and kingdom. Wearied by their strife, the aged chieftain at last determined on a step that would end their disputes ; and that was to give the whole of his dominions to the Church. Accordingly he rode to York, taking with him his largest drinking-horn, and, filling it with wine, he went upon his knees before the high altar, there drank off the contents, and then placed the horn upon the altar, to be held by the Church as title, in all time, to all his lands, tenements, and wealth, thus bestowed upon God and St. Peter." *

Henry II. "gave a horn of ivory containing the liberties of Inglewood Forest at Carlisle, where Ray saw preserved two elephant's teeth fastened in a bone like a scalp, which they call the horns of the altar." Those now in the upper sacristy look like the horns of a small deer, but Brane says, "two great unicorns' horns of great value, by an ancient custom, were placed upon the altar." †

At the west end of Ashby-de-la-Zouch Church, Leicestershire, there is a curious object called "a finger-stock or pillory," an old instrument of punishment—a contrivance to detain irreligious persons by the finger, so as to become the mark for reprehension and scorn. A correspondent of *Notes and Queries* (October 25, 1851), describing this quaint contrivance, says, "It is fastened at its right-hand extremity into a wall, and consists of two pieces of oak ; the bottom and fixed piece is three feet eight inches long ; the width of the whole is four and a half inches, and when closed, it is five inches deep : the left-hand extremity is supported by

* "Traditions and Customs of Cathedrals," 173.
† Parkinson's "Legends and Traditions of Yorkshire," 97.

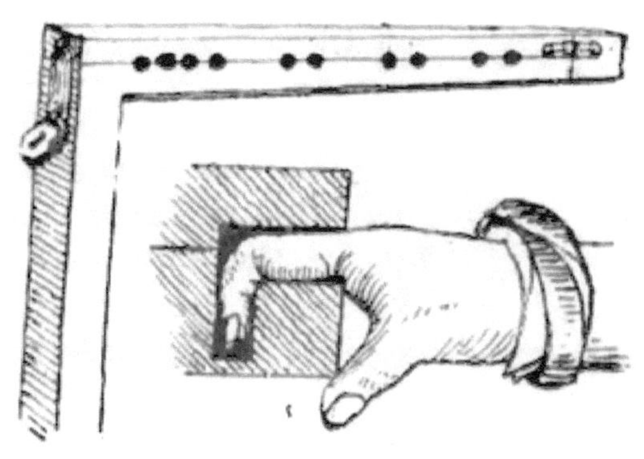

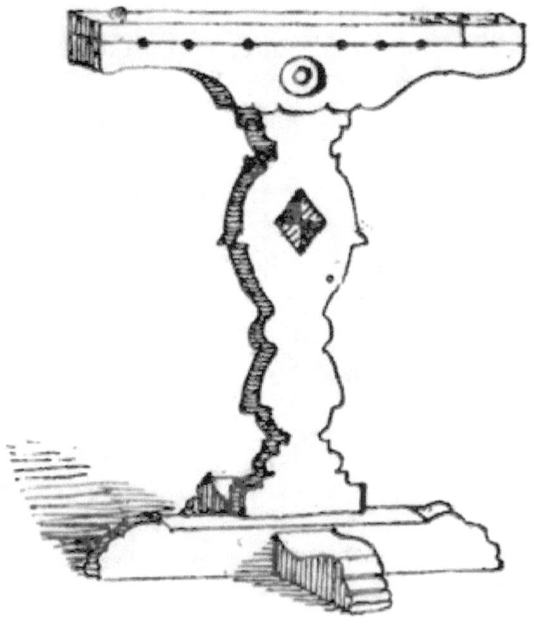

FINGER-STOCKS, OR PILLORIES.

1. Ashby-de-la-Zouche.   2. Littlecote, Wilts.

Page 335.

a leg of the same width as the top, and two feet six inches in length ; the upper piece is joined to the lower by a hinge, and in this lower and fixed horizontal part are a number of holes varying in size. The largest are towards the right hand. These holes are sufficiently deep to admit the finger to the second joint, and a slight hollow is made to admit the third one, which lies flat. There is, of course, a corresponding hollow at the top of the moveable part, which, when shut down, encloses the whole finger." With this curious instrument of punishment may be compared another one preserved at Littlecote Hall, Wiltshire, and which has long been an object of interest.

Winfarthing Church, Norfolk, was formerly renowned for the possession of " a certeyn swerd, called the good swerd of Winfarthyng." A chapel at the end of the south aisle was devoted to this sword, which "was visited far and near," especially for the discovery of "things that were lost," as of stolen or strayed horses. It was also efficacious in delivering wives from husbands who were distasteful to them, if they " would set a candle before that swerd every Sunday for the space of a whole year." Becon, in his " Reliques of Rome," asserts that he had "many times heard when a child," that the sword had belonged to a certain thief who took sanctuary in the churchyard, and afterwards escaped, leaving his sword behind, which in time came to be regarded as a relic of powerful virtue.*

St. Lawrence Church, Reading, once possessed a silver gridiron, containing a relic of St. Laurence.

Godwin and Britton, in their "Churches of London," speak of the four large syringes preserved in the vestry-room of St. Dionis Backchurch. These were at one time the only machines used in London for the extinction of fires. They

* Murray, Handbook for Norfolk, 1870, 186, 187.

are about two feet three inches long, and were attached by straps to the body of the person using them.

In the north porch of St. Margaret's Church, Westminster, between the outer and inner doorways, are kept with religious care two ancient parish engines, with their primitive hose and a few water buckets.

An interesting relic, too, belonging to the parish of St. Margaret, is the tobacco box in the keeping of the Past Overseers' Society. Its history is curious and interesting. The original oval-shaped box, made of common horn, and of a portable size for the pocket, was purchased, we are told in "Old and New London" (iii. 575), by a Mr. Monck at Horn Fair, Charlton, for fourpence, and from it he often replenished his neighbour's pipe at the meetings of his predecessors and companions in the office of overseers of the poor. In 1713 he presented it to the Society of Past Overseers, and in 1720 this body ornamented the lid with a silver rim. The next addition was a silver side-case and bottom in 1726. In 1740 an embossed border was placed upon the lid, and in 1746 Hogarth engraved inside the lid a bust of the Duke of Cumberland, with allegorical figures, and scroll commemorating the Battle of Culloden. In 1765 an interwoven scroll was added to the lid and an inscription: —"This box to be delivered to every succeeding set of overseers, on penalty of five guineas."

An additional silver case was next provided for it, and this in turn became enveloped in a third, fourth, and fifth case. In 1793, Mr. Read, a past overseer, detained the box in revenge, because his accounts had not been paid. Litigation ensued, and eventually the Chancellor directed the box to be returned to the Overseers' Society.*

At the Church of St. George the Martyr, Southwark, there is preserved a curious handbill, or *affiche*, printed in black

* See Mackenzie Walcott's " Westminster."

letter, which, it is said, "must have been promulgated previous to the suppression of religious houses in the reign of Henry VIII. It is surmounted by a small woodcut of St. George slaying the dragon and by a child." At St. Matthew's, Bethnal Green, there is a curious old staff used by the beadle, the head of which, in silver gilt, presents the legend of the Blind Beggar of Bethnal Green and his daughter, as in the old ballad.

At Barfreston church, Kent, during some repairs, was found imbedded in the mortar a pair of small scissors, not acting upon a rivet, as do those of the present day, but formed in one piece, like sheep-shears.* Hasted mentions at Stone-in-Oxney, in the same county, an altar of stone preserved "time out of mind in the church," with a basin hollowed in the top, and the figure of an ox carved on the sides, three feet four inches high. It had, he says, been turned out of the church and used as a horse-block, whereby it became cracked; but it was repaired and placed in the vicarage garden.

* "Notes on the Churches of Kent, Sussex, and Surrey," Rev. A. Hussey, 1852, 27.

INDEX.

A

Abbot's Morton, tradition at, 87
Abingdon, St. Helen's, Easter sepulchre at, 223
Acoustic jars, 70–74
Addelthorpe, low side **window** at, 211
Adderbury **Church,** tradition relating to, 24
Addington Church, **funeral armour at,** 169
Adel Church, sanctuary knocker at, 182
Adhelm's, St., Bell, 77
Alban's, St., Wood Street, hour-glass at, 203
Albrighton, church at, tradition relating to, **22**
Aldershot, funeral armour at, 169
Ale, church, 322–328
Alford, Lincolnshire, Easter sepulchre at, **227**
Alfriston, church at, 11, **85**
Alkmund's, St., Derby, well so called, 279
Allhallows Barking, **church of,** 19, **227,** 228
Allington, Wilts, low side window at, 213
All Saints' Church, Binfield, Berkshire, 240; Clevedon, 58; Derby, 302, 303; Hartley, Kent, 214; Hastings, 90; Northampton, 60; Norwich, **71;** York, sanctuary knocker **at,** 182, beacon lamp at, 207

Alphege, **St.,** Cripplegate, **192**
Altarnum, well at, 276
Alvingham, Lincolnshire, two churches in **one** churchyard, **232**
Amberley, Easter sepulchre at, 227
Ambleside, rush-bearing at, 328
Andrew, St., Undershaft, 301; Derry, 86; Greenstead, 240
Antony, St., **in Kerrier,** church of, 20
Ardley, low side window at, **217**
Armour, funeral, 165–170
Arundel Church, 154
Ashburton, acoustic jars discovered at, 71, 72
Ashby-de-la-Zouche, finger pillory at, 334, 335
Ashton-under-Lyne Church, **24,** 185
Astrology, 112
Attleborough, Norfolk, 245
Austin's, St., well of, Leicester, 280
Ave Bell, 95
Avening Tower, 79
Avington Church, **Hungerford, 262**
Aycliffe, Durham, **246**

B

Badingham Church, Suffolk, 240
Bagbury, legend relating to, 32
Baldock Church, funeral armour in, 168

Bampton Church, Easter sepulchre at, 226

Banners in churches, 170-173

Banns of marriage, 123, 124

Baptism, customs relating to, 111, 117 ; superstitions relating to, 115 ; by the midwife, 112

Barcheston, chained books at, 303

Barfreston Church, Wilts, 110

Barking lich-gate, 155

Barn Hall, legend connected with, 143

Barnard Castle Church, 211

Barnes, Surrey, Easter sepulchre at, 229

Barton Church, Lincolnshire, 93, 97

Basingstoke, church library at, 295

Baschurch Church, legend relating to, 6

Bath Abbey, 105, 299

Beacons, 207, 208

Bebington, cow charity at, 271

Beccles, church library at, 294 ; ringers' pitcher, 106

Becket, Thomas à, well of, at Derby, 279

Belfry rules, 89-92

Bells and belfries, 75-110

Bells, benediction of, 75-76 ; rung in storms, 76, 77 ; stolen, 79, 80 ; sacrilege connected with, 80, 83 ; submerged, 82-84

Bell rhymes, 99-103

Bellman, at funerals, 151, 152

Belton, Lincolnshire, 230

Benet's, St., Gracechurch, 302

Berkeley Church, Gloucestershire, 46

Bermondsey Abbey, 17

Berrington Church, legend relating to, 27

Berry Harbour, 155

Berwick, Sussex, 85

Bescars, land so-called, 330

Beurin's, St., Cornwall, right of sanctuary at, 173

Beverley Minster, right of sanctuary at, 176 ; well at, 282

Beverley, St. Mary's, beacon at, 208 ; library at, 286

Bicester, female churchwarden at, 243 ; church-ale at, 326

Bier House, 155

Bishop's Cleeve, Gloucester, 48, 108

Bishops, sugar-loaves presented to, 249

Blackpool, legend at, 84

Black Tom of Sothill, 104

Blaise, St., church of, at Arles, 74

Blisworth, low side window at, 217

Bloxham Church, tradition relating to, 24

Blythburgh Church, Suffolk, 200

Bobbing, custom for waking sleepers, 64

Bonchurch, well-dressing at, 279

Books in chains, 296-305

Boscastle Tower, 208

Bosham, Easter sepulchre at, 227

Boston Church, churching-pew at, 194 ; library at, 287 ; Easter sepulchre at, 227

Botolph, St., Aldgate, 220

——, Northfleet, 238

Bow Church, Cheapside, 101, 180, 206

Boxwell, low side window at, 212

Brabourne Church, funeral armour at, 169

Bradestone Church, Norfolk, curious custom at, 62

Branksea Church, Devonshire, curious pew at, 191

Branock, St., 15

Braunton, church at, legend relating to, 15

Bray Church, lich-gate at, 154

Bradsall Church, old reading-desk at, 303

Breedon Church, strange building legend relating to, 11

Brelade's Church, St., Jersey, 6

Brent Eleigh, Suffolk, 295

Brent Tor, Church at, legend relating to, 4

Brickleigh Church, funeral armour in, 166

Bride ale, 120; chair, 127; form, 191

Bride's dower, paid at church porch, 50; garters, 123

Bridget's Church, St., Chester, 58

Bridgnorth, St. Mary's, library at, 289

Bristan, St., 26

Bristol Cathedral, sweet smelling herbs strewn in, 53

Bristol, St. James's Church, 247, 249

Bristow Street, Edinburgh, meeting-house in, 74

Broadwater, Sussex, funeral armour at, 169

Brokenborough, Wilts, 94

Bromham, church library at, 293

Broughton Church legend, 6

Bryn-y-grog, church legend relating to, 12

Bucknell, Oxfordshire, low side window at, 216

Budeaux, St., Devon, female churchwarden at, 243

Bungay, storm at, 37

Burgh-by-Sands, tower used as fortress, 238

Burial customs, 128–152

Burial in erect posture, 135, 136; solemn, 137, 138; by torchlight, 139, 140; under church pillars, 144; head downwards, 136; in woollen, 145, 146

Burnley Cross and the demon pigs, 11

Burnley marriage custom, 123

Burnsall, Yorkshire, lich-gate at, 155

Burscough Priory, tradition connected with, 24

Burwell, Cambridgeshire, Easter sepulchre at, 228

Bury, Easter sepulchre at, 220

Bury St. Edmund's, church library at, 292

Buxton, well-dressing at, 279

C

Cadoc, St., church of, 86, 87

Caistor, Northants, 216

——, Lincolnshire, 237

Canterbury Cathedral, 49, 62, 167, 181, 282

Carhayes, St. Michael, funeral armour at, 169

Carlisle Cathedral, well at, 282, 283

Cartmel, Lancashire, chained books at, 300

Carw Gwyn Church, 15

Cashel, Rock of, 13

Casterton, Great, Rutlandshire, Roman camp at, 237

Casting the Nativity, 111

Castle Orchards, 5

Castleton church library, 290

Castor, Northamptonshire, 237

Catfield, hour-glass at, 205

Celibacy, 126

Chadderley Corbett, low side window at, 217

Chained books, 288, 296–305

Chalk Church, Kent, figures at, 324

Chambered porches, 44–48

Chapel-en-le-Frith, 262

Chapel Royal, hour-glass at, 204

Chatham Church, 261

Chelmsford church library, 290

Chelsea, chained books at, 304

Cheltenham parish church, 45, 110

Cherington church bells, 79

Cheriton, Easter sepulchre at, 226

Chesham Bois Church, 204

Chichester Cathedral, 25, 62, 109, 223

Chiddingford, Easter sepulchre at, 227

"Children of God," 112

Chiltern All Saints, Wiltshire, 126

Chrisom, 75, 147, 148

—— child, 148

Christ Church, Hants, 46, 48, 304

Christmas Eve custom, 104

Church acre, 4, 331

Church-ale, 321–328
Church Brampton, Northamptonshire, 80
Church-building legends, 1–15
Church discipline, 53–69
Church door, skin attached to, 43
Churchdown Hill, legend connected with, 2
Church-going rhymes, 63, 64
Church Hoppys, spot so called, 18
—— house, 326, 327
—— libraries, 284–295
—— osiers, 18
—— pigeon-houses, 67–69
—— pillar, burial under, 144
—— porch, 39–52, 125; deeds
signed in, 39–41; money pay-
ments in, 41; business transac-
tions in, 41, 42; refuge in, 44;
marriage in, 48–50; burial in,
50, 51; watching the, 51, 52
Churching-pew, 193, 194
Churchwardens, 241–250
Churchyard, 153–160
——, two churches in one, 231–
234
Cirencester Church, books at, 288
Claverley Church, Shropshire,
dog-whipper at, 62
Cleather, St., well at, 277
Clee, custom at, 331
Cleer, St., well of, 276
Clement, St., Danes, 114, 260
——, Eastcheap, 302
——, Sandwich, acoustic jars at,
71
Clerkenwell, 251
Clerks, parish, 150, 251–263
Cliffe Church, Kent, hour-glass
at, 204
Clock-holt, land so-called, 201
Clock, Jack of the, 197–200
Clock-keeper, 201
Coates, Great, Lincolnshire, 228
Cockerington, North, near Louth,
232
Cockfield, Durham, low side
window at, 211
Cock-fighting, 104
Colby Church, Norfolk, cham-
bered porch at, 46

Collingham Ducis Church, 68
Collumpton, Devonshire, 262
Compton Bassett, Wilts, 205
Consecration crosses, 108–110
Copford Church, skin nailed to
the door, 44
Coroner's inquest, 97
——, custom respecting dead
bodies, 250
Corpus Christi, festival of, 77
Corse Bell, 151
Coslany, St. Michael, Norfolk, 245
Coventry, Holy Trinity and St.
Michael Churches, 232
Cranley Church, Surrey, Easter
sepulchre at, 232
Cropredy, clock-keeper at, 202
Crosmere, legend relating to, 85
Cross, St., near Winchester, 48
Croston Church, 24
Crouch Hill, 24
Cubington, Warwickshire, low
side window at, 217
Cunmor, Oxon, chained books at,
304
Curfew bell, 92, 93
—— land, 93
Curst Field, 5
Cuthbert, St., 10
Cuxham Church, hour-glass at,
205

D

Dagtake Bell, 97
Danbury, storm at, 38
Darsingham Church, Lincoln-
shire, low side window at, 211
Daventry, Northamptonshire, bell
custom at, 102
David's, St., Cathedral, 62, 239
Dead, memorials of, 161–172
Demon pigs, 11
Denchurch library, 288
Denford Church, Northampton-
shire, 71
Dersingham, low side window at,
214
Devil's door, 116; knell, 104;
seat, 127

Discipline, church, 51–69
Diss, Norfolk, curious parish register entry, 44
Doddington, low side window at, 212, 213
Dog-noper, 60
Dog-whipper, 60–62
Dog-whipper's marsh, 62
Doncaster, election of church-wardens at, 244
Doncaster Church, library at, 289
Donington Church, tradition connected with, 22, 23
Doves, in church building, 11
Downton Church, Wiltshire, low side window at, 211
Dragon legends, 27–34
Drinking-Bush Hill, spot so called, 325
Dunchurch, low side window at, 217
Dun cow, milkmaid and the, 36
Dunstan, St., and Mayfield Church, 4
Dunstan, St., Church, Fleet Street, 198, 203
Dupath Well, 275
Durham Cathedral, 36, 62, 176; building legends relating to, 9; phantom army at, 26; custom on Corpus Christi Day at, 77; right of sanctuary at, 174, 176; sanctuary knocker, 182; Easter sepulchre at, 221

E

Easington, Oxon, parish clerk custom at, 255
Eastbourne, Easter sepulchre at, 227
East Dereham, well at, 283
Easter bells, 104
—— Eve, 215, 219
—— Day, 216
—— Sepulchre, 219–230
Eaton Mascott, strange story told of, 27
Ebchester Church, Durham, Roman camp at, 237

Eccles, pew arrangement at, 184
Ecclesfield parish, dog-noper at, 61
Eccleshall, low side window at, 217
Echingham Church, Sussex, bell tradition at, 83
Edmund's, St., well at, Oxford, 281
Egginton Church, chained books at, 303
Elsdon, Church, Northumberland, horses' skulls at, 74
Elkstone Church, Gloucestershire, church discipline at, 67
Elsfield, low side window at, 213, 216
Elvaston, Church-ale at, 323
Elvetham, pew at, 189
Elwick, low side window at, 211
Ely Cathedral, 214, 215, 217, 223, 231
Embleton marriage custom, 125
Endon, Shropshire, well-dressing at, 279
Epworth Church, 259
Ethelbert, St., well of, 283
Ethelburga's Church, St., Bishopsgate, 203
Euny, St., well chapel of, 276
Evesham, churches of All Saints and St. Lawrence, 232
Excommunicated persons, burial of, 159

F

Fairies and church building, 9, 10
Fairwell, Staffordshire, acoustic jars at, 71
Farley, Sussex, Easter sepulchre at, 223
Female parish clerks, 262, 263
Fennel strewn in churches, 331
Ferriby, South, Lincolnshire, consecration cross at, 110
Fillan, St., bell of, 78
Finger-pillory, 335
Fisherty Brow, legend connected with, 84
"Five Sisters," York Cathedral, 22

Flags in churches, 170, 171
Fleet Church, Lincolnshire, custom of waking sleepers at, 65
Flixton Church, hour-glass at, 204
Font, superstitions relating to, 115
Football match on Shrove Tuesday, 103
Forrabury church bells, 82
Fotheringay Church, 206
Foundlings, baptism of, 114, 115
Fountains Abbey, 72, 73
Frensham Church, Surrey, witches' cauldron at, 308
Frodsham Church, Cheshire, 97
Fulborne, near Cambridge, 233
Fulham Church, tradition connected with, 23
Funerals, handbell rung at, 151
Funeral armour, 165–170
—— feast, 138
—— garlands, 161–164
—— sermon, 138

G

Gabriel bell, 95
Garlands, funeral, 161–164
Garsington, low side window at, 217
Gateway of the Knight, Walsingham Church, 38
German's Cathedral, St., crypt at, 308
George's, St., Doncaster, chambered porch at, 48
Giles's, St., Northampton, low side windows at, 216
Gillingham, Dorset, 295
——, Norfolk, two churches in one churchyard, 232
Glasgow Cathedral, well at, 283
Gleaners' bell, 96, 97
Gloucester Cathedral, 25, 154
Glyssop Church, Derbyshire, bells stolen at, 80
Goddington, Oxfordshire, custom at, 97
Godrefarth church, legend at, 9
Godshill, church at, 3
Goltho, Lincolnshire, 243

Good Friday, 216, 230, 251
Goosnargh, land custom at, 39
——, dog whipper at, 61
Gorleston, Suffolk, 226
Gorton Church library, 292
Gosberton, Easter sepulchre at, 226
Grantham Church library, 299
Grasmere, rush-bearing at, 329
Gregory's Church, St., Norwich, 189
Gridiron, silver, at St. Lawrence, Reading, 335
Grimsargh, dun cow at, 37
Grundisburgh Church, knocker at, 183
Gunnislake Church, 239
Gunwalloe Church, 20

H

Hacsombe Church, horse shoe at, 308
Hadstock Church, skin on door of, 44
Hailsham Church, rush-strewing at, 331
Hall dog-pew at Northorpe Church, Lincolnshire, 191
Handsworth Church, near Birmingham, old customs at, 65
Hanmer Church library, 289
Hardwick-cum-Pasmore, female churchwarden at, 243
Harling Church, Norfolk, acoustic jars at, 70
Hart, low side window at, 211
Hartfield Church, lich-gate at, 154
Haslingfield Church, clock-keeper at, 201
Hathersage Church, belfry rules at, 91
Hats, smelling of, 318, 319 ; worn in church, 314–318
Hay strewn in churches, 331
Hayes, Kent, Easter sepulchre, at, 227,
Heart burial, 130–134

Heckington, Lincolnshire, Easter sepulchre at, 226
Hellesdon, Norfolk, low side window at, 217 ; Easter sepulchre at, 227
Hell-hole, spot so called, 83
Helston, well at, 277
Hempsted, hour-glass at, 205
Henry VII. Chapel, Westminster, 109
Henley, election of churchwardens at, 244
Hereford Cathedral, 27 ; library at, 299
Hexham Abbey Church, funeral armour at, 169 ; right of sanctuary at, 177 ; knocker at, 182
High pews, 191
Holbeach, superstition at, 310–312
Holme Church legend, 3
Holy Innocent's Day, muffled peal ring on, 103
Holy wells, 273–276
Holy Well Dale, Lincolnshire, 280
Hope Church, banns of marriage custom at, 124
Horkstow Church, sloping floor at, 239
Horncastle, Lincolnshire, Roman camps at, 237
Horn of Ulphus at York Cathedral, 333, 334
Horningham, bell custom at, 105
Hornsea Church, Yorkshire, 100
Hornsey Church belfry, 89
Horsham, Jack of the clock at, 199
Horse shoes, 308, 309
Horses' skulls, 74
Hour-glasses, 202–205
"Hung in the bell ropes," 124
Hurst, Berkshire, hour-glass at, 204
Husborne Crawley Church, funeral armour at, 166
Hyssington Church, strange legend attached to, 32–34
Hythe, Easter sepulchre at, 226

I

Ickburgh Church, Norfolk, female parish clerk at, 262
Iffley Church, Oxfordshire, consecration cross at, 110
Illtyd, St., bell of, 78, 79
Impington Church, Cambridgeshire, books at, 288
Ingham, Norfolk, low side window at, 211
Inkberrow Church, 10
Interment in church walls, 142
—— of hearts, 130–134
Ipswich, St. Mary-le-Tower, 247

J

Jack of Newbury, 96
Jack of the clock, 197–200
Jacques et les Innocents, Paris, 74
Jarrow Church, 126 ; Bede's well near, 280
Jersey Church bells, 82, 83
Jesus bells, 81
John, St., Maddermarket, Norwich, 245
John, St., well at Harpham, 281
John's Priory Church, St., Clerkenwell, 142
Judas bell, 104 ; candle, 104

K

Kenardington Church, fortifications at, 237
Kenwyn, Cornwall, anecdote relating to, 257
Keyingham, Yorkshire, holy well at, 280
Keyne, St., well of, 278
Kidderminster Church, legend connected with, 5
Kieran, St., tradition relating to, 14
Kilgrimol, Church of, submerged, 83

Kingsbury Church, Roman camp at, 237

King's Sutton, tradition relating to, 24; church-ale at, 325

Kingston-on-Thames, parish bull custom at, 265

Kirkheaton, custom of church-wardens at, 248

Kirton-in-Lindsey, Easter sepulchre at, 220

Kiss, nuptial, 119

L

Lambeth Church, tradition of pedlar and his dog, 18

Lancing, Easter sepulchre at, 227

Leake Church, legend relating to, 8

Ledbury bells, 87

Leeds Church, near Maidstone, acoustic jars at, 71

Leigh Church, Kent, hour-glass at, 205

Leigh-upon-Mendip, Somersetshire, bell custom at, 103

Lepers' gallery, 45; window, 209, 210

Lessingham Church, hour-glass at, 205

Les Tuzets, field so called, 9

Levan, St., lich-gate at, 155

Leverton, Lincolnshire, Easter sepulchre at, 223; church library at, 297

Lewes Church, Roman camp at, 237

Leybourne Church, Kent, heart-burial at, 134

Libraries, church, 284–295

Lightning, superstitions relating to, 37, 38, 77

Lilleshall Church, low side window at, 210

Lillington, low side window at, 217

Limerick bells, 85

Lincoln Cathedral, 25, 226, 297

Linton Church legend, 23; worm, 31

Llanbadarn Fawr, church at, 239

Llandulph Church, Cornwall, 90

Llangar Church, legend relating to, 15

Locks to pews, 189

Longbridge Devrill, funeral armour at, 169

Long Compton, Warwickshire, 97, 217

Long Melford, Easter sepulchre at, 225

Long Stratton, Norfolk, 94

Looe, Cornwall, 265

Louping Stone, 125

Lowestoft, low side window at, 211

Low side windows, 209–218

Ludham Church, 211

Ludlam, Mother, 309

Ludlow Church, weather-cock at, 206

Ludgvan, well at, 277

Luppitt Church, acoustic jars at, 71

Lych-bell, 151

Lych-gate, 153–156

Lychnoscopes, 209–218

M

Macclesfield Church, 228

Madeley, Shropshire, custom at, 156

Madron's, St., Church, 2; well, 274; bed, 274

Magic, church robbery traced by, 310–312

Maidservants, charity for, at Reading, 249, 250

Maismore, Gloucestershire, 243

Malmesbury Abbey, 77

Mancroft, St. Peter's, Norwich, 71

Mauthe Dog, 308

Margaret's Church, St., Westminster, 190, 194, 203, 231

Margaret, St., Pattens, 223

Market Overton, Rutlandshire, 237

Marriage ceremony, 118-127; seasons for, 118

Marie du Castel, St., Church of, 8

Mark's, St., Eve, watching in the church porch, 51

Martin's-le-Grand, St., **173, 178**

Martin's, St., Canterbury, **227**

——, Cliff, Kent, 216

——, Liskeard, 209

——, **Angers,** 74

——, **Carfax,** Oxford, 199

Mary Redcliffe, St., Bristol, **36,** 48, **48, 169, 224**

Mary, St., Bridport, **48**

——, Islington, **59**

——, Reading, **61**

——, Youghall, 73

——, Over, Cambridge, 97

——, Ottery, Devon, 109

——, Guildford, 211

——, Marlborough, 295

——, Woolchurch Haw, 185

Mary-le-Bow, St., Durham, 63

Maundy Thursday, 219

Mayfield, Church at, 4

Melton Constable, low side **window at,** 213

Mertsham, Surrey, 191

Mevagissey, bells at, 85, **257**

Michael, St., church of, at Cornhill, 37

——, Southampton, 304

——, St. Alban's, 205

——, Gloucester, 91

——, Queenhithe, 205

Mickleham, Sussex, curious **pew** at, 191

Middleham Church, church **dis-** cipline at, 59

Middle, Shropshire, **church** library at 293,

Midwife, baptism by, **112, 113**

Midwives' pew, 194

Mildred's, St., Poultry, weather- cock at, 205

Miller and his men, Jack of the clock so called at Exeter, 200

Minehead, Somerset, 272

Mint, right of sanctuary in, **178**

Misterton, Somersetshire, female parish clerk at, 262

Mitton **Church, sloping floor at,** 239

Moorin, St., church of, tradition relating to, 19; well of, 20

Mordiford Church, legend con- nected with, **32**

Moresby Church, Cumberland, Roman camp at, **237**

Morris dancers, 325, 330

Morrow mass bell, 96

Morwenstowe, church at, 19, 279

Mortality, bills of, 252, 253

Mother Ludlow's Hole, **309**

Muffled Peals, 102, 103

Murdered body, bleeding of, **130**

N

Narburgh, Norfolk, **228**

Nativity, casting the, **111,** 112

Needle, St. Wilfrid's, at Ripon, 312, 313

Neot, St., Church **of, 13; well of,** 277

Newington Church, **Kent, acoustic** jars at, 72

Newport Pagnell, **chained** books at, 303

Nicholas Church, **St., Gloucester,** 182; Ipswich, 72

Night, burials at, 139, 140

Ninnie, St., well of, 278

North Hinksey, Berkshire, 216

North Moor, Oxford, hour-glass at, **205**

Northorpe Church, Lincolnshire, hall dog pew at, 191

Northwich Church, Cheshire, marriage custom at, 123

Norwich Cathedral, 200, 201, 222

Nunnington Church, old tomb at, 28

Nun's Well, St., 276

Nuptial kiss, 119

O

Oakington, Cambridgeshire, **216**

Offchurch, Lincolnshire, **low side** windows at, **217**

Offerings at marriage, 122, 123
Okebrook, church-ale at, 323
Old Deer, church at, 6
"Old Moll," 16
Ore, Sussex, Easter sepulchre at, 227
Ormskirk Church, tradition relating to, 24
Oswald, St., 10, 11
——, church at Gruseley, marriage custom at, 50
Otterington, Yorkshire, legend connected with, 8
Ouen's, St., Bay, bells heard at, 83
Our Lady of Barking, 19
Our Lady's Well, 281
Over Church, Cheshire, tradition at, 8
Overbury Church, Worcestershire, pigeon house at, 68
Overstrand, Norfolk, two churches in one churchyard, 232
Overy, St. Mary, Church of, legend connected with, 16, 17
Owthorne Church, legend at, 23
Oxen in church building, 23

P

Panburn bell, 102
Pancake bell, 102, 103
Parish bulls and cows, 264, 272
—— clerk, 150, 251, 263
Parson's bell, 97
Parting-stool, 126
Parvise, keeping school in the, 46, 47
Paschal candle, 215
Passing bell, 87, 89, 149
Patrick, St., 13 ; well of, 283
Patrington Church, Easter sepulchre at, 226
Paul's cross, 55 ; Jacks, 199
—— Cathedral, St., 173, 223
Peculiarities, curious church, 231, 241
Pedlar and his dog, 18, 19
Pedlar's acre, 18, 19

Pembroke College, Cambridge, 110
Penance, public, 53–59 ; rules for, 54, 55
Penzance, custom of churchwardens at, 248
Peover, Chester, 241
Perry Trough, spot so called, 8
Pershore Abbey Church, bell stolen at, 80
Peter's, St., Oxford, 48, 295
—— Ropsley, 214
—— Upton, near Newark, 71
—— Cornhill, 206
—— Dorchester, 226
Peterborough Cathedral, 63
Petting-stone, 125
Pevensey, Sussex, Easter sepulchre at, 227
Pews, 185–196
Phantom nun of Holy Trinity Church, Micklegate, 34
Pierre-du-Bois, St., Guernsey, 240.
Pigeons in church towers, 67–69
Pigs in church building, 10, 11, 15
Piskie's Well, 278
Plympton St. Mary, church of, legend connected with, 4
Pollard worm, 30
Porchester, Hants, 237
Portsmouth, weathercock at, 207
Prentice's bracket, at Gloucester, 25 ; pillar, at Roslyn, 25 ; window, at Lincoln, 25
Prestmell, Lancashire, curious entry in parish register, 248
Prestwich, election of churchwardens at, 244
Pudding bell, 96
Pulborough, lych-gate at, 154
Pulham St. Mary Magdalen, Norfolk, cow charity at, 268
Pulpit, spot so called in Cornwall, 7 ; sounding boards, 74
Purton Church, skeleton in walls of, 142
Putney Church, 23, 227
Puxton, Somersetshire, hour-glass at, 205

R

Race-horse, bells rung in honour of, 104
Raleigh, Nottinghamshire, bell legend at, 84
Randwick, Gloucestershire, 243
Raveningham, Easter sepulchre at, 226
Raydon, Suffolk, low side-window at 216
Reading, St. Lawrence Church, charity custom at, 249
Reepham, three churches in one churchyard, 232
Relics, curious church, 333
Ribbesford Church, Worcestershire, 241
Right-of-way through churchyard, 160
Ringers pitcher, 105, 106; pot, 106
Ringwold Church, 93
Ripon Cathedral, St. Wilfrid's Needle at, 312
Rochdale Church, legend at, 3
Rochester Cathedral, 43, 45
Roche, St., bell of, 277
Roman camps, churches within, 237-238
Romford Church, bell legend at, 85
Rostherne churchyard, lych-gate at, 155
Rothersthorpe Church, low side-window at, 212
Rougham Church library, 294
Round churches, 234, 235
—— towers, 235, 236
Ruan's, St., Well, 277
Rugby Parish Church, tower used as stronghold, 238
Rumbald, St., figure of, at Boxley Church, 313
Runcorn, rush-bearing at, 330
Rushbearings, 330, 331
Rushes strewn in churches, 330-332
Rustington, Easter sepulchre at, 227

S

Sacombe Church, hour-glass at, 204
Salford, chained books at, 301
Salehurst, Easter sepulchre at, 227
Salisbury Cathedral, 25, 109, 177, 298
Sanctuary, burial without the, 157
—— knockers, 174, 182, 183
——, right of, 173-183
Sanctus bell, 93, 94
Satanic agency, 1-15
Saundersfoot, church at, sloping floor at, 239
Sauveur, St., Guernsey, sloping floor at, 240
"Savyne Croft," spot so called, 11
Savoy, hospital of St. John the Baptist in, 178, 179
Saxby, All Saints, Lincolnshire, 239
Scallenge-gates, 153
Scape-begotten child, 113
Scawthorp, excommunication at, 60
School in the parvise, 46, 47
Scotter Parish, Lincolnshire, disipline at, 60
Sefton, Lancashire, well at, 280
Selby Abbey Church, 46, 66
Sennan, St., Cornwall, 214
Sepulchre's Church, St., City, 45; Cambridge, 235; passing bell at, 89
Sepulchre, Easter, 209-230
Sermon bell, 96
Sexes, separation of, in church, 192
Sexhow, worm at, 28, 29
Shelsey Beauchamp, 205
Sherringham, low side window at, 213
Sheviock, tradition relating to, 21
Shottesbrooke Church, tradition relating to, 21
Shriving bell, 102; pew, 195
Shrove Tuesday, 93, 102, 103

Shurdington Chapelry, Gloucestershire, consecration cross at, 110
Sister churches, the, 23
Sites for churches, stories relating to, 2–15
Skipton Church library, 291
Skulls of horses in churches, 74
Slaugham, Sussex, Easter sepulchre at, 228
Sleepers in church, waking, 64, 65
Slingsby worms, 28
Smarden parish, Kent, dog whipping at, 61
Smock, marriage in, 126
Smoking in church, 319, 321
Sockburn, legend relating to, 29
Solemn burial, 137, 138
Sompting, Sussex, Easter sepulchre at, 227
Southwold Church, Jack of the clock at, 200
Speaking stone at St. David's Cathedral, 38
Sprowston Church, low side window at, 213
Spur money, 97–99
—— peal, 124
—— Sunday, 124
Spurring, 124
Staindrop Church, low side window at, 211
Stalham Church, hour-glass at, 205
Stampford Peverell Church, horse shoe at, 308
Standon Church, Herts, sloping floor at, 239
Stanground Church, Hunts, Easter sepulchre at, 227
Stanford-le-Hope, low side window at, 211
Stanley, St. Leonard's Church, church pigeon house at, 67
Stanningfield Church, figure of horse shoe at, 308
Stanton, St. John, Oxon, Easter sepulchre at, 226
Stanwell, Middlesex, Easter sepulchre at, 225

Staunton, Nottinghamshire, two churches in one churchyard, 232
Stephen's, St., Walbrook, Easter sepulchre at, 219
Strange tales, 26–38
Stillborn children, burial of, 157
Stoke Charity, Hants, 228
Stoke Lyne, Oxon, 228
Stoke-upon-Tern, Church at, 6
Stolen bells, 79, 80
Streatham Church, 188, 189
Strasburg Cathedral, 73
Straw strewn in churches, 331
Submerged bells, 82–84
Sudbrook, near Lincoln, 262
Superstitions, church, 306–313
Sutton Courtenay, library at, 295
Swaffham, Cambridgeshire, 231, 289
Swansea, Easter sepulchre at, 228
Sweet bells at Dewsbury, 104
Sweet herbs strewn in churches, 331
Swindon Church, peculiar tower, 238
Swithin, St., legend associated with, 51
Swavesey, low side window at, 217
Syringes, at St. Dionis Backchurch, 335

T

Talland Hill, legend at, 7
Tawstock, lich-gate at, 155
Temple Church, 114, 226, 235
Tewkesbury, pews at, 187
Thorpe-le-Soken, inscription at, 324
Thorpe, near Norwich, two churches in one churchyard, 232
Thornton-le-Moor, legend relating to, 8
Thunderstorms, bells rung in, 76, 77
Ting Tang, bell so called, 97
Tissington, well-dressing at, 279
Tofts, the, spot so called, 8

Tolpuddle Church, Dorset, **rhyme** relating to, 99

Tong, Shropshire, church library **at,** 295

Torchlight, burial by, 139, **140**

Totnes Church library, 293

Tottenham Church, chambered porch at, 46

Towednack Church, **legend connected with, 9**

Towers, round, **235, 236 ; used as** fortresses, **238**

Traditions, church, 16–25

Trefethin, legend connected with, 86

Trelystan, Montgomeryshire, half-timbered church **at,** 141

Trimley, Suffolk, two churches in one churchyard, **232**

Trim-trams, 153

Tring, Easter sepulchre **at, 226**

Trophies of **war hung in church, 170, 171**

Troutbeck, lych-gate at, **155**

Trysull, Staffordshire, dog **whip-per** at, 61

Tunstall church bells, 83

Turton, chained books **at,** 299

Twickenham, cow charity, 266

U

Udimore Church, **legend relating** to, 9

Uffington Church, **Berks,** consecration cross **at,** 110

Ulphus, horn of, at **York Cathedral,** 333, 334

V

Virgin chimes, 104 ; garland, 162

W

Wakefield Bridge, **226**

Wakerell bell, 94

Walpole, St. Peter's, **Norfolk,** sloping floor at, **240**

Walsham, North, 232

Walsingham Church, tradition relating **to,** 38

Waltham, **St.** Lawrence, church at, Easter sepulchre, 227

Walton, West, tradition connected with, **22**

Walton-on-**Thames, Easter** sepulchre at, 223

Wandsworth, Easter sepulchre at, **229**

Wantage, two churches in one churchyard, 232

Warburton, rush-bearing at, 330

Warrington Church, seats at, 191

Wartan Crag, Lancashire, 127

Waverley Abbey, witches' **cauldron** at, 309

Weathercocks, **205–207**

Wedding peal, **105** ; psalm, **120** ; sermon, 120

Well-dressing, 279

Wells, cathedral, 103, 134, **298**

Wells and well chapels, 273–283

Wendover Church, legend relating **to,** 7

Westbury - on - Severn, two churches in one churchyard, 232

Westgate, Exeter, clock at, **200**

Westminster Abbey, 43, 69, 131, 167, 168, 179, 180 ; **sanctuary** at, 173

Wettesall, low side window at, **217**

Weybridge, Easter sepulchre at, 229

Whalebone, St. **Mary Redcliffe** Church, 36

Whipping dogs out of church, 61–63

Whitby Abbey Church, **curious** tradition at, 35 ; bell legend at, 84

Whitchurch, library at, 292

White sheet, worn at public penance, 53-55

Whitsun ale, 325

Whitwell, low side window at, 217

Wickham, West, Kent, Easter sepulchre at, 227
Wigtoff, Lancashire, chained books at, 296, 297
Willingale Doe, Essex, two churches in one churchyard, 232
—— Spain, two churches in one churchyard, 232
Wimborne Minster, church library at, 299
Winchester College Chapel, 217
—— Cathedral, 227
Wine-drinking in church, 120
Winfarthing Church, curious relic at, 335
Wingrave, Buckinghamshire, 331
Winston, low side window at, 211
Winwick Church, legend relating to, 10
Wishing wells, 274
Witchcraft, 37, 307, 308
Witches' cauldron, 308, 309; meadow, 7
Withburga's, St., Well, 283
Withernsea Church, tradition relating to, 23
Witney, Easter sepulchre at, 221
Wolstan, St., and the devil, 27
Wolvercot, hour-glass at, 205

Woodchurch, Cheshire, 271
Wooden churches, 240
Woollen, burial in, 145–146
Worcester Cathedral, 27, 43, 80
Worfield Church, 6, 240
Wonders, tales of, 26–38
Worksop parish, dog whipper of, 61
Wootton Wawen Church, chained books at, 303
Worldham, East, hour-glass at, 205
Worth, lych-gate at, 154
Wrexham Church, legend associated with, 12
Whittle, Essex, Easter sepulchre at, 226
"Wrong side of the church," 157
Wyke, Hants, Easter sepulchre at, 227

Y

Yarmouth, Great, parish church, 67, 127, 222, 304
Yaxley Church, Suffolk, bells at, 94
York Cathedral, 22, 69, 144

LONDON : PRINTED BY WILLIAM CLOWES AND SONS, LIMITED,
STAMFORD STREET AND CHARING CROSS.